Challenge and Change in the Curriculum

This Reader is one part of an Open University integrated teaching system and the selection is therefore related to other material available to students. It is designed to evoke the critical understanding of students. Opinions expressed in it are not necessarily those of the course team or of the University.

Challenge and Change in the Curriculum

A Reader edited by Tim Horton and Peter Raggatt for the *Purpose and Planning in the Curriculum* Course at the Open University

HODDER AND STOUGHTON

in association with
The Open University

British Library Cataloguing in Publication Data

Challenge and change in the curriculum.
  1. Curriculum change
  I. Horton, Tim   II. Raggatt, Peter
  375'.001   LB1570

ISBN 0 340 28774 8

Typeset in 10/11 pt Baskerville (Monophoto) by Macmillan India Ltd.,
Bangalore.

Printed and bound in Great Britain
for Hodder and Stoughton Educational,
a division of Hodder and Stoughton Ltd,
Mill Road, Dunton Green, Sevenoaks, Kent,
by Richard Clay (The Chaucer Press) Ltd, Bungay, Suffolk.

Contents

Part Three   Reforming the Curriculum

Preface

This Reader is one of two collections of papers published in connection with the Open University course E204, entitled 'Purpose and Planning in the Curriculum'. E204 is primarily intended for those with a professional interest in examining major curricular issues affecting primary and secondary schools as well as institutions providing education and training for students after school.

The readings in this collection examine questions about the role of formal education in a social and cultural context, the translation of values into guidelines and frameworks for practical implementation and problems associated with change and renewal in the curriculum. The companion volume, entitled *Planning in the Curriculum*, focuses on analyses and proposals at the level of the institution.

This Reader has been compiled during the preparation of a course on curriculum studies that includes several teaching elements. Nevertheless, we believe that this collection of papers, addressed to important contemporary concerns in education, contains coherent and important analyses of curricular issues.

It is not necessary to become an undergraduate of the Open University in order to take E204. Further information about the course may be obtained by writing to: The Admissions Office, The Open University, PO Box 48, Walton Hall, Milton Keynes, MK7 6AB.

General Introduction

During the past two decades, the study of the curriculum has undergone a considerable revolution. Although the foundations for distinctly curricular approaches to educational enquiry were laid earlier this century, only recently have *curriculum studies* achieved a formal status in the work of many colleges and departments of education. To what should we attribute this change? No single explanatory factor is sufficient and we need to look at a conjunction of problems that needed urgent attention. The first issue concerned the distance, or even the divorce, between theory and practice in education. Teacher education was extremely heavily weighted on a 'front-end' model where attention to theory largely preceded any practice in the craft of teaching. As a form of apprenticeship, this was profoundly unsatisfactory for students who would later look back on the period with disdain. They were not the only losers however. Teacher educators all too often became distanced from points of stimulus – the work of schools and colleges.

The second problem pursues the first. Increasingly, serious doubts were raised about the capacity of the established disciplines within the field of education, such as psychology, philosophy and sociology, to explain the dynamics of formal education. Inter-disciplinary approaches were first adopted, albeit rather tentatively.

The third problem was presented by the pressure from social changes, 'outside' education. Many educators shared a desire to review practice but were uneasy about selecting methods of procedure. The separate pressures for innovation were numerous; they included forecasts of future employment needs as many traditional industries declined. At the same time, other educators believed that curricula based on such criteria would have undesirable effects upon the life chances of pupils.

Curriculum studies developed, therefore, out of a search to reconcile partial theories about education, a new commitment towards finding a body of theory that was informed by practice, and a wider movement to renew the form and content of education. Over time a new body of academics, researchers and, significantly, teachers, has emerged, which is not identified strongly with any single discipline in education. The record of the curriculum movement is not without its disappointments and failures. Nevertheless, some of the new styles of enquiry it has produced seem likely to survive the period of economic expansion with which they were closely identified. This collection of readings gives attention to the lessons of the first phase of the curriculum re-form movement and anticipates the new tasks ahead. Whether at the level of the individual or society, education is necessarily concerned with change and a practitioner's theory is necessary to give understanding to these dynamic processes. The field of curriculum studies is littered with many tentative propositions but one suggestion about the curriculum task made by Denis Lawton in this collection would meet with a broad measure of support – ' . . .

each generation has the three-fold task of efficiently learning the knowledge acquired by previous generations, adding to it or modifying its interpretations, and finally passing this revised knowledge on to the next generation'.

This task of identifying 'worthwhile' knowledge provides the theme of the first part of this collection. The writers acknowledge the contribution of philosophers to the moral and ethical questions involved here but face up to practitioners' questions. What traditions of thought inform current practices? How are these traditions sustained? What implications might particular selections from all available knowledge have for the respective statuses of the pupil and learner?

The theme of the second part of the collection is the public curriculum. This draws attention to education as a national enterprise. The term 'public curriculum' emerged at the time of the 'Great Debate' on education which began in 1976. The Debate culminated in a set of specific proposals, some of which are now codified in statute. The recommendations appeared to some like old wine in new bottles, but this belies the true significance of the exercise. It reminded those in education that the state is not reluctant to review, admonish and redirect the work of schools and colleges. Its formal involvement with teaching and learning has a history stretching back over a century, but the autonomy accorded to professionals is licensed only.

To liberal thinkers the level of attention accorded in the Debate to the 'productive needs' of society may seem narrow, but the establishment of frameworks about the main things pupils should do and learn may have advantages, focusing discussion about education on content rather than sets of overt or covert controls deemed to operate upon teachers. Further, it classifies the rights pupils and students can expect to have within the education system. For example, it is practically worthless to select an aspect of a literary tradition, say, as worthwhile unless we can decide through public discussion whether or not everyone should have access to it, whether its acquisition can be left to chance or whether formal institutions are best able to impart understanding.

The final part of this collection is concerned with innovation and change. Prior to the Great Debate the will to innovate provided a stimulus for curriculum studies while economic growth held out some promise for satisfying desires. Yet in retrospect some of the models used to explain how education systems work seem woefully inadequate. The new phase of curriculum development is, it is to be hoped, more realistic. Sponsors of the early, large national curriculum projects promoted the idea of adoption through dissemination and yet failed, in large measure, to graft on new teaching approaches to established methods in schools and colleges. The trend now is to emphasize adaptation through evaluation and review. To some zealots of reform, this may appear initially as an over-cautious and piecemeal approach, but the early signs are not discouraging. Although change of this kind may seem chaotic, the call to teachers to apply their professional wisdom in order to re-appraise the totality of their activity may have a more enduring effect on curricula.

Innovation on these lines has alerted teachers to issues formerly masked by the rhetoric of individual teacher autonomy. The struggle between contending aspirations and ideas about the purposes of education do not lie exclusively outside school gates and college walls. Innovation is not simply a technical problem of mastering resources and coping with physical constraints, for it engages teachers with sets of value questions no different from those confronted in departments of state or local education offices. Changes in education are not just responses to challenge but themselves unlock a new set of challenges and goals.

Part One   Selecting from Culture

In his preface to *Culture and Anarchy*, Matthew Arnold wrote of culture that it is a 'pursuit of our total perfection by means of getting to know, on all the matters which concern us, the best which has been thought and said in the world'. Arnold's eloquence conveys the idea that culture is more than a legacy of the past but is, through our desire to improve, active in the present. All the efforts of mankind, he suggests, are directed towards the improvement of culture. Of course, what constitutes the 'best' in culture is open to much argument and dissent. If 'quality' in culture provides one reason for making selections from it there are others. Individually our span of years on earth restricts what we can accumulate from available knowledge. In consequence we provide 'short-cuts', ostensibly to enhance a fuller appreciation of culture. This provides some justification for schooling, but it is by no means certain that formal education is, or can be, the most efficient way to acquire cultural understanding.

Malcolm Skilbeck examines ideologies as sets of beliefs and values in society which contain relatively distinct views on what is best in available knowledge. Each set – progressivism, reconstructionism and classical humanism – does not provide finite conceptions of the purpose of education and sub-variants are clearly discerned.

However, Skilbeck's analysis points up the fact that beliefs about worthwhile knowledge contain, explicitly or implicitly, ideas about how learning should be organized. His own undisguised allegiance to re-constructionist ideas stands in some contrast to the views of G. H. Bantock. Bantock suggests that in Christian societies two quite distinct strands of cultural experience have emerged – the culture of the upper classes based particularly on their ability to read and write and the culture of the ordinary people or 'folk' based largely on their traditions of oral communications. Bantock proceeds to deplore first the watered-down versions of an intellectually-based culture provided for the bulk of the population who require a curriculum aimed at practical common life and, second, the stranglehold of examinations upon the cultural tradition of the upper classes.

An alternative radical tradition is represented by John White's article, in which he asserts that education's purpose of providing a good society, one free of the desire for status, demands that all young people should have some acquaintance with the higher culture. White rejects what he sees as the vagaries of some progressivist rhetoric as firmly as he supports arguments for guaranteeing that each child should study certain disciplines of education.

Denis Lawton shares White's view that pupils and students should share a right to have access to a common cultural curriculum. However his analysis of disciplines as different forms of knowledge leads to somewhat different conclusions. Knowledge, he argues, is not a unified whole but consists of logically different ways of enquiring into, understanding or experiencing 'reality'. However, although disciplines provide some basis for planning the curriculum this does not imply the curriculum should be discipline-centred. A detailed critique of Lawton's views on a common curriculum is provided by Uldis Ozolins. Ozolins suggests that Lawton ignores the socializing effect of schooling particularly outside the formal syllabus laid down. The effect of these covert practices and processes is to differentiate between and exclude pupils on a social class basis. The tradition of a working-class culture is best understood by reference to the history of inter-class struggle – a struggle which is continuous in the life and work of schools.

Gerald Grace supports Ozolins' contention that the conventional structure of the curriculum is alienating to working-class pupils. Drawing upon research in London schools, he argues that the shift in pedagogy towards forms of 'integration' provides an indicator, not only of doubts about the classifications of worthwhile knowledge in society, but also, more widely, of a moral crisis in society's structure of power and control.

Gabriel Chanan too acknowledges that confusion surrounds the issue of how to prescribe what pupils ought to know and think. His particular emphasis is upon education not only for cultural transmission but, importantly, also for 'cultural criticism'. Chanan's particular recommendation is that the curriculum should be focused around adult predicaments – particularly those activities that contribute to the sustaining of life. In this way, school would become a kind of supervised cultural centre where activities were fostered for direct benefit of the community. Chanan's attention to the notion of self-help in small communities may provide a solution to the paradox highlighted in Daniel Boorstin's analysis of communications in Western societies. He points out that the larger the distance to be covered in order to communicate, the greater the power of technology to reduce the required time. Societies' emphases in sponsoring aeronautics and electronics have achieved little in bringing us closer to our neighbours. Such analyses of contemporary cultural forms may call into question Arnold's optimism about the efforts of mankind to make improvements in existing culture.

1.1 Three Educational Ideologies

Malcolm Skilbeck

Part 1 Progressivism

The starting point for educationists subscribing to what we are calling a progressivist ideology is not the postulated requirements of a pre-established, adult-centred cultural system. Rather, it is a conception of children's unfolding nature, their interests and their developmental needs. The central metaphor in this school of thought is growth. In thinking about this ideology, though, you should not fall into the trap of equating 'child-centred education' with the rejection of adult views and values. [. . .]

The child-centrism of the progressivist ideology is frequently traced back to Rousseau's imaginary biography of the pupil Émile [1911], from infancy to adulthood. Certainly Rousseau inspired a new movement in education through some of his famous slogans, such as: 'The wisest people are so much concerned with what grown-ups should know that they never consider what children are capable of learning. They keep looking for the man in the child.' And, 'having taken pains to make the child bad we complain about his badness'. And, 'in the schoolroom the scholar listens to the verbiage of his master as he listened in the cradle to the babble of his nurse . . . leave him in ignorance of both'. This movement, away from fixed views about what children should learn, continues to the present day and is one of the most important influences in the thought of Piaget. [. . .] Rousseau, on his own admission, drew heavily on his predecessors, so that many of his ideas about a curriculum built upon the emerging individual qualities and talents of children were not original in the latter part of the eighteenth century. Nevertheless, the emergence of the romantic movement in eighteenth-century Germany, England and France, of which Rousseau was one of the leaders, was undoubtedly a decisive factor in the popularization of the view that, in education, transmitting a cultural heritage must be made subservient to 'discovering' and 'following' the developing impulses of the individual child. [. . .]

In educational theory, Rousseau's *Émile* is the most striking and fully worked out example of the romantic iconoclastic attitude towards the values and rules of traditional culture, and the social institutions in which the traditional culture expressed itself. Thus the curriculum Rousseau envisaged for the pupil Émile was situationally based, and some of Rousseau's boldest proposals for the organization of learning arise from unpremeditated encounters between the pupil and various adult members of the rural community in which he was depicted as growing up. It is not mathematics or

Source: THE OPEN UNIVERSITY (1976) E203 *Curriculum Design and Development*, Unit 3 *Ideologies and Values*. Milton Keynes: The Open University Press, pp. 28–41.

language in any formal sense that the boy is taught, but mathematical understanding and linguistic skill are developed, by an artful and well-informed teacher, through the educational exploitation of the situations of everyday life. This approach, now familiar through the work of progressive primary schools was regarded by Rousseau's contemporaries as revolutionary and highly destructive of traditional values in education and life.

This conflict between the classical and progressivist ideology is very apparent in contemporary educational thought and practice at all levels from primary school to university. Rousseau's *Émile* is a long and difficult book to read, and it may be safely assumed that few detractors of modern theories of child-centred education have ever either read it or pondered over the paradox that, although Rousseau made devastating attacks on the traditional arts and sciences, the régime he proposed for the pupil Émile was highly structured, orderly and disciplined, with the pupil's spontaneity and expressiveness contained within a well worked-out developmental programme. During childhood, Émile's freedom to develop was conditioned by the tutor's constant surveillance of every situation into which he entered – a far more pervasive form of control than is normally available even in fully residential schools. During adolescence, with a mind and spirit toughened by the régime of direct experience of physical nature, the pupil was led into the systematic study of literature, philosophy, history, Euclidean geometry, and so forth, and the modes of political experience expressed through the urban and national institutions of his time. Many advocates of the progressivist ideology claim to have reconciled *freedom* (in the sense of the pupil's spontaneity and choice) with *order* in the sense of a clearly articulated logical sequence of learning tasks. But such a reconciliation is exceedingly difficult. [. . .]

The progressivist ideology [has] not, of course, followed Rousseau in all respects. Rousseau demanded the isolation of the pupil during infancy and childhood from all influences save those the tutor could control. This indicates not only a high degree of confidence in the wisdom and judgement of the teacher but also a suspicion of the influence of other people and agencies. Rousseau put forward the extreme position. His followers have been more modest, or more realistic, in recognizing that they cannot achieve total control over the child's environment.

However, the main respect in which modern progressivist ideology differs from Rousseau is the importance now attached to the very *communitarian* elements which Rousseau studiously avoided. The school as a community and working in close and active relationship with the wider community of which it is a part now forms the setting for much progressivist educational thinking. This was not so in Rousseau's theory. The cultural choices made for and by Émile were made in the deliberately restricted setting of a very small and intimate primary group – mostly no more than the one-to-one relationship of pupil to teacher. Furthermore, the substance of the decisions reflected the values and insights of the tutor (Rousseau), an individualist and a revolutionary very much at odds with the world of his time.

Translated, by his followers Pestalozzi and Froebel, into a wider and more normal educational setting and falling under the influence of nineteenth-century socialism and the prevailing idealistic philosophy, Rousseau's original theory has come to be *communal* as well as *individualistic*. This means that the progressivist ideology in education now accepts that man is not an isolated individual whose education prepares him to enter into combat with his life and times, but fundamentally a social being, who not only has to learn to live in harmony with others but whose very development is conditioned by social relationships. [. . .]

In the latter part of the nineteenth century, romantic communitarianism split into two broad streams of educational thought and practice: (i) the kindergarten, child development and activity movements in the emerging national school systems of the old and new world; (ii) the progressive education movement, which came to fruition in a relatively small number of independent and private schools, mainly in Western Europe and North America. It is in the latter group of schools that the communitarian ideal has been most fully explored, in a way that parallels the classical ideal of community which finds expression most fully today in the English public schools.

Communitarianism in education includes the conviction that a single, unified community can be formed from the collection of teachers and pupils that comprise the school; that this community can be and should be more or less isolated from what are taken to be the harmful effects of modern society; that the life of the community is capable of being articulated through norms and rules, which over time can become self-correcting and, to a considerable extent, tacit, but which always remain open to modification through conscious, corporate action. This is an ideal which lies behind some of the independent progressive schools like Summerhill and Dartington Hall in England, and John Aitkenhead's Kilquanity House School in Scotland. [. . .]

A form of life grows in these communities. It is a complex whole, not reducible to a pedagogical régime, a régime of order, of control, and so forth. It bends academic, social and emotional elements; hence, the 'curriculum' of the communitarian institutions is much broader and much more complex than the activities of the classrooms or the subjects listed in the time-table. The major tasks of the communitarian school are to nourish the sub-culture it has itself created, to induct newcomers, foster the values it professes, and to build up a secure base from which its members can challenge and confront the wider society.

The concept of 'preparation for adult life', which Rousseau vehemently denounced as a proper target for education, has an ambiguous place in the communitarian ideology; on the one hand, the life of the community is seen as a worthwhile end in itself, and childhood is not merely a preparation for adulthood; on the other hand, the community's values are pitted against those of the wider society and pupils are encouraged to reform, change or modify that society, and not simply to fit into it. Thus it is of great functional significance that the whole way of life of the communitarian school should be highly idiosyncratic and indigenous to the institution. [. . .]

The progressivist ideology casts the school into a critical and creative role, and its curriculum is best viewed as part of a strategy of social renewal. It is not surprising, therefore, that prominent progressive educationists, like Michael Duane, former head of Risinghill School, London, Tim McMullen, former warden of Countesthorpe College, Leicestershire, and R. F. Mackenzie [former head of Summerhill Academy, Aberdeen] should find themselves strongly opposed by certain parents and other interest-groups who correctly perceived that these kinds of schools are throwing out a fundamental challenge to a whole established way of life. [. . .] As they have become older and more firmly established, the progressive schools have come to accept more of the values and practices of the larger societies of which they are a part, and have reverted to concern for individual child growth and development in place of messianic campaigns for the conversion of the whole society. Conversely, where they fail, their leaders may become more radical, like Mackenzie. . . .

Part 2   Reconstructionism

Whereas classical humanism and romantic communitarianism are a familiar part of the British educational scene, reconstructionism has never been as conspicuous in this country as in the United States and, now, in the developing world. President Nyerere's essay 'Education for Self Reliance' and Tanzania's programme of rural socialism are better examples of the reconstructionist mentality than can be found in recent British thought or practice, although parallels could be found towards the end of and shortly after the Second World War, when education was widely discussed in the context of social reconstruction.

Maybe the relative decline of reconstructionism in advanced industrial societies and its rapid rise in third world and other developing societies points to a relationship between educational theory and the socio-political context from which it develops. Stable, traditional societies which are generally satisfied with their institutions and policies do not throw up radical educational doctrines whose intent is to reconstitute the whole social order. Putting this point rather more cautiously, it is only in periods of great social upheaval or crisis that reconstructionist thinking finds a ready audience among educators.

In the twentieth century, the most powerful and influential educational theorist in the reconstructionist school is the American John Dewey (1921, 1929). [. . .] Dewey's theory cannot be summarized easily. We are concerned here primarily with its social aspects, and in particular with the analysis that Dewey and his successors made of the relationship between school and society.

What is distinctive about the reconstructionist ideology in education is:

(*a*) The claim that education, properly organized, can be one of the major forces for planned change in society. (Nyerere argued this, as have advocates of comprehensive education in Britain.)

(*b*) The claim that educational processes should be clearly distinguished from certain other social processes, such as political propaganda, commercial advertising, or mass entertainment, and that the former should, if necessary, enter into conflict with the latter in pursuit of worthwhile ends or goals.

(*c*) The aspiration to make a new kind of man, especially a new kind of citizen, 'better' and more effective than the average present-day citizen. (This has been peculiarly an aspiration of Communist education, but parallels can be found in Britain among religious and moral educators, for example Archbishop Temple and Bertrand Russell.)

(*d*) An interest in a social-core curriculum in which prevailing social norms and practices are analysed, criticized and reconstructed according to rationalistic, democratic, communitarian values. [. . .]

(*e*) A conception of learning and the acquisition of knowledge as active, social processes involving projects, problem-solving strategies guided but not dominated by teachers. (The reconstructionist ideology shares this conception of active learning with the progressivist.) [. . .]

(*f*) The elevation of teachers and other members of a carefully selected and highly trained élite of educators who are designated the agents of cultural renewal. [. . .]

(*g*) The relative neglect of difficulties and of countervailing forces – a characteristic feature of all kinds of utopian thinking, of which reconstructionism is one of the recognizable strands. [. . .]

These characteristics are neither exhaustive nor definitive of any particular educator. They are presented to help you identify a movement in educational theory which has become very influential throughout the developing world in particular, even though it may seldom be acknowledged as a distinctive standpoint. [. . .]

Reconstructionism is a movement in educational thought which starts from a sense of deep dissatisfaction with existing arrangements and tendencies in society. Nyerere's critique of the persistence of the colonial educational heritage is one example of this. Reconstructionist writers usually talk about the 'crisis of the age' or an impending or actual social and political disaster on a grand scale. [. . .] Ironically, in Western educational thought, it was Plato who first gave significant form to the reconstructionist mentality and thus became the founder of this movement, just as his thought was instrumental in founding classical humanism, against which reconstructionism has frequently directed its sharpest criticism. Plato thought education both could and should provide the foundation for a revolutionary society, and justified the comprehensiveness of his reform measures by invoking a grave political and social crisis in the Athens of his day.

[Twentieth-century reconstructionist] thinkers have stressed the impetus towards basic cultural change, including change in individual and social values, provided by the key modernization processes of science, technology, industrialization and democracy. Except for the latter, towards which he was exceedingly hostile, these factors played no part in Plato's thinking. The modern reconstructionists have not only shown how these factors have basically transformed the tasks facing modern societies, including their educational systems, they have also reversed Plato's assessment of democracy, treating it as the chief moral and political inspiration for the new social order they advocate. However, both ancient and modern exponents of the ideology have agreed that education is a key process in lessening social conflict and in developing new patterns of life.

Modern reconstructionists, under the influence of Enlightenment ideas and those of nineteenth-century democratic theory, grandiosely envisage the progressive social and economic amelioration, and the intellectual and spiritual advance, of humanity as a whole. The pursuit of perfectibility requires the lowering of one of the most serious barriers to human improvement, namely the theological doctrine of original sin. This doctrine has played a large part in traditional approaches to justifying harsh punishment in schools. The rejection of the concept of original sin is an essential part of the expressionist movement in education. Significantly Rousseau assailed it, replacing it with the doctrine of innate human goodness. [. . .]

Reconstructionist theory has been deeply influenced by the Enlightenment assertion of man's rationality and by that movement's elevation of the cultivation of rationality as a primary goal of all education. Yet modern reconstructionists are not so naively confident as were the enlightenment thinkers about the inevitability of social and cultural progress given the sustained application of science to human affairs. Rather, they have argued that a steady and indefinitely extended amelioration can be achieved through large-scale attempts to plan and organize individual and social experience according to agreed ends and using agreed procedures. Hence [. . .] there is a concern for planning structures, for participation, concensus and the pursuit of ends common to a whole population. Science, not least science as a costly, highly organized intellectual enterprise, need play only a relatively minor part in the process. From an educational standpoint what is important is not the production of scientific élites or even the training of a whole populace in scientific techniques, but the deliberate cultivation of rationality, of problem-solving procedures, adaptability and flexibility and a generalized capacity to face up to the problems of practical life.

Reconstructionism is an open thought-system, capable of absorbing a very wide range of influences and new possibilities for action. Consequently, all the thinkers in this tradition have been interested in the interaction of ideas and changing social and cultural environments. There are many uses of the term 'environmentalist' which are relevant to an analysis of reconstructionism. We have noted one: the readiness of these thinkers to modify their ideas as circumstances change. A more popular use of the word 'environmentalist' in education refers to the contrast drawn between 'environment' and 'heredity' as influences in shaping human behaviour. Human nature is usually described by reconstructionists as 'plastic', 'malleable', having 'potential for growth'.

Similarly, in considering social institutions and traditions, reconstructionists stress their fluidity and modifiability. You might compare the classical humanist's interest in classifying human beings into fairly rigid categories with both reconstructionism and progressivism, which dispute this categorizing. [. . .] Clearly these beliefs affect attitudes towards such matters as common-core curricula, mixed-ability grouping, and even the use of different forms of pupil assessment.

Reconstructionists are acutely conscious of the vulnerability of man and his social institutions to manipulation, whether commercial or political. Reconstructionism reached its height in Britain and the USA during the period of economic depression and during the totalitarian movements in the thirties and forties. In their anxiety to develop educational strategies and procedures fit to meet the challenges of some of the great crises of the twentieth century – war, depression, fascism and commercial manipulation – the reconstructionists took a strong interest in the techniques of mass propaganda. The American educationists G. S. Counts and T. Brameld, and the German sociologist Karl Mannheim, who moved to England in the 1930s, all used and advocated the use of propaganda as a counter to the apparatus of persuasion and manipulation used by political and commercial propagandists. Mannheim's argument, that the totalitarian movement in Europe in the thirties had seized and maintained power partly through their capture of the national propaganda machinery, was an interesting one. Despite the warning of John Dewey that propaganda was self-defeating for an educational theory which was based on the idea of cultivating reflective inquiry, some of the reconstructionists were prepared to use against their ideological enemies these very propagandist weapons that they had themselves so effectively developed. [. . .]

More successfully than any other theory, reconstructionism, I believe, has identified a number of tasks which confront educationists in periods of rapid, large-scale cultural change. Justifiable though it may be in some circumstances, the attempt by teachers to transmit established and settled knowledge loses credibility when the world which gave rise to these orderly bodies of knowledge is itself changing rapidly.

Focus in the curriculum on the characteristics, trends, problems and dislocations of contemporary culture as distinct from the past is a relevant and vital concern, since the very meaning and significance of past ideas and achievements has become highly problematic in a rapidly changing world. While willing to learn from the progressive tradition, the reconstructionists have become impatient with its apparent aimlessness and disregard of events which could destroy or drastically change the whole fabric of society, including the schools themselves. New cultural selections and definitions of task are required; new teaching procedures and a new core of socially unifying values are advocated, simply because the pace and scope of social change has accelerated so rapidly during the century.

The reconstructionists have perceived, in my view correctly, that patterns of culture would continue to emerge in the industrialized societies. This process will accelerate now that a large part of the developing world has become committed to varied forms of industrialization and urbanization. However, the reconstructionist ideology is not simply a form of adaptation to changing social circumstances. The mapping out of ideal futures, culture patterns and model social situations has for long been part of the programme of utopian reformers, among whom we shall number several reconstructionist thinkers. H. G. Wells and Julius Nyerere, among reconstructionists, illustrate the tendency very well. It is characteristic of these models of future culture that they should be:

highly generalized and schematic

heavily moralistic in tone

visionary and utopian in the sense that intractable problems are made to vanish

emphatic on the value of rationality and considerateness in all human dealings

built around a notion of world government and the disappearance of national wars

anti-class, egalitarian

democratic and communitarian

cultivated, in the sense of providing scope for aesthetic and intellectual development

scientifically humanist in outlook

flexible and capable of planning their own development.

Critics have been vehement in denouncing the 'man-making' assumptions and the general abstractness of the reconstructionist theorists. What objections would you make to this approach to education? Would you agree with D. H. Lawrence who, in an essay on the eighteenth-century Enlightenment leader, Benjamin Franklin, attacked Franklin's programme for educating the populace through practical, useful studies fitted to the creation of a commercially minded democracy as an alternative to the religious, aristocratic and aesthetic strands in the colonial society of his own day?

Critics such as Leavis and Bantock in our own times have been equally hostile to the man-making mentality which reconstructionism exhibits. Lawrence's criticism (in *Studies in Classic American Literature*) is one-sided. Yet it exposes one of the obsessions of enlightenment thinking that pervades much twentieth-century reconstructionist educational theory, namely the conviction that man can choose for himself the kind of life, society and culture he wants. You may care to ask whether such a conviction dominates contemporary approaches to curriculum planning.

Part 3   Classical humanism

Classical humanism is the oldest and traditionally the most esteemed of the three ideologies we have selected. Since the time of the Athenians (fourth and third centuries BC) it has been advanced as a belief in the value of a refined cultural heritage, whose custodians are a class of guardians. Matthew Arnold (1932) referred to them, in biblical language, as the remnant, T. S. Eliot (1948) as the élite, consisting of mandarins, academics, political and cultural leaders and selected teachers. Many different strands of classical humanism could be identified, but élitism of one kind or another has always been part of it.

This is an important feature to note because élitism is usually associated with some claim to social power and the élites constitute groups or corporations. Elitism is a claim both to a special kind of knowledge or skill and to certain privileges or rights to action. The nineteenth-century Oxford Professor of Greek, Benjamin Jowett, believed that the classics he taught were a means of preparing leaders of the home and colonial civil service.

Whatever the content of the classical humanist heritage – and it has shown a remarkable capacity to change and adapt, from mathematics and philosophy, to theology, to classical languages, to literature, for example, according to changing cultural circumstances – it has been the task of the guardian class, including the teachers, to initiate the young into the mysteries of knowledge and the ways in which knowledge confers various kinds of social power on those who possess it.

In the writings of the Athenian philosopher Plato, especially in his two educationally significant treatises, *The Republic* and *The Laws*, classical humanism tended to become a static ideal. It was assumed that the quest for knowledge could, in principle, ultimately yield permanent truths which transcended all actual political and social situations. The guardians were given the task of sustaining and transmitting these truths, or at least of training the young in the quest for these truths, and at the same time they were to provide the young with appropriate styles and graces for effective political and social leadership.

In the twentieth century, the knowledge content of classical humanism is not static, but it is still held to confer leadership rights. Invariably, in classical humanist doctrine, the potential leaders are given a different and separate education from that of the masses. The common school and the common curriculum play little part in this tradition, except possibly in the education of very young children.

Once a decision is taken about the proper content of schooling, or the appropriate institutional structures – notably universities and grammar schools – it is characteristic of classical humanism that a firm tradition is established and beliefs and practices, which might be of quite recent origin, are sanctified and rigorously enjoined on all who would seek to be educated. Grammar schools in twentieth-century England are a case in point. As noted above, the tradition has shown itself capable of change, but the principle of continuous adjustment and adaptation to circumstances has never been admitted.

It has been characteristic of classical humanism to attack innovativeness in other theories while accommodating its own tenets to the changing needs of the social leaders in whose education it has always proclaimed an overriding interest. The Black Papers are classical humanist in orientation, although there are much more cogently argued forms of the theory, for example the writings of Matthew Arnold, T. S. Eliot, F. R. Leavis, G. H. Bantock and the American scholar Irving Babbitt.

Classical humanism has drawn significant distinctions between the classes who are to be educated. These distinctions usually relate to either intellectual potential or social class or both. For example, Plato outlined, with unparalleled vigour and detail, the framework of nurture and schooling within which a cultural heritage was to be communicated to the mass. Only a tiny élite in Plato's scheme was to be granted freedom to pursue inquiry untrammelled, and this only after a basic commitment to the stable values of the state had been thoroughly inculcated. Plato was prepared to resort to tricks and deceit in order to select and to maintain the purity of his élite. In the twentieth century we have adopted more scientific forms of selection, but they are far from perfect, and the evidence is overwhelming that social class remains a major determinant of élite membership. This mass – minority distinction, and the emphasis on a curriculum which reinforces differences within an orderly, hierarchically structured régime, has always characterized educational theorists in the classical humanist tradition. Professor Bantock, for example, advocates a form of schooling which accepts the classical dichotomy between high culture and mass culture.

Bantock (1968) wants a curriculum that gives less prominence, for the masses, to literacy, and to what he calls 'a watered-down version of the same culture that is thought adequate for the brightest'. Instead of watering down 'high culture', which is appropriate only for the élite, Bantock advocates a radically different curriculum for the masses. For them he proposes a wide range of activities based on the 'primary experience', the 'face-to-face interests of the folk': hence his antipathy to the common-core curriculum, one of the tenets of faith of democratic ideologists who aim to develop a common consciousness of social and political life through core studies.

In Bantock's view the concept of the 'common core' curriculum

denotes the imposition of an abstract educational provision, derived from social and political principles of little relevance to the situation, on the living reality of children with their immense range of interests and capacities, deficiencies and handicaps, all of which need careful consideration in order to serve their best interests (1968, p. 62).

It is, of course, important to relate the curriculum to the 'best interests' of children. (It would be odd to relate it to their worst interests, or to ignore their interests.) However, by 'best interests' Professor Bantock, like all writers in the classical humanist tradition, has in mind not just the individual psychology of children but a conception of what ought to interest them. This turns out to be the folk culture, which is different in quality and form from the high culture which it is the prerogative – and responsibility – of intellectuals to safeguard.

Thus when he says that the 'common core' curriculum denotes 'the imposition of an abstract educational provision, derived from social or political principles of little relevance to the situation', what Bantock is afraid of is that what *he* regards as unsatisfactory principles will prevail. His own theory is part of an action programme which idealizes a certain kind of culture and clearly has social and political implications.

Important questions are raised here. Clearly it is neither desirable nor possible to educate everyone in the same way. Differences in intelligence, interest, aptitude for studies and many other factors in the learning situation point to the need for a differentiation of studies. However, the mass – minority distinction can be an extremely crude one which fails to recognize either difficulties of classification or the wider social consequences of sharp dichotomies which are built into the educational process. It is not being suggested in this unit that any one ideology is superior on all counts to all others. (How does one go about demonstrating such superiority?) Rather, we are aiming to raise the broader social, political and cultural issues which lie behind apparently straightforward educational recommendations.

As mentioned above, the classical humanist tradition in education has shown a remarkable capacity to accommodate itself to social change. One of its central curriculum concerns has always been the preservation and transmission of the values and contents of particular sub-cultures, for example Bantock's 'high' and 'folk' cultures. 'High' culture has not always meant the esoteric achievements of the intellect. For example, in the classical world a variety of high cultures were valued. The distinctive ways of life of those occupying leadership positions in society were transmitted and preserved through different kinds of educational programmes – hence the 'culture' of the farmer, the knight, the doctor, as well as those of the politician and the intellectual, all formed distinct educational traditions.

The changes since that time have, however, one thing in common: the orientation is always towards achieving or recapturing a standard which was built up at some time in the past. For the classical humanists there is a sense in which things are never as good as they have been in the past: first we had the age of gold, then that of silver, and now we live in the age of iron. Like all traditional doctrines, classical humanism sets for the present and future generations of learners a standard designed for them by their forefathers. The standard constitutes both an ideal to be striven for and a heritage to be transmitted.

Consequently, in education, classical humanism has been associated with clear and firm discipline, high attainment in examinations, continuity between past and present, the cohesiveness and orderly development of institutions and of the myths and rituals engendered by these institutions, and it has been associated with predefined views about what it is fitting to do, feel, think, and with standards of performance in all spheres. Education may be active but is always primarily an assimilative process: induction into institutions; acceptance of defined values and standards; initiation into clearly articulated modes of thought and action.

References

ARNOLD, M. in WILSON, J. DOVER (ed.) (1932) *Culture and Anarchy*. Cambridge: Cambridge University Press.
BANTOCK, G. H. (1968) *Culture, Industrialisation and Education*. London: Routledge and Kegan Paul.
DEWEY, J. (1921) *Democracy and Education*. New York: Macmillan.
DEWEY, J. (1929) *The Quest for Certainty*. New York: Milton, Balch and Co.
ELIOT, T. S. (1948) *Notes Towards a Definition of Culture*. London: Faber and Faber.
ROUSSEAU, J. J. (1911) (trans. FOXLEY, B.) *Émile*. London: J. M. Dent and Sons Ltd.

1.2 The Culture of the Schools

G. H. Bantock

The discipline of the school

The school is heir to a very long-standing tradition, implicit in the whole Christian heritage, which sees in man an antagonism of forces. It is, of course, inevitably a moral agency; the notion of education, as Professor Peters has recently pointed out, has a value assumption built into it. And the morality it has inherited, both implicitly and explicitly, is essentially one of conflict. Accordingly, the child is thought of – or was thought of until recently – as being a bundle of urges and impulses, many, if not most, of an undesirable nature. Therefore he must be submitted to a regimen of discipline, so that he can be helped to control the more destructive part of his nature and give rein to the better, more constructive side. Various ways of expressing this would be to say that he must overcome the burden of original sin by which he is by nature oppressed; that he must conquer impulse and passion by reason; or that he must keep the Id under restraint through proper Ego control, aided by the Super-ego. The aim, fundamentally, has been to produce a moral, rational being, capable of self-direction and self-responsibility, latterly to take his place as a free citizen in a free society. This picture of the child as a conflict of forces has been modified but not finally repudiated by 'progressive' ideas in education; but of this I shall say more later.

It is clear, for instance, that the gains of the school are long term. Before even their more tangible results – in the guise of examinations and certificates – become apparent, a good deal of disciplined work has to be undertaken. The pupil has to subordinate immediate satisfactions – playing out, hobbies, and so on – to later benefits. The work itself often conveys no immediate enlightenment in compensation, and it is not always as well adjusted to the psychological development of the pupil as it ought to be; it makes demands, that is to say, that the pupil can only imperfectly accommodate. It runs contrary to the interests and expectations of many homes and, at best, is supported there as an element whose function it is to procure future pecuniary benefits in terms of better jobs and the like.

All this [. . .] implies a very serious inroad on 'natural' inclinations and propensities. Here lies at least part of the explanation for the fact that the classroom is nearly always a scene of some tension and conflict; and why concepts like 'discipline', 'rewards', 'punishments' make their way into the traditional pathways of the school. Of course, it is quite true that in fairly recent years, in the state system at any rate, attempts in some sectors of

Source: BANTOCK, G. H. (1968) *Culture, Industrialisation and Education*. London: Routledge and Kegan Paul, Chapter 2.

schooling have been made to work in terms of a rather different set of assumptions, in line with a rather different ethic. Here the key lies, not in the imposition of restraints, but in their lifting. This stems from a different tradition of human assessment – one which asserted the 'natural goodness' of men and blamed their shortcomings, which are all too observable, on to the corruptions of the society into which they are born (how men ever become corrupt originally, if they were born good, was never satisfactorily explained). This line of educational thinking, which stems from Rousseau via Pestalozzi and Froebel, implied that natural impulse was a good thing, and urged a much less authoritarian role for the teacher: he should, according to Froebel, be 'passive and protective, not active and interfering'. He was to *follow* the child's spontaneous interests, teach through situations rather than by instruction, use the discipline of things rather than that of people. In this way one would inevitably fall into line with children's psychological development, and would thus match the logic of material with the growth of mind and body. It is an attractive theory, but, of course, it does not entirely work. Sin gets in somehow and the projected harmony of inner being and outer world breaks down. Authority is still needed, as even the most cursory study of Rousseau's *Émile* (1911) indicates; but the authority tends to be one of manipulation rather than that of direct intervention. It is still the teacher who must prepare situations – and, moreover, the *right* situations in the correct order. It becomes clear that it is only certain impulses that can be encouraged; it is still 'moral' rather than 'natural' man that we are concerned about. Learning of this intellectual complexity cannot be made entirely attractive – there is inevitably an element which may well be regarded as drudgery involved.

The purpose of all this discipline [. . .] is very much to induce *understanding*. There are obvious exceptions to this. Physical education, various arts and crafts, a variety of practical skills (domestic science and the like) emphasise doing rather than pure cognition; though, even here, of course, there is usually an intellectual, theoretical element. But the central core of the school curriculum emphasises learning of an intellectual sort – properly conceived, that is, because it often degenerates into memory work. English, a modern language, history, geography, social studies, technical subjects, mathematics, the sciences – these are the disciplines that play a major role in our schools. In their full development, they constitute the modern guise of 'high' or 'minority' culture. For less able children they appear in watered-down versions; attempts are made to integrate them in projects, so as to give a real-life orientation and appeal. They are displayed in their practical applications – French, for instance, appears as spoken rather than literary French. But the core remains scientific, technical, social and humanistic. The aim implicit in the curriculum, or explicit in government reports of the last hundred years, is to help children to learn to *think*. The emphasis is pervasively on cognition – certainly rather than on affectivity. It is, indeed, explicitly the aim of the comprehensive school, towards which we are inevitably moved by government intention, to provide a common core curriculum of mainly intellectual work for at least the first two or three years of the secondary stage; and, with minor modifications, this common element is provided for all children except the badly retarded who require remedial help. Again, treatment may differ from level to level, approach may alter, range and depth of study within the framework may vary; but, in all cases, what is done shares one broad characteristic – *it nowhere seriously touches those cultural experiences in terms of which a considerable majority are going to spend the rest of their lives.* Even the arts which are practised have practically no roots in the community at large and, therefore, exist largely as hot-house exercises. Where will school leavers find the opportunities to pursue any interest they may have found in *practising* modern educational dance, pottery, drama, even art and music? There are adult education classes – but these attract only a tiny percentage, mostly drawn from the middle classes. There are local art, orchestral and drama societies – the latter usually for ephemeral West End successes rather than for serious drama. Even these, moreover, are usually middle-class preserves; they are in no way integral to the cultural life of the community, but represent groups (often cliques, with its slightly pejorative implication) of interested parties who meet as strangers, sharing little common life experience except where their mutual hobbies are concerned. I do not want to deprecate the devoted efforts of extra-mural lecturers, society secretaries, producers and similar workers. But the totality of their efforts is still marginal to a central and healthy cultural tradition. The bulk of the population find their interests in football matches, bingo, the milder forms of gambling, like football pools, and the communications of mass media. Whatever is done in school in the name of 'creativity' – and all honour to what *is* done – has no real roots in the life of the community, and tends to wither in the out-of-school environment. The mass media comprise the real cultural life (apart from 'hobbies') of most members of the community; and they play little part – except as peripheral 'aids' to conventional subjects – in the cultural life of the school. Folk music clubs alone offer wider possibilities.

But there are a number of children who go to schools who are nevertheless perfectly capable of making sense of the culture of the school, and who are going to make some use of what they learn afterwards. It is unfortunately true, however, that they are not always given the opportunity for understanding, making sense, in any real way. The subjects are treated, not as means to a complex understanding of our common life, but as means to getting through examinations. The tutelary deity of our schools for the more intelligent (both Alpha and Omega) is called G.C.E. Examinations play an inescapable role: structuring the culture of the school. [. . .]

[GCE examinations] have come to seem restrictive rather than releasing for several reasons. As instruments of social mobility, means through which the school has come to take on its major role in the distribution of life chances, they have come to exercise a disproportionate amount of educational attention. Pupils want to pass; teachers measure their 'success' in terms of the number of passes their pupils attain. Whatever the idealists may say about learning for learning's sake, understanding and the production of the 'thinking being', the schools have very largely substituted their own realistic goal of learning for the examination's sake, and success gained in terms of the number of A- and O-levels. A recent survey in a South of England Grammar School (King, 1965) indicated to how little an extent the staff had succeeded in conveying their own values and ideals to their pupils; 'disinterested learning' is still what the grammar school, in general, considers itself as pursuing – at least, this tends to be the stated opinion of the staff, however little some of them may be concerned with anything other than the examinations. Their pupils apparently don't even pay lip service to the wider purpose; they know the rat race is on and they act accordingly.

There are two further objections on rather more fundamental, ideological grounds. Some forms of testing have been criticised on the grounds that they tend to favour children from middle-class background. Such children acquire a fuller and better vocabulary and are thus more able to cope with verbal intelligence tests, which have in the past played a considerable part in the eleven-plus selection examination, for instance. The answer here, I would have thought, is fairly clear. The school cannot revolutionise society (*pace* John Dewey) and must make the most of what is offered it. If some children come to school better equipped verbally than some others, I cannot think that this provides an excuse for holding them back in the often rather doubtful hope that these others will catch up. Vocabulary is clearly fundamental to progress in school subjects – without the ability to handle the relevant concepts, children are quite unable to acquire the various disciplines, whatever might be posited about their innate 'natural' abilities. The fact that there is thought to be a certain amount of 'wastage' does not provide an excuse for creating further wastage. It is possible to direct other criticisms against intelligence tests, but this is not altogether a reasonable one. As verbal ability is so strong a factor in scholastic success, any clue as to children's abilities to handle language should provide a useful guide as to future attainment. The objection is based on social and political rather than educational grounds.

The other objection is made on social grounds also. Examinations, it is argued, stress competition rather than co-operation; they foster the good of the individual participant rather than that of the group, 'good' here implying the ability to get ahead. This criticism rests on the ethical proposition that what we want is a less competitive, more co-operative form of society. This proposition, like most such, is of so vague a nature that it is really not possible to pronounce one way or another. What we need to define much more closely is what it is we are supposed to co-operate about; there are certainly some things that we ought not to be co-operative about, as the Nazi régime would clearly and instantly illustrate. I am reminded of T. S. Eliot's dictum: 'Fortunate the man who, at the right moment meets the right friend; fortunate also the man who at the right moment meets the right enemy'. (Eliot, 1948). Of course, it is arguable that this is a vague pronouncement like the other, that we need to define these 'right moments'. This is true; what is important in the remark is the realisation that conflict can be as 'creative' as co-operation. Education is not politics; in politics a major aim lies in the elimination of conflict lest such antagonisms should come to take on a more dangerous and disruptive appearance leading to armed force and the break-down of civil (and civilised) life that implies. But in education, the rubbing of one mind against another contains important cultural possibilities. The non-streamed class, for instance, is another political rather than educational desideratum. Bright children benefit from contact with minds of equal intensity. There are other ways of meeting the specifically educational criticisms which, not unjustly, are directed against streaming than that of simply abandoning it *in toto*.

The main objections against examinations, then, are educational ones. Examinations undoubtedly provide incentives for pupils who, quite naturally, do not possess the foresight to see the more far-reaching benefits of the education they receive. On the other hand, they distort the nature of the subject matter and tend to substitute success in the examination for the clarification which the study of a subject should bring about. But they remain essential instruments of allocation in a society that requires so many gradations of expertise for its running. They are instruments of efficiency – and, in a society geared in large measure to efficiency, they are obviously here to stay. Any assessment of the nature of the culture of the school, then, must give them a central place in diagnosis. They form the nearest equivalent we have to the old initiation ceremonies of primitive tribes, the *rites de passage* which marked the difference between childhood and participation in the adult occupations of the tribe.

Academic subjects

My assumption all along, of course, is that subjects matter for those who can cope with them. Underlying my comments has been a view of the possible nature and function of the conventional school subjects which I must now make more explicit. 'Subjects', today, in some circles, are rather at a discount – as can be gathered from that hoary old cliché which is trotted out with considerable frequency, especially by primary school teachers: 'I teach children, not subjects.' It is as well to realise that there is no such process as simply 'teaching children'; it is always necessary to teach them something. The verb 'teach' requires a direct as well as an indirect object. Once we are forced to ask 'What do you teach?' the answer will usually fall within one of the recognised subject areas, whether the teacher likes it or not. There are, obviously, ways of breaking down what are termed 'subject barriers' so that the interconnection between different subjects is seen; but as soon as one puts it this way, the basic necessity of recognising subjects as such is at once apparent; only in terms of defining vertically various areas of study does the horizontal arrangement of the cross-subject project make any sense; it relies, to become viable, on the mastery within various subject fields of certain elementary classifications and concepts, which then ˌbecome employable within the new arrangement.

And, indeed, classification by 'subject' is not an arbitrary device imposed for the greater bewilderment of the young, an unnecessary perversity thought up by academics for the purpose of staking a claim to their own territorial rights, but simply, in the early stages at least, the most fruitful and convenient mode of organising knowledge so that it can be profitably studied and can lead on to new understanding. The world presents to us an undifferentiated mass of data which only the mind can organise into manageable proportions, through a series of models and conventions which make thinking possible, let alone fruitful. Subject areas are made up of these models and conventions: experts may argue as to which are precisely the *most* convenient and the *most* fertile; but, all are agreed that some such organisation is essential to allow experience to be handled intellectually at all.

And it is learning to think, or otherwise behave, within an important subject area that forms an essential element in any true education. Here I am implying a wide definition of subject area – using it to refer to conventional academic or practical or artistic subjects; hence my reference above to 'otherwise behave'. All that is learnt in school, at whatever level, implies discipline, ways of organising material, conventions of behaviour or activity. We only reduce the chaos of the world to some sort of order by learning relevant concepts and modes of organisation; otherwise we could never grasp the flux of experience.

Where the more conventional academic subjects are concerned – the ones that make up the bulk of the school time-table for practically all our children, at least for a considerable time during their school career – it is, of course, not the ability to parrot facts that constitutes the essentials of education, but the capacity to handle facts, to understand their interrelations, to see the interconnections between fact and theory, to distinguish between relevant and irrelevant argument, to handle the concepts relevant to the subject with confidence and to see how they fit into the structure of knowledge concerned, to come to an understanding of boundaries, to see the links with adjacent disciplines, and so on. Application rather than accumulation is the key to modern attitudes to learning; hence the emphasis on problem solving rather than on the acquisition of facts. It is more the pity that conventional examinations do not necessarily examine those features of subjects which are within the grasp of children of the age concerned.

References

ELIOT, T. S. (1948) *Notes Towards a Definition of Culture*. London: Faber and Faber.
KING, R. (1965) 'Grammar School Values', *New Society*, 1 July 1965.
ROUSSEAU, J. J. (1911) (trans. FOXLEY, B.) *Émile*. London: J. M. Dent and Sons Ltd.

1.3 The Curriculum Mongers: Education in Reverse

John White

There was, not so long ago, what might be called a radical tradition in secondary education in this country [the UK]. Remnants of it still exist here and there – although, ironically, the longer Labour has been in power the more the tradition has disintegrated. How and why this disintegration has come about is what I wish to investigate here.

It may seem odd to talk of the decay of radicalism in this way. Isn't it true, on the contrary, that there has scarcely been a time of such rethinking as in the last few years? And not only by theoreticians. Teachers themselves have never before been involved on such a scale – helping to forge new curricula on the committees of the Schools Council or in their local curriculum development groups; introducing interdisciplinary studies; removing the impersonality and mechanicalness of traditional education by tailoring courses more to individual pupils' needs, and pressing for school counselling services to strengthen pastoral care; breaking down the barriers between school and community; promoting action research in the classroom; revolutionising teaching by team-teaching and new audio-visual aids, language laboratories, teaching machines . . .

Why do I speak of the decline of radicalism at a time when our schools are being revitalised in every way? To put it as I think R. H. Tawney might have put it: radicalism in educational, as in industrial, reform is essentially about *ends*. The 'new' thought in education has avoided ends and substituted an obsessive devotion to means. All the colourful new departures I have mentioned are only machinery: like any machinery they can be put to bad ends as well as good, serving reaction as efficiently as reform. This, briefly, is why the radical tradition is disintegrating; our very fascination by machinery has made us forget what we are about.

What are the ends, as the radical sees them? Very briefly, a good education system is one designed to help create a good society. A good society is one in which desire for *status* – power, wealth, prestige – is no longer the mainspring of social life, where no more reverence is paid to the bank manager than to the boilermaker; each is seen as contributing equally to the common good.

But this is not in itself sufficient. We may respect the boilermaker as a man, even though he leads a life cut off from higher culture, from art, the sciences and philosophy. This is nothing more, so far, than the Christian ethic, without its transcendental trappings. Radicalism is grounded in this Christian ethic but goes beyond it: it claims there is no necessary connexion between a professional career and access to the higher culture. This connexion exists *de*

Source: *New Society*, 6 March 1969, No. 336.

facto, but is not rationally based. If most children will later have to do jobs which are not intellectually demanding, there is no reason why they should be taught only those things which will make them efficient workers – and perhaps efficient consumers and law-abiding citizens as well.

For men are not only workers or consumers or good citizens: they are also *men*, able, if taught, to contemplate the world of a poem or a metaphysical system as well as to enjoy more easily accessible pursuits. If, as Tawney said, we think the higher culture fit for solicitors, why should we not think it fit for coalminers – those 'other inhabitants of places of gloom'?

The radical's aim in education to help produce a society in which everyone is acquainted with the higher culture entails more specific objectives in the schools. For it follows from this that every secondary school child, unless good reasons can be produced to the contrary, should be initiated into those forms of experience which together constitute this higher culture – the arts, mathematics, the human and physical sciences, philosophy . . . i.e., very roughly, activities whose nature, unlike cookery, say, or cricket, is utterly incomprehensible until one begins to engage in them. It follows from this, too – and this is merely another way of making the same point – that every secondary school child should be given a compulsory curriculum in at least these forms of thought. None should be allowed to drop any of these disciplines until he is sufficiently inside it to understand why its devotees are devoted to it.

This would mean in practice that every child should carry all these disciplines to something like sixth-form level. However much some individuals may race on past this point, in the same time as it takes the average child to reach it, still no one should normally leave school without having attained this basic understanding of the disciplines. If he is 'less able' at one of them – mathematics, say – then, far from being allowed to give it up in favour of something with which he can cope, he should be given *more*, perhaps differently oriented, teaching in the discipline, so that he *becomes* able at it. Ability in this context is not a given thing, but a goal.

This, then, is what radicalism implies in practice. All secondary schools must provide a compulsory curriculum in the higher forms of thought to all normal children. If they fail to do so voluntarily, they must be made to do so. This is no more than a spelling out of what I take to be the comprehensive ideal.

Here, I imagine, many will part company with me. Surely progress is incompatible with coercion, uniformity: isn't this scheme a return to the bad old days of close state supervision of curricula? Or perhaps it is an attempt to introduce state control on the French pattern, where according to the much scorned legend, at five past twelve on a certain day, each third form history class in each lycée in the land . . . Progress means not uniformity, but diversity – diversity for each school to work out its own curricula as it sees best: for how can there be progress without experiment, without thought?

At this point the objector may point to the achievements of the 'new look' in secondary education with which I began. But let us take stock. If one accepts the radical view of the good society – that is, if one agrees that all men should be equipped to follow the higher cultural activities if they so choose, then how *can* the schools be left to teach what they want? If one school insists on compulsory games or metalwork, but not on compulsory physics or poetry-appreciation, then one cannot rationally both allow it to do so and at the same time oneself desire the radical end. For this way the end will never be attained – or if it is, it will be in spite of the school's efforts, not because of them.

There is no logical escape. Given the end, there must be public control over the curriculum, a public guarantee that no child shall be deprived of access to the higher culture. But this does not necessarily mean detailed state supervision of syllabuses on the French pattern.

First, as long as there is public control over what children are expected to have learnt by the time they leave school, there is room for all sorts of new techniques and experiments in methods of getting them to this end and there are infinitely many routes to the same destination.

Secondly, there is no reason why public control of the broad framework should be in the hands of the *state*, if by this is meant the government of the day. A Teachers' General Council is clearly another possible alternative, and no doubt a more desirable one. Just as the British Medical Council controls professional standards in medicine, so a general council of teachers could do the same for teaching—provided that there is sufficient common agreement about the ends of education.

I argue that all children must be compelled to study certain disciplines – history, physics, and so on. This does not imply that they must be taught these things by coercive methods – namely, by threats of punishment. Clearly there are more efficient and more benevolent ways of teaching them. There is no necessary connexion between compulsion and coercion. But this connexion is often made, at a not-too-conscious level, in a person's conceptual scheme – and constitutes a quite understandable, if not quite valid objection to the radical point of view I have propounded. [. . .]

There has been such a barrage of anti-radical opinion directed at the teaching profession that the original issue – that to do with ends and the nature of a good society – has been obscured. No doubt much of it is just a continuation of more ancient anti-radical thinking. But the result, if not the intention, is a confusion in the minds of many teachers, which does not so much turn them against questioning ends as prevent them from even seeing that there are questions to be raised about them. It channels their desires to improve the system wholly into the task of remodelling its machinery.

One fashionable line now being preached from educationists' pulpits is this: the very notion of there being aims, or objectives, in education, is a hopelessly muddled one. Educational theorists have talked far too long about such woollinesses as 'self-realisation' or 'the whole man'; teachers should forget all this claptrap and direct their thinking to the actual teaching situation, making sure that what they are doing is presented in such a way that children understand and want to learn.

Now there is some truth in this: some statements about the aims of education have often been intolerably vague. But it does not follow that we should give up talking about aims altogether. It is difficult to see how we rationally could do this. It may make sense to tell a teacher to pay attention to immediate classroom problems and forget the nonsense about *pseudo*-aims. But unless he is to be as blinkered as a slave, carrying out his master's orders punctiliously and holding it no business of his to inquire what their purpose is, he cannot but connect his present actions with larger, more long-term purposes.

Not all statements of aims are so vague as to be useless as a guide to conduct. The radical's aims are clear enough. The creation of a good society entails that all be initiated into the disciplines of the higher culture. The more teachers see each other as engaged in the *same* task, under the aegis of this shared, explicit radical rationale, the more one will be justified in talking of teaching as a united profession; the more atomistic they become, the more their horizons become restricted to the here and now, the more they will become like slaves.

A large share of the responsibility for turning the teachers' attention recently from ends to means must be attributed to the Schools Council, which [. . .] has been enormously active in promoting new ideas about curriculum reform. It may seem paradoxical that a body set up by the government specifically to get teachers to think more about curriculum ideas – both by having a majority of teachers on the central committee of the council and by setting up local curriculum development groups among teachers – should be the object of such a complaint. But I believe the complaint is justified. For in scarcely any of the innumerable working papers, reports and bulletins which have poured out from the council since 1965 has there been any consideration of the overall rationale of the curriculum. There have been papers on specific topics—science for the young school leaver, sixth-form curricular reform, Certificate of Secondary Education exams in different subjects, French in the primary school. But very little on the larger issues.

In a way, this omission is understandable in the light of the council's own official objective of upholding and interpreting 'the principle that each school should have the fullest possible measure of responsibility for its own work, with its own curriculum and teaching methods based on the needs of its own pupils and evolved by its own staff . . .' For it is not the Schools Council's job to get teachers to think out what shall be a *common* curriculum for all schools; this would fly straight in the face of its own terms of reference. It is by its constitution committed to an anti-radical position.

There is a further paradox here. On the one hand, as I have said, the Schools Council is committed to uphold the principle that every school should have its own curriculum, evolved by its own staff. On the other hand, most of its publications – at least its earlier ones have propagated a similar view about what curricula ought to be like.

Take, for instance, the repeated theme that subject barriers must be broken down and that the curriculum must be 'integrated'. Now, in one sense of the term, an integrated curriculum is highly desirable. But what I would like is a curriculum unified by a rational principle. The separate disciplines should be seen as fitting people to be members of the good society. This does not entail – though it does not rule out – any fusion of the disciplines. But 'integration' in the Schools Council sense has nothing to do with any such rational principle. It seems in many cases to mean the virtual disappearance of the disciplines, their swallowing-up in topic-based courses which may well keep school-leavers happily occupied, but seem to be more of a barrier than a help to their acquiring the higher culture.

Another depressing feature found in these papers, as in the Newsom report [Central Advisory Council for Education (England), 1963], is the emphasis on vocational education. There is everything to be said for vocational education, if this means that on leaving school everyone is intellectually equipped to understand what any vocation, 'professional' as well as non-professional, involves. But the only vocations which, in either the Newsom report or the Schools Council's papers, are to influence the curriculum of the young school leaver are those in manual or service industries. Why only these? No one can rationally prejudge that any normal child will never be able to hold down a professional career, so there is no good reason to cut him off from this. True, the economy needs non-professional workers; but there is no good reason to shape most children's education with only economic ends in view.

Reference

CENTRAL ADVISORY COMMITTEE FOR EDUCATION [ENGLAND] (1963) *Half our Future*. London: H.M.S.O.

1.4 Knowledge and Curriculum Planning

Denis Lawton

Education is concerned with the transmission of culture to the next generation; curriculum planning is concerned with the selection of knowledge for transmission and the principles by which the selection is made. I have re-stated the argument in this way to emphasize the crucial position of knowledge in the educational process – a point which tends to be obscured by some kinds of sociological discussion. [. . .]

Schools and the transmission of knowledge

I should like to begin by taking up [. . .] Bernstein's division of knowledge into common-sense knowledge and non-common-sense knowledge, and his suggestion that schools are concerned with various kinds of non-common-sense knowledge. If we mean by common sense the kinds of knowledge and view of reality which are 'picked-up' informally rather than learned system-atically this is a very useful distinction. If informal induction by family and peer group into common-sense, everyday reality were regarded as sufficient, then clearly schools would be quite unnecessary. But unlike many pre-industrial and pre-literate societies, our culture has become so complex that informal learning is insufficient for at least two reasons: the wide range of knowledge (and its rapid growth) which is regarded as necessary for a general understanding of our culture; and the need for education to lay the foundation for specialized vocational training. [. . .]

Before proceeding with this analysis it would be as well to emphasize one point. In accepting the useful distinction between common-sense knowledge and school knowledge, I am not suggesting that they are completely different or that there is no connection between them. I would suggest that school knowledge or academic knowledge is an extension and refinement of common-sense reality.

The history of mankind is the long story of men interacting with the environment, interpreting the interaction in various ways and acquiring a degree of mastery over the environment. The accumulation of many generations' interactions with the physical environment (and with other people) is called knowledge. Each generation thus has the three-fold task of efficiently learning the knowledge acquired by previous generations, adding to it or modifying the interpretations, and finally passing this revised knowledge on to the next generation. If a culture is reasonably simple

Source: LAWTON, D. (1975) *Class, Culture and the Curriculum*. London: Routledge and Kegan Paul. Chapter 5.

everything may be regarded as common sense, but as skills and technology become more and more complex, more specialized learning becomes essential.

[. . .] The key to human learning is the power to generalize: every incident of experience is unique, but if we regarded all events as unique, learning would be impossible. We only learn by seeing relationships, and in order to see relationships, we need concepts. Concepts are formed by making particular incidents or things into classes: we conceptualize by classifying. [. . .]

Knowledge and the disciplines

But thinking does not stop at the point of making single concepts or single generalizations. Just as we link unique events by analysis to form concepts, so we link some concepts together and exclude others to form conceptual systems. Part of the learning process is concerned with seeing which kinds of concepts and generalizations are related to each other or fit together, and which do not. For example, quite young children learn that it is regarded as inappropriate to talk of a 'naughty lawn-mower' – the word 'naughty', and others conveying moral disapproval or approval, have to be collocated with some kind of intention, whereas lawn-mower belongs to a technology-set of inanimate, non-feeling objects. That kind of distinction in language is acquired early on in the world of everyday reality, but slightly more complex examples would take us into the kind of conceptual network which we call *disciplines*.

[. . .] If we ask the question 'Why disciplines, or why different forms of knowledge?', I suggest that there are four kinds of answer which we should examine:

1. Because reality is like that.
2. Because different sorts of questions are being asked.
3. Because children develop in that way.
4. Because disciplines promote more economical learning.

(1) Disciplines justified in terms of the nature of reality A naïve, realist point of view is that the world exists 'out there', with certain fixed characteristics, and man's search for knowledge is a simple cumulative process of gradually uncovering more and more of 'Nature's secrets'.

[. . .] But even in those branches of science concerned with the physical world, it is increasingly difficult to regard knowledge as uncovering 'the truth': it is a much more complex process of puzzle-solving within theoretical frameworks created by scientists. [. . .]. In the social sciences the 'human contribution' by way of theories and ideologies is even greater. Thus 'reality' is a combination of man-made and natural phenomena. [. . .]. Facts do not 'speak for themselves', they only 'speak' in some kind of meaningful context – which is always man-made. The extent to which reality is man-made or 'natural' is a point which sharply divides philosophers and curriculum theorists. Phenix (1962, pp. 273–80), for example, is firmly committed to the 'realist' position, that is that there is a real objective world which we gradually discover, classify and reduce to meaningful knowledge. [. . .] Phenix has stated the realist position in an extreme form – some would say an extravagant form. Nevertheless there are many who would agree with him. Unfortunately Phenix's statement is not only extreme but also does less than justice to the case for disciplines. What should be contrasted with nominalism is the view that the way in which we have come to conceptualize the world *does* eventually get at the real essence of things even if our methods of classification are developed for a variety of reasons, including some social or political ones. [. . .]

But the rejection of the extreme kind of realism put forward by Phenix does not mean that we have to take up an equally extreme kind of nominalist position: a *via media* is much more fruitful. In other words, the kind of nominalism which suggests that classifications are mere conventions does not necessarily cut out the existence of meaningful constraints on mere conventions, that is given that one could classify things differently for different purposes, there are still limits imposed by the nature of the universe. There is something about the world that both makes classification possible and yet prevents some kinds of classification. There are limits which are imposed not by man's traditions or conventions but by the nature of reality. These kinds of distinction may be very important for curriculum planning because questions about disciplines relate to questions about purposes or the questions being asked (see 2 below), whereas for an extreme realist (or essentialist) the questions being asked are, logically, irrelevant, i.e. the 'real world' simply 'exists' out there, and all we have to do is find out about it. It seems much more likely that our classifications of reality expressed in the disciplines are partly conventional (i.e. they could be rearranged) and partly 'real'.

(2) Different disciplines ask different questions This leads us to the second argument in support of basing a curriculum on disciplines, namely that the various disciplines are asking different kinds of questions and making different kinds of statement. Thus the 'same' landscape will be seen in different ways by a geologist, who might be interested in the rock formations, a historian who analyses its importance in the result of a significant battle, or an artist who wants to paint it. Different kinds of question are being asked, which leads to different kinds of methods of procedure and different end-results. It is clearly important that *at some stage* [. . .] pupils should come to see the differences between disciplines, and the curriculum is an important means of organizing this. Unfortunately, in the past, schools have often only succeeded in differentiating between disciplines at the cost of ignoring the relationships between them.

(3) Disciplines and the nature of human learning The third argument in favour of basing a curriculum on disciplines concerns the view that *children learn in this way*. This argument might be closely connected with the work of Piaget. [. . .] The last chapter of *The Development of Logical Thinking from Childhood to*

Adolescence (Piaget, 1958) is extremely relevant in this connection. [. . .] Piaget's work certainly provides some support for the view that the process by which children classify experience is not simply the result of the social norms of the culture they happen to be born into: there is something in human mental structure that facilitates certain kinds of conceptualization. There is evidence about a human predisposition to categorize in certain ways not only in the fields of mathematics and science, but also in moral development (Kohlberg, 1964), and also the 'deep structure' of linguistic categories referred to by Chomsky (1966) in his work on children's acquisition of language. A child's development is neither simply a matter of socialization into cultural norms nor is it a question of automatic maturation. It is a very complex process of the interaction of a developing child with the social and physical environment.

There is [. . .] a good deal of evidence to justify the view that children do have predispositions to categorize reality in certain basic ways. But the emergence of knowledge is the result of a complex set of interactions between a unique individual (who possesses certain psychological predispositions to classify experience), the 'real world', and the set of interpretations of the real world which we refer to as culture. The basic predispositions referred to, do not correspond exactly with our own cultural constructs – the disciplines. [. . .] There is, however, enough evidence to suggest that children's understanding of reality will be enhanced by being able to make, at some stage in their development, those distinctions which correspond to some extent with 'disciplines' however defined. This does *not* mean, of course, that we should necessarily organize the whole curriculum on disciplines or subjects. But the discipline factor should not be ignored. [. . .]

(4) Disciplines and efficient learning Finally I should like to consider the fourth argument in favour of basing learning on disciplines or forms of knowledge – the suggestion that *learning by means of disciplines is made easier or more efficient.* [. . .] This psychological argument has been put forward by such curriculum theorists as Phenix (1962) to support his more philosophical views. Such arguments ought, however, to be related to empirical enquiry. There has been a good deal of speculation and discussion along these lines but rather less research. Much of what research has been done stems from the ideas of Bruner: 'Every subject has a structure, a rightness, a beauty. It is this structure that provides the underlying simplicity of things, and it is by learning its nature that we come to appreciate the intrinsic meaning of a subject' (Bruner, 1970, p. 314). Bruner has also given examples and evidence to support this view of the importance of structure in learning: 'Grasping the structure of a subject is understanding it in a way that permits many other things to be related to it meaningfully. To learn structure, in short, is to learn how things are related' (Bruner, 1965, p. 7).

[. . .] Similarly, Ausubel (1959, p. 79), in a critical review of some exaggerated versions of child-centred education and informal learning, appeals for more structure:

Even more important, however, is the realisation that in older children, once a sufficient number of basic concepts are consolidated, new concepts are primarily abstracted from verbal rather than from concrete experience. Hence in secondary school it may be desirable to reverse both the sequence and the relative balance between abstract concepts and supportive data. There is good reason for believing, therefore, that much of the time presently spent in cook-book laboratory exercises in the sciences could be much more advantageously employed in formulating precise definitions, making explicit verbal distinctions between concepts, generalising from hypothetical situations, and in other ways.

Whether or not these examples of discipline structures are 'real', or imposed by the culture, seems to be less important than the fact that they are necessary for efficient learning. [. . .]

How many disciplines?

If the suggestion that education should be based not only on knowledge but on the separate disciplines or forms of knowledge is accepted, it is necessary to see exactly what these disciplines are. There is some variety in the kind of responses given to this question – the answers range from three to eight or more categories. But this apparent contradiction may be less disturbing than appears at first sight – as usual in such discussion and in such classifications there is a difficulty of defining exactly what is meant by discipline. Considerable work has been done in this field by the American curriculum theorist J. J. Schwab (1962). Schwab puts forward four bases for classifying disciplines: first, the *subject matter*; second, the characteristics of the members of the particular *community of scholars*; third, the syntax they use, that is their *methods* of procedure and modes of enquiry; and finally the *kinds of knowledge* they are aiming at. Clearly such a four-fold system of classifying is likely to produce scholars working in disciplines which are partly 'real' and partly 'man-made'. There are real distinctions but the actual number of discrete areas or communities of scholars is *to some extent* fluid and the barriers arbitrary. [. . .]

Schwab (1962) [. . .] puts forward the view that there are three *kinds of disciplines*. He refers to these as the investigative disciplines (roughly mathematics and the natural sciences), the appreciative disciplines (the arts), and finally the decisive disciplines (the social sciences). Peterson (1960), on the other hand, recommends a curriculum of general education based on four main modes of intellectual activity: the logical, the empirical, the moral and the aesthetic.

H. S. Broudy (1962) has developed a curriculum plan based on five groups of disciplines which he derives from the theoretical work of Tykociner.

1 Bodies of knowledge that serve as symbolic tools of thinking, communication and learning. These include the language of ordinary discourse, of logic, of quantity, and of art.

2 Bodies of knowledge that systematise basic facts and their relations. These

disciplines (the sciences) give us a way of speaking and thinking about the world and everything in it; a way structured by the conceptual system that characterises each discipline.

3 Bodies of knowledge that organise information along the routes of cultural development. History, biography and evolutionary studies serve this purpose by giving some kind of order to the past.

4 Bodies of knowledge that project future problems and attempt to regulate the activities of the social order. Tykociner cites agriculture, medicine, technology, and national defence as examples of the former, and political science, jurisprudence, economics, and management as examples of the latter. We have also developed sciences to guide dissemination of knowledge, e.g. education, mass communication, journalism, library science, custodianship of records and relics.

5 The integrative and inspirational disciplines which create syntheses or value schema in the form of philosophies, theologies, and works of art.

Perhaps the best-known work on the structure and organization of knowledge in England is that of Paul Hirst (1966). Hirst states that all knowledge that man has achieved can be seen to be differentiated into a number of 'logically distinct domains or forms'. Hirst suggests that knowledge is possible only because of the use of patterns of related concepts in terms of which our experience is intelligible:

That there are distinct forms within knowledge can be seen by the logical analysis of the whole domain. These forms can be distinguished from each other in three inter-related ways. First, within the domain there are distinct types of concepts that characterise different types of knowledge. . . . Second, these concepts occur within different networks whose relationships determine what meaningful propositions can be made. . . . Third, the domains can be distinguished by the different types of test they involve for the truth or validity of propositions.

According to Hirst there are about seven forms of knowledge:

1 Mathematics and formal logic.
2 The physical sciences.
3 The human sciences, including history.
4 Moral understanding.
5 The religious form of knowledge.
6 Philosophy.
7 Aesthetics.

What all the above theorists have in common is much more important than the differences between them. First of all they agree that disciplines are distinguished from each other not only by their content, subject matter or substantive form, but also by the rules, concepts, and methods of validation. Secondly, they agree that education should be concerned with learning about the differences between disciplines and also the relations between disciplines. [. . .] Thirdly, the theorists seem to be agreed that education should include an understanding of all the disciplines. The concept of the educated man is closely connected with an appreciation of the full range of the different kinds of knowledge and educative experiences.

Thus we are provided with two important criteria for curriculum planning: the principle of adequate *coverage* of the disciplines, and secondly the importance of achieving adequate *balance* between the disciplines. If education in schools is concerned with the transmission of a general understanding of the world and a general basis for later vocational specialization, then care should be taken in the construction of school curricula to ensure that important kinds of knowledge are not neglected or ignored and also that too much specialization in one area does not take place at the expense of other areas.

References

AUSUBEL, D. P. (1959) 'Human growth and development'; reprinted in DE CECIO', J. P. (ed.) (1963) *Human Learning in the School*. New York: Holt, Rinehart and Winston.

BROUDY, H. S. (1962) 'To regain educational leadership', *Studies in Philosophy of Education*, No. 11.

BRUNER, J. S. (1965) *The Process of Education*. Cambridge, Mass.: Harvard University Press.

BRUNER, J. S. (1970) 'Structures in learning' in HAAS, G., WILES, K. and BONDI, J. (eds) (1970) *Readings in Curriculum*. Boston: Allyn and Bacon, 2nd edn.

CHOMSKY, N. (1966) *Cartesian Linguistics*. London: Harper and Row.

HIRST, P. H. (1966) 'Educational theory' in TIBBLE, J. W. (ed.) (1966) *The Study of Education*. London: Routledge and Kegan Paul.

KOHLBERG, L. (1964) 'Development of moral character and ideology' in HOFFMAN, M. L. (ed.) *Review of Child Development Research*, Vol. 1. New York: Russell Sage Foundation.

PETERSON, A. D. C. (1960) *Arts and Science Sides in the Sixth Form*. Oxford: Oxford University Department of Education.

PHENIX, P. H. (1962) 'The Use of Disciplines as Curriculum Content', *Educational Forum*, No. 26.

PHENIX, P. H. (1964) *The Realms of Meaning*. Maidenhead: McGraw Hill.

PIAGET, J. (1958) *The Development of Logical Thinking from Childhood to Adolescence*. London: Routledge and Kegan Paul.

SCHWAB, J. J. (1962) 'Disciplines and schools' in *The Scholars Look at the Schools*. Washington D.C.: National Education Association.

1.5 Lawton's 'Refutation' of a Working-Class Curriculum

Uldis Ozolins

The focus on what is being taught in our schools should be a welcome one: a decade of considerable structural change in education [. . .] has passed, and we are still beset with immense problems of inequality and seeming lack of effectiveness particularly in relation to the participation and retention of working-class pupils.

The last decade has however also brought more understanding of this situation, particularly from the application of cultural analysis to explore the phenomena of school culture, youth sub-culture and the widespread resistance to schooling. Behind much of the writing in the cultural analysis tradition is a clear concern that if schools are going to do more than merely provide the site of cultural conflict and heightened attempts at social control, the content of schooling will need to be substantially changed in the direction of providing 'really useful knowledge' to all pupils in our schools.

I will examine here the work of Denis Lawton, who has long been prominent in curricular debates in Britain and elsewhere, but who is also one of the few such theorists to address himself to the question of a 'working-class curriculum'. Lawton is most interesting for us in that he attempts a genuine synthesis of sociological, philosophical and pedagogic considerations in curriculum planning, and is keen to make explicit the principles upon which we can base a curriculum for all children. For Lawton, curriculum can be defined as 'essentially a selection from the culture of a society' and debate should proceed on just which aspects of our culture should be selected for transmission by our schools. [. . .] For Lawton, the notion of a working-class curriculum does immense harm in educational thinking (especially in pointing to an alleged 'middle-class curriculum') and serves only to take us away from the only viable democratic alternative (in his eyes) – a *common curriculum*.

I will assess Lawton's case in his book *Class, Culture and the Curriculum* (1975) and subsequently point to alternative considerations that seriously question Lawton's stance. [Page numbers in brackets in the subsequent text refer to Lawton's book unless otherwise indicated.]

The thesis

For Lawton, drawing a curriculum from aspects of working-class culture would be nonsensical for two interrelated reasons: first, that it is extremely

---

Source: JOHNSON, L. and OZOLINS, U. (eds) (1979) *Melbourne Working Papers*. Melbourne: University of Melbourne.

difficult to identify a strictly working-class culture that is viable and which stands apart from the dominant culture in British society today. And second, Lawton believes that the desire for a working-class curriculum (and opposition to the 'middle-class' curriculum of current schools) fundamentally misconstrues the relation between class, culture and knowledge. The transmission of *knowledge* is and should be the school's major function, and most of this knowledge can be characterized as *classless* knowledge.

Let us take each of these in turn.

A viable working-class culture?

Lawton takes a great deal of care in addressing himself to the question of whether a distinct working-class culture can be said to exist in contemporary Britain. He first of all looks at Bantock's *Culture, Industrialization and Education* (1968) as an example of the *wrong* way of thinking about working class and education. Bantock's concern is to point to the limits inherent in the modern attempt at mass education, particularly mass secondary education:

> According to Bantock, public or mass education has so far been a dismal failure, and this is largely because we have attempted to force a literary culture down the throats of the masses whose tradition is an oral one. (p. 13)

And this failure has come about because of ignorance of two quite distinct cultural traditions, whose origins pre-date the industrial revolution but whose heritage is still very much with us:

> There has been the culture of the upper classes based particularly on their ability to read and write. And there has been the culture of the ordinary people or 'folk', based largely on their traditions of oral communication. (Bantock, 1968, p. 3)

The chasm between high culture and low culture cannot be crossed by a common school curriculum, Bantock argues, and in particular the traditional academic curriculum is not suited to the masses of working-class children. Any attempt at such a common curriculum would result only in a dilution and bastardization of the high culture.

Although he introduces (rather arbitrarily in Lawton's eyes) some arguments from psychology, linguistics and heredity, Bantock is eager to stress that it is quite specific *cultural* differences that are crucial. The working class, with its long non-literary tradition, should have a curriculum which responds to this specific tradition: Bantock suggests such a curriculum should be aimed at practical common life, be concrete and specific rather than abstract, and should include aspects of television, film and popular press. It should not neglect the education of the emotions, be concerned with preparation for leisure, and finally it should avoid the usual concentration on reading: music and drama, art and craft should be developed in a suitable way for working-class children.

Lawton's concern with detailing Bantock's proposals foreshadows his attempts to deal just as critically with those on the 'left' who propose a distinct curriculum for the working class, and his criticisms of Bantock will in time be turned on this latter group. Why, asks Lawton, are we to accept Bantock's absolutely clear cut distinction between a working class and an upper class? Who will classify children as belonging either to the 'high' culture or the 'low' culture? Who will sort out the exceptions? On another tack, should not Bantock's 'practical concerns' (for example the media) be the concern of *all* pupils? And finally, is not all of Bantock's argument merely taking the child's destiny as 'given', and in fact *forcing* a certain destiny on a child because of her or his class background?

Bantock is wrong basically because he misperceives the reality of working-class culture today. Basing his insights largely upon the work of E. P. Thompson (1968), Lawton now argues that the process of industrialization had the most profound and destructive effects upon the traditional folk culture of pre-industrial life, the folk culture that is Bantock's basic building-block for his curriculum for the masses. E. P. Thompson has analysed the making of the English working class as involving four stages:

(a) destruction of traditional ways of life, especially of what we would now call cultural pursuits
(b) changes of work relationships, especially for craftsmen, and the loss of meaning of dignity in work-alienation
(c) reduced standard of living
(d) the growth of a conflict view of society, partly due to (b) and (c) above, but also due to deliberate political oppression, backed up by the economic ideology of *laissez-faire* (p. 34)

These processes had a traumatic effect upon the traditional culture – the loss of traditional rhythms, rituals and pastimes, the decrease of autonomy in work, changed family relationships, often extreme poverty, the forces of the state used to crush any resistance. According to E. P. Thompson (1968), these forces resulted in a political and social 'apartheid'.

Lawton now takes his next step: did not these dreadful forces result in a working-class culture

which was inferior or damaged in some ways? Writers as different politically as Bantock on the one hand and Cole and Postgate on the other, seem to assume that working-class culture was 'damaged' in some respects by the transition . . . Cole and Postgate talk of the working class being psychologically 'diseased'. They justify the use of this term by the supposedly irrational aspects of working-class life – such as turning to prophetic and Messianic religions, and their behaviour at public meetings, such as Chartist gatherings, which amounted to mass hysteria. To account for this 'irrational' behaviour, Cole and Postgate suggest that living conditions were so bad that 'escapist solutions were adopted on a wide scale'. (p. 41)

Lawton's aim here, it would appear, is not the denigration of working-class life, but rather an attempt to lay to rest the ghost of cultural relativism, the argument propounded by such authors as Midwinter that 'any sub-cultural values, attitudes and activities are just as good as any others – they are different but equal' (p. 28).

It is here that Lawton most vigorously criticizes the curricular assumptions of Midwinter that the traditional academic curriculum 'is irrelevant to the community, its children and both their needs' (Midwinter, 1972, p. 13). Lawton fears that the question of relevance begs far too much:

if an environment is an extremely limiting one, then to base the whole curriculum on 'relevance' to it may be to 'sell the children short' in a dangerous way. (p. 28)

This is even more the case when we deal with cultural extremes such as the 'culture of poverty', but it is here that Lawton's analysis becomes distinctly uneven and indecisive. Following Oscar Lewis and Maria Ossawska (1971), the particular poverty of Mexico City is characterized by

lack of privacy, gregariousness, alcoholism, physical violence, a more permissive attitude to sex, family solidarity, and a generally fatalistic attitude towards life accompanied by a distrust of authority. (p. 41)

But in asking whether such an analysis can be applied to contemporary Britain, Lawton begins to hedge his bets quite dramatically. [We lack, he suggests] 'a clear distinction between the twentieth-century working-class and the twentieth-century poor or severely disadvantaged' (p. 42). Moreover,

perhaps the analogy of health and disease applied to culture by Cole and Postgate is more misleading than helpful. It would be more in keeping with general anthropological thinking to avoid such blanket distinctions or value-judgements and talk, instead, of specific strengths and weaknesses of particular cultures for specific purposes. (p. 42)

Thus, the 'culture of poverty' can be seen as an adaptive process to an experience of extreme deprivation, and working-class adjustment in the early nineteenth century 'may have been effective in as much as it facilitated survival' (p. 42). But Lawton will not let this rest:

But we also have to ask whether, in the long run, certain communities have found themselves in cultural dead-ends, living in a way which limits opportunities outside the sub-culture? (p. 42)

Here is one clue to Lawton's thought: opportunities *outside* the sub-culture mark the degree of 'disease' or 'weakness' or 'inferiority'. But what is meant by such opportunities? Lawton engages in some rapid social engineering:

If we now want to abolish poverty must we destroy the culture of poverty? I would suggest that it is difficult to see how a culture can survive without its social and economic environment, therefore the culture of poverty should eventually disappear; but it should be stressed that this is *not* the same as working-class culture. (p. 43)

For presumably, Lawton does not foresee the immediate disappearance of the 'social and economic environment' that produces the working class. [. . .]

But perhaps these vagaries suit Lawton's argument well enough. Certainly, they allow him to 'suggest' a 'disease' or inferiority of at least some aspects of working-class culture, and leave this sufficiently vague ('opportunities' blocked off) to be threatening without being pointedly offensive. And by such analysis Lawton can also avoid any substantial analysis of the working class in the contemporary social structure. As a sop, he offers us also Cole and Postgate's observation that *middle-class* culture suffered a serious decline in the nineteenth century as well – in music, painting, architecture, as well as in social attitudes such as the spread of avarice, ruthlessness, selfish individualism and so on; again, a reminder that we *can* make judgements about cultures and should not be afraid to face up to them (p. 42).

Lawton seems almost relieved to talk of more contemporary issues which seem decisive for his case. In a brief survey of leisure patterns and patterns of cultural pursuits, Lawton argues that there are mostly insignificant differences between the social classes in the way most people spend their free time, in their range of media habits, and their cultural interests. The evidence that we are moving towards a common culture in the Raymond Williams sense (Williams, 1961) Lawton regards fairly optimistically.

As a final, perhaps surprising, argument that we are moving towards a common culture, Lawton argues that the strictly conflict view of society which attended the emergence of the urban working class has not in fact been carried over into twentieth-century working-class political life and consciousness. Following the work of Mann (1973), Lawton points to the 'hegemonic nature of capitalist society' as having diffused potentially revolutionary consciousness. The rise of the Tory-voting worker, for example, would indicate that class and political divisions are now more blurred and complex than ever before: deferential and oppositional attitudes are in some tension.

To talk of a working-class culture which today is vibrant, healthy, self-consciously assertive and an alternative to the dominant culture of the society seems to Lawton to be palpably contradicted by the evidence. And to base a school curriculum upon selecting out from a sub-culture elements that are in themselves suspect would be educationally irresponsible. Our attention must clearly be on a common curriculum.

Classless knowledge

The reality of a common culture, based on evidence of universal leisure pursuits, media patterns, cultural interests and common orientation to work and politics, are also used by Lawton to point us in another direction, one which he hopes will dispel the plausibility of a working-class curriculum and put us well on the way to a common curriculum. What Lawton is concerned to stop is the persistent argument that our schools are profoundly middle-class institutions, and that the curriculum they transmit can be essentially described as a 'middle-class' curriculum. Lawton's argument here is very broad and sweeping. Even though he admits schools may in some sense be considered 'middle-class' because of the background or socialisation of the teachers, he nevertheless is insistent on opposing the view that '*everything* that the school offers is middle-class culture and, therefore, of no value to working-class children'. He meets the issue head on:

in terms of high culture it is very misleading to see art, music and literature as middle-class, and . . . even more ridiculous to see science, mathematics and history as middle-class. (p. 51)

Lawton does admit that working-class children often have considerable difficulty in mastering the academic curriculum of secondary education, and is well aware that very often the forms of secondary schooling have been shrouded in middle-class rituals and assumptions. He is painfully aware of middle-class bias in teachers when they teach and label working-class children, and he agrees with Jackson and Marsden (1962) that some schools are misguided in their emphasis on 'middle-class manners, etiquette, and lower-level middle-class values'. But – and this is the crux of his argument – 'it is quite different from saying that the *knowledge* that grammar schools in the past have tried to transmit is middle-class' (p. 49).

Lawton's antecedents must be traced back carefully here: when we start discussing knowledge, Lawton argues, we must be philosophically literate and not confuse questions of a social nature with questions of basic epistemology: we must look to the way knowledge itself is structured and organized to enable us to understand how it can be transmitted through the school. And these questions cannot be reduced to questions of the social valuing or organizing of knowledge (we will witness his attack on the knowledge 'relativists' shortly) – what we need is attention to the analysis of knowledge itself, and for this Lawton relies upon the work of Hirst.

[. . .] As Lawton himself says, Hirst does not talk of a curriculum as a selection from the culture, and cultural factors seem to have little place in Hirst's view of how to organise education. For Hirst, the aim of education is essentially intellectual: the central objectives of education are the 'development of mind', and that development can best take place if thought of in terms of development of forms of knowledge'. For Hirst, and now for Lawton, the structure and organization of knowledge is universal rather than culturally based. And while sub-cultures may pose problems in terms of the *means* of education (how do we get *this* across to *these* children?), their existence does not suggest alternative *ends* for education.

Much of the rest of Lawton's book consists in a rather more leisurely exposition of these points: he writes on the nature of disciplines, of how we can understand the 'forms of knowledge' (Hirst says there are seven such forms, another author has proposed six . . .), and emerges in the end with his own fundamental forms of knowledge which can serve as the basis for a common curriculum, with each pupil having access to at least a basic understanding in each area. Lawton's six basic areas are:

1 mathematics
2 physical and biological sciences
3 humanities and social science (including history, geography, classical studies, social studies, literature, film and TV and religious studies)
4 expressive and creative arts
5 moral education
6 inter-disciplinary work

(p. 88)

But what has happened to class and culture? Lawton certainly does have worries about some aspects of a common curriculum. For a start, would such a curriculum be *received* by all pupils as common? It is possible that children from different backgrounds and of different levels of ability will receive a common curriculum in a highly differentiated way (p. 50). Lawton does want to say that the evidence of a common culture should warn us that extreme fears of this happening may well be over-exaggerated. But he is also aware that much needs to be done in changing teachers' attitudes – this he sees as by far the major barrier to the teaching of the common curriculum.

But that is all. This is the status of sub-cultures: they represent problems to be overcome. Having defined a curriculum in the beginning of his book as a selection from our culture of elements to be transmitted by the school, we are now on the slippery slopes of *classless* and *transcultural* knowledge in which the forms of knowledge must determine our curriculum. But for our analysis, what becomes most marked here is not so much a new view of knowledge so much as a serious contracting of the possible scope and aim of a school: whereas previously in the discussion the role of the school seemed at least to be up for serious debate, it is now asserted that there is only one aspect of culture that school can deal with, and that is a closely defined set of forms of knowledge. It is no help here to say that these are selections from our present day culture: the selection shows far more affinity to the traditional grammar school curriculum than to any present-day 'common culture' that Lawton has identified. Indeed, Lawton's description of what our contemporary culture looks like and what are its most important features and forces is nowhere to be found: he has no analysis of our culture, or of class relations within it. We can only remark on the rapidity with which his discussion on class and culture evaporates; his proposal of a common curriculum in the end seems to owe little to that discussion.

There is only one more enemy for Lawton to face: those who it seems, cast doubt on the forms of knowledge themselves. A chapter is devoted to strenuously opposing the notion of class bias in many of our forms of knowledge, especially as espoused by Marx, Mannheim, Berger and Luckmann and the contributors to *Knowledge and Control* (Young, 1971), particularly Young, Esland and Keddie. While he sees these authors as posing serious questions about the social organization of knowledge he wishes most of all to counter the extreme relativist tendencies he sees in their work, particularly in *Knowledge and Control*. [. . .] Lawton welcomes Young's study of the way certain forms of knowledge come to be enshrined in school curricula and how processes of selection are controlled and regulated. The important question of the status of different forms of knowledge is also noted, but Lawton draws back from Young's most radical implications:

It is, however, foolish to ignore the possibility that there may well be important characteristics of certain kinds of knowledge which are not irrelevant to their inclusion in or exclusion from school curricula. My main criticism, is, then, that Young's persuasive arguments in drawing our attention to some of the social factors in curriculum organization should not blind us to the fact that there may be other important factors as well as those he has dismissed: it is at least possible that some kinds of knowledge are superior in some meaningful way to other kinds of knowledge. (p. 62)

Specifically, Lawton goes on to rebut Young's view of the arbitrariness and artificiality of subject boundaries, the view that all knowledge is socially contracted, and Young's seeming implication that all rationality is merely a convention.

Bernstein is seen as another supporter of Lawton's basic position, through his emphasis on schools being concerned with non-common-sense knowledge, rather than with the common-sense knowledge of everyday life. This is used by Lawton to begin his defence of the fundamental role of disciplines in human knowledge as the organizing systems of the basic forms of knowledge, and we are quickly again within Lawton's six areas of curriculum. But not before Lawton makes one final, strange bedfellow: Freire. Lawton does not want to say that there is no connection between common-sense and non common-sense knowledge; rather, school knowledge must be seen as an extension and refinement of everyday knowledge: a 'gap' between the two merely indicates poor teaching. The real world of the child is certainly the beginning point of education. And he concludes –

Those curriculum theorists who advocate situation-centred learning (Freire, 1971) do not contest the importance of 'disciplines' – they argue for making them relevant to the 'situation' of the majority. (p. 71).

And Lawton would 'agree completely' with this emphasis. But one fears that Lawton by now is really agreeing with too much. Certainly his representation of Freire's work does an unconscionable degree of violence (through co-option) to Freire's thought; the aims of education for Freire are very different from what Lawton would have us accept with his common curriculum.

Critique

I want to set out cryptically a four-stage critique of Lawton's main thesis, pointing to serious lacunae in his argument. From this critique I will draw implications of what a worthwhile working-class curriculum may look like – a curriculum quite different from the meagre scraps that Lawton himself offers as examples of such a curriculum.

1 *Hegemony.* Lawton gives us, in the end, a reified view of schooling. The school is locked into performing one function: the transmission of knowledge. Totally ignored is the concomitant of this – that which the school teaches its pupils in its very process of selection, grading, testing and patterns of relationships. These concerns are only weakly covered by the notion of a 'hidden curriculum'. Lawton *does* point to some non-curricular problems: he wonders if a common curriculum will be *received* in a common manner, and he is aware that teachers' attitudes towards working-class children can be quite prejudicial. But he sees these as largely problems of making teachers aware of

their own hidden biases, and then working towards innovative techniques for teaching the basic disciplines, including using the everyday culture of the child as an occasional or more than occasional starting-point.

Lawton ignores much of the socializing effect of schooling, a socializing effect that relates the child very directly to notions of authority, of legitimacy and meritocracy, and to pervasive attitudes towards work and future life-chances conveyed by the school. Whether this is conveyed directly (civics, religious education) or implicitly (the hierarchical structure of school, the definition of 'success' and 'failure' at school), it is evident that the school is far more than a passive agent without an impact on basic political and social attitudes.

To make a plausible case, Lawton must at least suggest what are the non-curricular aspects that are part of a school's process of transmission. Implicitly, he does recognize this, but he refers only to such matters as 'middle-class manners, etiquette, and lower-level middle-class values' (p. 49). Far more non-curricular learning goes on, much of which is very directly connected to the patterns of social, political and class relationships that powerfully shape our society; it is only by evading some essential argumentation on these points that Lawton can so blithely formulate his curriculum based on the 'forms of knowledge'. But worse, Lawton forgets much that he himself had written in his earlier chapters on class: he mentions there that powerful hegemonic forces have done much to break down a viable, oppositional working-class culture. But he has failed to ask the vital question of what part the schools themselves may have had in this process. And of course, no possibility of counter-hegemonic forces is entertained.

2 *Hegemony and the disciplines.* The previous point may seem far removed from considerations of curriculum, but I want to now focus directly on the curriculum and ask: do the basic disciplines and the organization of knowledge *themselves* contribute to hegemonic processes? Lawton certainly had such an argument before him in *Knowledge and Control* (Young, 1971), in the work primarily of Bourdieu (whom he ignores) but also from Keddie and Young. Bourdieu in particular is concerned to show how it is that the academic curriculum itself serves as an instrument of differentiation and exclusion: it is not that pupils are taught vastly different sorts of curriculum nor that teachers may have prejudicial outlooks on their pupils; rather, it is that a common curriculum, 'effectively' taught, will itself be a biased form of education. In *Knowledge and Control* Bourdieu discusses the education of élites, and the way in which education of certain forms encourages cultural homogeneity among élites by emphasis on an academic curriculum. This curriculum serves to distinguish the élite and (because they fail to master it) severely restricts and rationalizes the life-chances of the working-class pupils. Elsewhere, Bourdieu (1974) has amplified these views in two directions: first, that the school works in a biased manner by demanding of *every* child what only some children can give – a certain orientation to the culture of the school and the academic curriculum, a certain 'cultural capital' that reflects the cultural level of the home and provides the children of *some* families with the

essential skills and attitudes ('cultural ethos') that lead to success in school. It is these children who are rewarded in school when their social gifts are interpreted as natural ability and interest. Secondly, the curriculum of the school cannot be treated as a neutral object: some elements, particularly the letters, humanities and social sciences, are peculiarly dependent on the child's cultural capital. They are taught by a pedagogy which makes continual, *implicit* demands on a child's own social and cultural skills – the skills of subtlety, nuance, taste and manner which some children acquire 'naturally' from their own cultural milieu *and which are not capable of an explicit pedagogy.*

3 *Work and social destiny.* Despite his insistence on the need for a common curriculum, Lawton tells us surprisingly little about what he expects the consequences of such a curriculum to be. Nor, apart from the most occasional references to educational failure, is there much concern with the present outcomes of schooling. To propose a common curriculum, Lawton must be willing to argue that it will serve the interests of all students, or at least that it will serve their interests more than will the present [. . .] curriculum. No such case is made out by Lawton.

Lawton's common curriculum is solidly based on the forms of knowledge, but this concern with formal disciplines and bodies of knowledge only makes sense if the disciplines are to be pursued further at a higher level of education. Indeed the point about disciplines is that they *do* lead somewhere – into the substantially rigorous, abstract, subtle bodies of knowledge of the type enshrined by our university specialization. [. . .]

But what of a curriculum for early leavers? It seems that the same will do for all: four years of mathematics, history, science, social studies and 'moral education' will give the pupils the same sort of knowledge that six years of the same study will give – only the amount and, perhaps in the last year or two, the intensity will vary. This is the school, in Bourdieu's terms, seemingly offering the same to everyone.

[. . .] Lawton's common curriculum shall in the end only assist those who stay longer in school and take most advantage of the academic rewards it offers; apart from his desire to produce a few more good sixth formers, Lawton is silent on the destiny of the majority of pupils and how relevant the common curriculum is to their needs; questions of relevance are indeed entirely eschewed.

Let us take seriously the question of work. The point is not merely that Lawton's common curriculum ignores the work destinies of many of its pupils: once again, it should be pointed out that the school is an active, deliberate agency in relating pupils to work. Some kinds of work are highly valued and implicitly and explicitly celebrated in the curriculum itself: cerebral work, work of a theoretical and scientific kind, work which is usually non-manual. For this kind of work, the school serves the function of providing work training (no matter how elegant and non-utilitarian its rationalizations). Other kinds of work are sometimes denigrated, sometimes pointed to as punishment, but usually ignored.

Many teachers would assert that it is not their function to prepare pupils for work here and now, but rather (echoing Lawton) to raise expectations. It is here that the curriculum is far more replete with hopes than with actual objectives: teachers 'hope' that the curriculum of the first three or four years encourages pupils to stay on at school; for those who do not stay on, there is the 'hope' that it has given them 'a basic education'.

This is not to deny that many teachers today are worried about employment prospects for their pupils. Where this is allowed to intrude into the curriculum there is an almost desperate attempt to quickly teach the 'right' attitudes or manners or skill at letter-writing which may enable the pupil to land a job at all. But teachers are quite divorced from the world of work and can offer little advice beyond this: work-experience programmes, although not common in many schools, lack an integration into the rest of the school (and Lawton does not seem to think them worthwhile as part of his common curriculum; once again, school is work experience for some pupils, the rest are ignored).

4 *Class and culture.* Lawton's usage of the concepts of 'class' and 'culture' should not go unremarked upon. On the concept of 'class' Lawton will be the first to admit that he is not propounding a comprehensive theory of class or even taking his application of the term in any theory beyond its most general sociological usage.

A very static view of class emerges from Lawton's work – he talks only of the 'working class' and the 'middle class' (with a few hints of an 'upper class'), and from time to time he seems to suggest that these classes are moving closer together in some sense but he does not talk of the relations between them. [. . .]

The notion of class is essentially a *relational* concept, but Lawton's evasion of present-day class analysis and concentration on such symptoms as media habits renders him unable to give any coherent account of what a working-class curriculum may be. It is precisely in such a class analysis that we can find the starting point for a working-class curriculum: rather than just a study of working-class culture and working-class life, it must be a study of the relations of the working-class to the rest of society; the forces by which this relationship is created and maintained, and the ways in which this relationship can be investigated, questioned, and eventually transformed.

We shall return to this argument shortly.

Lawton's restricted account of 'culture' is similarly debilitating: most seriously, it prevents him from being able to recognize the implications of cultural factors, as they affect schooling and educational outcomes. One example of this, already mentioned, is his inability to see the nature of the academic culture which children must face in the school; but not only cannot he see cultural factors in educational failure, he also seems unaware of cultural factors in the matter of resistance to schooling. He is quite concerned to show that the intelligence of low-achieving children has often been underestimated (by curricular planners as well as by practising teachers), but not at all concerned with the persistent cultural factors that shape resistance as an active force in the school, quite apart from the processes of teacher labelling or just plain bad teaching.

As Willis (1977) points out, the curriculum and its method of transmission themselves become focal points of attack by a culture of resistance. These factors also point to the consideration that hegemony is not always complete, but continually needs to be reasserted by new patterns of school organization.

Towards a working-class curriculum

I want to take seriously the concepts of work, class and hegemony in giving us three points of orientation in beginning the immensely difficult and complex task of thinking about a working-class curriculum. But these concepts do not just serve as points of orientation; I want to argue that a relation to work, to one's class position and to domination over others *is* taught in our schools. There are schools in our education systems which do actually perform a most active, persistent and quite conscious function in terms of training their pupils for work, equipping them with the right attitudes and beliefs to hold their 'place' in society and to acquire the resources to enforce compliance and respect from others. These schools teach their pupils about work, class and hegemony and teach it extremely well: they are precisely the schools (both private and state) that are heirs to long and successful academic and social traditions. They teach the sons (and often the daughters) of the well-to-do and the ambitious the tools of hegemony: how to manipulate and control social institutions and cultural norms for one's own end, and how to celebrate one's cultural superiority.

This tradition of schooling cannot claim that its own curriculum has been unconcerned with problems of power and control in society. If we ask: what kind of curriculum is most suited to those who will be the controlling figures in society, the answer historically seems to be: a curriculum which first of all camouflages this power behind other attributes – being cultured, being knowledgeable, being educated itself – while equipping its recipients with the skill and the perspectives of cultural arrogance and manifest destiny. Cultural superiority masks and stands in for economic and social superiority.

It is in making these sorts of relationship explicit, open for debate and counter-suggestion, that the working-class curriculum must begin. For a start, what skills, what power of analysis, what kinds of understanding of oneself and of society are needed to not only be able to work in production, but to survive and begin to see viable ways ahead for oneself and one's class? What does an auto-worker need to know? Or a bus driver? Or a secretary? How are women placed in production? The working class has been politically articulate for more than a century – how can schools help to improve this articulation?

The central axiom of a working-class curriculum (not of the Lawton kind) must be that it takes seriously the destiny and life-chances of its pupils, and the first step would be to try to reverse the present position in which a majority of often ill-equipped young adults are ejected into production (or unemployment), while the school reserves its choicest plums for those who stay on to the sixth form. It simply will not do to consider so much education as 'enough' for people who will 'only' become factory workers: the consequences of such a view is to systematically deny the resources of the school as being relevant to children who will not go on to higher study. The benefits of education would thus be restricted to only one class (or those who aspire to that class).

The most immediate response necessary is a changed relationship between work and school, but work experience programmes are still barely integrated into the ongoing processes of the school, and our career-advice services are still geared to align one's skills, talents and preferences· with present job opportunities. In this process, finding and holding a job are the limits of career advice. An objective for working-class schools and their curriculum would be to show that work is planned, organized, constrained, negotiated and distributed; that one is part of a pattern of employment, and that not all considerations of work relate to personal talent, desire or liking (and there could well be lessons here for the supposed 'autonomous' professions, or the 'unattached' intellectuals). In sum, that the forces that shape employment and work can be examined and understood.

Such an endeavour would go well beyond merely fitting pupils to their 'inevitable' jobs; it would involve as much questioning of work as accustoming a pupil to it, as much pointing to alternatives and wider fields of work possibilities as concentrating on just the pupils' own preferences, based perhaps on severely restricted acquaintance with work. The greatest obstacle to this is teachers' extreme distance from other forms of work; a learning process for teachers will have to precede their being able to effectively teach about work.

The purpose of a working-class curriculum would not only be to study these phenomena (and actually experience some work), but also to help pupils to articulate their response. The forms of articulation whether in speaking, writing or other presentations are a particular and important task for curricular and pedagogic innovation, and nowhere more so than in a curriculum which looks to the outcomes of schooling as involving the ability to be politically and socially articulate. Certainly the 'basic skills' are a fundamental part of such education, but as Freire (1971) points out, *pace* Lawton, such skills are often best developed in a very explicitly political and personal context. One example of such an approach is the curriculum proposed and taught by small groups of part-time 'educators' with estate adolescents in England, described by Robins and Cohen (1978) as including the following basic areas of study:

1 literacy and communication skills
2 self-health, social biology and sex education
3 history of working-class life and struggle, local, national and international
4 studies in applied science and technology.

The working-class curriculum sketched here does not seek to jettison all vestiges of traditional subjects and disciplines. But it does assert to itself the right to make its own selection, a selection principled on very different considerations from those of Lawton and Hirst. It does not seem that analysis of class, work and hegemony excludes analysis of the traditional historical, economic or social studies type; indeed, it should be noted that concern with working-class history and such related areas as women's history has noticeably increased in our higher learning institutions: never before, at the highest level of our 'forms of knowledge', has class and culture been so extensively discussed, documented and theorized. Mathematics and science teachers also need not fear for their job: on Bourdieu's criteria, they should be the *last* traditional subject teachers to feel that they are irrelevant to working-class interests. Certainly it makes no sense to talk of control of one's destiny and ignore such powerful bodies of influence on human affairs as the natural, biological and mathematical sciences.

Final considerations

I want to finally mention two questions that would seem to arise about this proposed curriculum: first, the question of locality and universality – would such a curriculum be tied to at least beginning much of its study in the local community, and what are the implications of this? And secondly, the question of student interest: would it be a curriculum any more likely to secure student interest and response than a mere academically straight curriculum such as Lawton's?

1 *Local studies.* Often the starting point of 'relevant' curricula (for example Midwinter) is the study of the local community – urban studies, community studies, the street, the street-corner, the '97 Bus' are almost the staple diet of such curricular reform. Their rationale is simple: the curriculum must speak to the child's experience, and the most immediate experience is that of the family and the local community. Lawton points to one of the potential shortcomings of this approach: if the environment is an extremely limited one, little can be learnt by basing the curriculum upon that environment (though much, I suspect, can be learnt from comparison).

I think Lawton is quite correct in warning us that a curriculum constructed largely around local community life *may* be very limited, but profoundly wrong in his conclusion – to warn us off local studies as being in the end fit subjects for curricular development. It may be that whether we use the '97 Bus' is a tactical question – a sort of fly-paper approach to curriculum, catching the interest of pupils and so on. Lawton himself is not averse to these initial tactics for his own curriculum, so that here at least a suggested working-class curriculum could be compatible with Lawton's common curriculum.

The problem with the '97 Bus' is not that such study cannot lead into insights of a suitably profound, universal and knowledge-producing nature (Lawton's fears): questions about who uses the bus and why (or who doesn't use it and why), the actual areas it runs through – why are factories in one part of the city? where do the workers live? how did the city develop like this? what were the forces that shaped it and shape it now; all these questions can be asked and answered in quite a complex fashion. But in the end, many of these questions and much of this analysis is at such a remove from the '97 Bus', that it would be contentious to say that we were on about the bus any more. What we are on about may be social studies; it may be urban analysis; it may be class analysis with a view to making a social critique and locating our pupils' lives and their destinies within it, and there is nothing restricted and nothing parochial and limiting about this curricular process; certainly, far from Lawton's fears, pupils are not being 'sold short' under such a curriculum.

When I say that this does not appear to be a curriculum in any way restricted or narrow, I am also implying that the sorts of knowledge, understanding and articulation sought in this curriculum are not only relevant to working-class kids. In the questions it poses, and in the kind of understanding it attempts and the control over one's life that it asserts, it is a universal curriculum, a worthwhile curriculum for any school to adopt. [. . .]

2 *Student interest.* The local community is often the focus in initiating new curricula because it is meant somehow to capture the interest and imagination of working-class pupils in a way that topics more culturally distant could not hope to do. But many teachers are sorely disappointed: they find that the study of the local evinces no more interest from their pupils than do Egyptian tombs or quadratic equations, and often a sleepy boredom (or noisy chaos) greets all three. [. . .]

Whether or not a working-class curriculum evinces any more initial interest from pupils than any other type of curricula cannot be answered *a priori.* What should be said is that there is no suggestion that a working-class curriculum should be any easier or more sensational or more immediately engaging; the only point is that it be better. I suspect that this will depend above all on the extent to which a relationship between work and school can be successfully established and nurtured, so that the school constantly informs the pupil about work and promotes understanding and reflection on it.

Conclusion

We are only at the beginning of being able to define and elaborate a viable working-class curriculum. The purpose of this preliminary argumentation has been to show that it is neither philosophically nor educationally an incoherent concept of curricular development. Certainly attempted 'refutations' such as Lawton's should not deter us.

Summing up Lawton, to a great extent he was addressing the educational and political 'right' rather than making any profound critique of the 'left'. The common curriculum *does* go against the traditions of a stratified education system and a preserved sanction of élite education. Many of Lawton's arguments are attempts at convincing these elements that such a curriculum can be educationally responsible as well as being essentially democratic. If we witness the extraordinary depth of resistance to com-prehensivization and the horror expressed at giving all pupils a similar educational programme, Lawton's fears of such a curriculum's acceptance are certainly not groundless.

But as a critic of the working-class curriculum, he is much less convincing; he was scarcely fair to writers such as Midwinter who have gone some way towards defining a working-class curriculum. His analysis of both class and culture are immensely disappointing, as a few strong insights evaporate into a proposal for a curriculum which even in his own terms has little to do with the realities of class or the force and pervasiveness of culture. And he is politically ingenuous: he presents his idea of a common curriculum with very much the feeling that it is a philosophy whose time has come, but it is only arrived at by systematically ignoring class and culture conflict on a massive scale. Lawton *does* ignore it: he seems to hope that if one keeps one's eyes closed, the forces of industrialization and cultural hegemony will do their work. Lawton now *opens* his eyes and finds, behold, a rather academic sort of curriculum standing almost untouched, now ready for common consumption by an (almost) classless society. But the working-class will not wither away like this. Lawton denies the destinies and the needs of working-class pupils. And this is to deny them a great deal: cannot the school actually respond to this destiny and these needs?

References

BANTOCK, G. H. (1968) *Culture, Industrialization and Education.* London: Routledge and Kegan Paul.

BOURDIEU, P. (1971) 'Systems of education and systems of thought' in YOUNG, M. F. D. (ed.) *Knowledge and Control.* London: Collier-Macmillan.

BOURDIEU, P. (1974) 'Schooling as a conservative force: scholastic and cultural inequalities' in EGGLESTONE, J. (ed.) *Contemporary Research in the Sociology of Education.* London: Methuen.

FREIRE, P. (1971) *Pedagogy of the Oppressed.* Harmondsworth: Penguin Books.

JACKSON, B. and MARSDEN, D. (1962) *Education and the Working Class.* London: Routledge and Kegan Paul.

LAWTON, D. (1975) *Class, Culture and the Curriculum.* London: Routledge and Kegan Paul.

MANN, M. (1973) *Consciousness and Action among the Western Working Class.* London: Macmillan.

MIDWINTER, E. (1972) *Priority Education.* Harmondsworth: Penguin Books.

OSSAWSKA, M. (1971) *Social Determinents of Moral Ideas.* London: Routledge and Kegan Paul.

ROBINS, D. and COHEN, P. (1978) *Knuckle Sandwich.* Harmondsworth: Penguin Books.

THOMPSON, E. P. (1968) *The Making of the English Working Class.* Harmondsworth: Penguin Books.

WILLIAMS, R. (1961) *The Long Revolution.* London: Chatto and Windus.

WILLIS, P. (1977) *Learning to Labour.* Farnborough: Saxon House.

YOUNG, M. F. D. (1971) *Knowledge and Control.* London: Collier-Macmillan.

1.6 Curriculum and Pedagogy

Gerald Grace

[Gerald Grace's analysis of curriculum and pedagogies draws upon his research in ten inner city comprehensive schools in London. In the text of his article below he refers to these schools by letters and quotes from a few of the 105 interviews conducted with teachers in the schools.]

The dominant principles upon which the curriculum and pedagogy of working-class schooling in the nineteenth century was based were those of 'civilizing', 'gentling' and 'making competent' an increasingly urban population. Civilizing involved the transmission of appropriate selections of secular and religious culture from those *with* civilization to those without it; gentling involved socialization in acceptance of the given social order and of the forms of its relationships; and making competent involved the production of a range of skills required by an expanding industrial economy [. . .]. These principles were in some tension in so far as different fractions of the Victorian middle class gave different emphases to them. However, despite such intra-class struggle as to which principle should be accorded priority and, while the contents of the curriculum might vary, its *structure* and the *mode* and *social relations* of pedagogy remained constant for long periods. A sense of order derived from the apparent certainties of the time. The superiority of the forms of knowledge to be transmitted; the logical necessity of the structure of the curriculum; the self-evident requirement for a strongly teacher-directed pedagogy and the clear need for 'discipline of mind and body' gave to this schooling enterprise a self-confidence which is physically manifest in the assertive architecture of the London Board schools.

Such certainty and such self-confidence at both societal and at school level is hardly a feature of the contemporary situation. A pervasive sense of order at both levels has been replaced by a pervasive sense of crisis, particularly tangible in the centres of metropolitan cities.

At school level, the superiority of the forms of knowledge to be transmitted no longer goes unchallenged. Yesterday's work of civilization has become today's work of cultural domination. The socio-historical relativity of knowledge is asserted and claims are made for the inclusion of other cultural traditions, other languages, logics and understandings, including those of an indigenous working class. The conventional structure of the curriculum, far from being regarded as a logical necessity derived from the given boundaries of knowledge, is frequently seen to be an alienating and meaningless collection of arbitrarily defined contents. A pedagogy based essentially upon teacher transmission within ordered hierarchies of subject groupings and

---

Source: GRACE, G. (1978) *Teachers, Ideology and Control, a study in urban education*. London: Routledge and Kegan Paul, Chapter 10.

pupil groupings is criticized for generating intellectual and social *passivity* for the majority.

If, following Bernstein (1977, p. 85), we say that 'curriculum defines what counts as valid knowledge, pedagogy defines what counts as a valid transmission of knowledge and evaluation defines what counts as a valid realization of this knowledge on the part of the taught' then it is apparent that *in contemporary urban working-class schools in particular, there exists a crisis of validity in all of these areas.* Uncertainty and disagreement exist over what is to be considered an appropriate curriculum, pedagogy and mode of evaluation. [. . .] Bernstein (1977, p. 111) reminds us that Durkheim saw changes in pedagogy as indicators of a moral crisis and has himself suggested that a move away from traditional 'collection' curriculum towards integrated forms 'symbolizes that there is a crisis in society's basic classifications and frames and therefore a crisis in its structures of power and principles of control'.

While these issues are clearly constituted at the level of theory and also at the level of conflicting educational ideologies, their constitution *at the level of the cultural transmitters in the situation of crisis* (that is inner-city teachers) has been relatively unexamined. What constructs of crisis exist at this level? What curricula and pedagogic forms are advocated as solutions to crises? What are the underlying principles and intentionalities of such solutions? What is the reality of autonomy and constraint within present curricula and evaluation procedures?

Contemporary teachers in urban working-class schools, unlike their nineteenth-century predecessors, are at least active (or potentially active) partners in processes of curriculum formation and change and they have a wider area of pedagogic discretion than was previously the case. It becomes crucial, therefore, to know what kinds of epistemological and pedagogical models are salient for such teachers and what principles guide their day-to-day activities. [. . .]

Defending traditional disciplines

While the majority of teachers designated by their headteachers as outstanding were committed in theory [. . .] to various measures of curricula and pedagogic change, a minority of generally senior teachers saw their role as that of defenders of traditional disciplines and excellencies against the attacks of an educational progressivism which utilized relevance as a central notion for change which appeared to them to be most strongly located in departments of English in inner-city schools. The general position adopted by this group of teachers was that the traditional curriculum enshrined 'the best that has been thought and known'; that it made available to the pupils a richness and width of cultural experience which would not otherwise be available to them; that its essential disciplines were concerned with the inculcation of rationality, order and precision and that such experiences and such disciplines were as necessary for the pupils of the inner-city as for any other group of pupils. These teachers were hostile to a contemporary emphasis upon relevant curriculum or community curriculum because they read in this the provision of a special (sub-standard) curriculum for urban working-class pupils. They were hostile to discussions concerned with notions of middle-class imposition of values, meanings and knowledge, claiming that such argument was either 'merely political' or analytically unclear. *For such teachers the crisis of the urban school was that these ideas had gained so much ground,* particularly among younger teachers and especially in English departments. A senior teacher at School E epitomized this position:

The arguments at the moment about knowledge and the curriculum being remote from the pupils and not sufficiently relevant, I would reject. The curriculum in my view is relevant enough . . . we will soon be teaching only about the immediate environment of the child. German, for instance, is being abandoned next year as a second language, on the grounds that it is irrelevant.

I think the danger of reducing the curriculum to the immediate world about the child is that you can produce no inspiration for the child. I think English departments in comprehensive schools must bear the blame for much of the ambivalence about the curriculum at present. They are totally absorbed with the immediate environment – the idea of teaching Shakespeare, for instance, is out. This has the effect of rubbing kids' noses in their environment.

English departments are the most trendy and progressive. They seem to have almost a policy (or, at least a unified approach) to these questions. There is more liaison between English departments and they have a very active professional group. I think it is true to say that there is *an alternative form of education* being espoused by English departments in London. They see themselves as the van of educational innovation. Invariably the largest department, they can exert a powerful influence, yet they are unwilling to accept responsibility for declining standards of competence in the basic language skills, especially reading.

It may be remembered that in an earlier period of urban working-class schooling the special mission of the teacher of English had been recognized by various writers. Teachers of English constituted as 'preachers of culture' and purveyors of sweetness and light had been seen to be the crucial agents of harmony, of social integration, of anti-urbanism and of the uplifting work of civilization. Now, by a number of teachers in this inquiry, English teachers were seen to have adopted a very different special mission: a mission which appeared to them to be generally *subversive* of standards and dangerously focused upon the grimness of the urban environment and the pervasiveness of conflict and exploitation within it.

The notion that the contents of the traditional curriculum could 'free' the working-class child from a world of cultural, social and economic limitations ran through the discourse of such teachers. The traditional contents of the curriculum were seen to provide 'windows to other worlds' and to provide the means whereby pupils could *escape* both imaginatively and (for a minority) actually, from the grimness of inner-city living. Constructs of the curriculum as ultimately *a path to individual freedom through escape* had their own biographical locations. Those who most strongly maintained this position and were most critical of progressive English departments had personal bio-graphies of scholarship success from working-class origins. For them the curriculum as path to individual freedom had a real and personal validity and they saw their work in an inner-city school as essentially concerned with *reproducing* their own biographical experience in as many children as possible. Progressivism was seen to be a threat to this possibility and a betrayal of working-class children. [. . .]

The 'need' for structure

Defence of the traditional curriculum and of traditional forms of pedagogy was often associated with a diagnosis of need for structure in inner-city schools. [. . .] Notions of structure feature significantly in teacher discourse but carry a variety of meanings. The notion can stand for a particular framework of social relations; a sequence of prepared material for lessons; the existence of indicators demarcating 'right' and 'wrong' (morally and academically) or a particular organization of curriculum and pedagogy. The central meanings, however, appear to be those of *'boundary'* and *'certainty'*. That the educational experience of inner-city children should be such as to provide both a sense of boundary and a sense of certainty, was thought to be crucial by a number of teachers. Boundary features and features of certainty were seen to be in dissolution as a consequence of social and economic change in inner-city areas and, also, as a consequence of more frequent family 'breakdown' in those areas. Thus, some teachers argued against curriculum and pedagogic change on the grounds that change was already *a too frequent occurrence* in the lives of the pupils and that a countervailing experience of the familiar and the structural should be provided by inner-city schools. The school was thus cast as some form of *sanctuary against the world* and not to be merged with it in forms of community education or in being more relevant.

In general, this group of teachers provided realizations of the principle of 'things must be kept apart' which Bernstein (1977) has suggested as a fundamental feature of traditional curricula and pedagogic arrangements. They also provided realizations of a strongly individualistic ethic, in terms of notions of individual freedom, liberation or escape for working-class children, as made possible by existing curricula arrangements. They rejected the validity of alternative curricula models and particularly the view whereby curriculum became the means for a *social group* to become conscious of its situation of oppression and exploitation. This was 'political'.

'Being relevant' and 'being interesting'

Many teachers saw the problem of the urban school as essentially one of boredom with and alienation from the traditional contents and structure of the curriculum and traditional modes of pedagogy. Such boredom and such alienation was most visible among the less able pupils who formed the most challenging and resisting section of the school population. Concern about such pupils was a salient but not exclusive feature of liberal reformist thinking among the teachers. Notions of *relevance* and notions of *interest* were utilized frequently in the teachers' discourse but were accompanied by uncertainty as to the principles being invoked or the means of their realization. In particular, many teachers appeared to be convinced that the curriculum was not sufficiently relevant, without being very explicit as to what being more relevant would involve. They appeared to register an *intuitive sense of disjuncture* between the curriculum and their pupils' present and future lives, a sense which they encapsulated as 'not relevant'. Such an intuition was registered by a young and outstanding teacher of modern languages at School H:

I think education is the way by which the working class can one day be made more active in the democracy. That's why I teach in a school in this area and not in a middle-class area. I make active decisions about my teaching because of these ideas. But I often question the validity of teaching modern languages to those with needs in other directions. I'm sceptical about teaching languages to inner-city children, it seems somehow irrelevant to their experience when they have far more basic problems that we should be considering.

Some teachers were uncertain of the relevance of modern languages, of algebra or of Shakespeare in an inner-city school and yet, at the same time, they were reluctant to advocate what they intuited as an inferior curriculum for their pupils in which these items would be absent. There were various manifestations of curricula change in the ten schools which ranged from the addition of subjects such as sociology, economics and computer studies, through curriculum projects such as the humanities project, Nuffield science and new approaches in mathematics and modern languages, to the creation of new curriculum categories such as integrated studies, community education, social education and learning for urban living.

In examining the ways in which the schools and the teachers had responded to ideas of 'being more relevant' and 'being more interesting' it is apparent that various and sometimes contradictory principles were implicated. These included the use of principles of relevance to the conditions of contemporary society and economy (which legitimized the inclusion of sociology, economics, computer studies, technology, and so on); relevance to a particular ability category of pupils, especially less able (which legitimated social education); relevance to being responsible and competent citizens (which legitimated forms of community service); relevance to a particular community or locality (which legitimated community education) and relevance to a particular social category of pupils: in this case inner-city working-class pupils (which legitimated for some teachers inclusion of 'working-class history' and 'working-class literature' as well as an emphasis upon community rights). For some teachers being relevant implied essentially curricula and pedagogic change designed to modernize and make more efficient the educational experience of the pupils. For others being relevant was a necessary response to a growing resistance from among the tougher elements of the school's population to the contents and mode of the traditional curriculum. For a minority of young radical teachers being relevant was finding connections with urban working-class life experience, both historically and contemporaneously, in order to facilitate the development of a group consciousness and sense of identity.

If a central principle of the curriculum of urban working-class elementary schools in the nineteenth century was that of 'civilization', it can be argued that a central principle of their contemporary successors is that of 'relevance'. In the same way that principles of civilization for an urban working-class population implied various selections of curriculum contents and various emphases in pedagogy, so, too, do contemporary principles of relevance. Their current realizations in urban schools provide an important area of inquiry for urban education.

Within the present study a dominant liberal ideology of relevance could be discerned in most of the schools, an ideology concerned with modernization, efficiency, overcoming boredom and producing responsible citizens. Such principles of relevance had affected the constitution of all the subjects of the curriculum and had, in some cases, found a particular institutionalized expression in forms of community and social studies. Against this dominant liberal emphasis was counterpoised in some schools an alternative principle of relevance. This principle implied that an understanding and appreciation of the socio-historical and cultural experience of working-class life should be a central preoccupation of the curriculum of urban schools. As such, it represented the *antithesis* of the founding purposes of such schools.

'Being integrated'

Older and more conservative teachers in this inquiry were concerned to preserve traditional curricula arrangements for, among other things, the sense of boundary which they implied. Young teachers in at least five of the schools, were concerned, on the other hand, to promote notions of an integrated curriculum which would remove a sense of boundary in favour of a 'relational idea'. As with the notion of relevance, the notion of integration was a powerful constituent of liberal school reform, though signifying a variety of motives and intentions. At School A under a previous headteacher, integrated studies (including history, geography, religious education, English, mathematics and science) had been an important feature of the time-table and its position legitimized by the creation of a head of department status. At Schools B, C, E and F various forms of curriculum integration were in process. As a general pattern the idea of integration involved, in Bernstein's (1977, p. 93) terms 'the subordination of previously insulated subjects or courses to some relational idea'. This might be 'discovery', 'the Creation', 'London living' and so on. The logistics of integration required minimally a team of co-operating teachers, a continuous 'space' on the time-table, adequate physical space and resources for an active pedagogy, for example work sheets, audio-visual aids, reference books. These minimal requirements often presented in practice, *major* obstacles to those attempting to introduce measures of integration.

A call for 'revolution' in curriculum arrangements, 'away with traditional subject barriers', epitomized one approach to the introduction of integrated studies. There was in the discourse of teachers associated with this approach an emphasis upon the need for 'wholeness', 'naturalness', 'meaning', 'perceiving relationships' and obtaining greater 'freedom and enjoyment'. Problems of alienation in urban schools were seen to be related to a lack of meaning and involvement in the curriculum, arising out of the distorting effects of arbitrary subject barriers. If these could be removed then an important part of the problem would be removed. A different quality of learning and a different quality of relationships would be realized.

The strongest advocates of curriculum integration tended to be teachers from colleges of education, rather than university departments of education. In some senses, their own less strongly bounded subject identity was a crucial element in their involvement with the development of integrated studies and its institutional-ization in the schools' time-tables. It must be noted, however, that those who most strongly advocated integration with its central notion of the 'relational idea' did not themselves characteristically engage in theorizing which related pedagogic forms to wider cultural or socio-political forms; or the constraints of the curriculum with any wider structure of constraints. However, at a more pragmatic level the pioneers of integration had experienced in their efforts for change, the reality of constraints arising within the school and it was such constraints which tended to preoccupy their thinking.

While integration found justifications in a language of educational principle, it also found justifications in a language concerned with notions of order. [. . .] The head of integrated studies at School A observed that 'the system has facilitated administrative control'. The value of the greater knowledge which a team of teachers working with first year pupils for consolidated periods of time could acquire about them, was commented upon in a number of schools. Motives here were various. There was an expressed concern to give first year pupils entering large urban comprehensive schools a sense of security by continuing a mode of pedagogy already familiar to them. At the same time, some teachers observed an increase in the difficulty of teaching first year pupils within a traditional curriculum structure: 'each year the first year are creating more and more problems. There are more maladjusted children, more children with really quite bad behavioural problems. They are beginning to come in unmanageable instead of developing into being unmanageable' (head of English, School J). There was a sense, therefore, in which the development of Integrated Studies appeared to be *necessitated* by an intake of pupils less tractable and amenable to traditional structures. *Integrated studies, from this viewpoint, provided a necessary 'space' within which socialization procedures for the secondary school could be undertaken.*

Attempting integration raised many questions at the level of school politics: of the distribution of power in the existing curriculum structure; of the varieties of ideological conflict; of strategies for change; of the provision of resources and of the general possibilities of school arrangements being otherwise. While these questions were being considered initially at the level of the school, they carried with them, as Bernstein (1977, p. 145) has put it, 'the potential of making visible fundamental social contradictions'. The realization of such potential, however, seemed conditional upon radical changes in the consciousness of liberal curriculum reformers, changes which would link more explicitly curriculum structures with social structures.

Developing alternatives

A small group of inner-city teachers in criticizing the curriculum and pedagogy of their schools and in advancing arguments for change, utilized a different vocabulary and pattern of discourse to that of the liberal majority. Although sharing with the liberal curriculum reformers the language of 'relevance', 'integration' and 'active pedagogy', these terms carried messages different from those of liberalism and were articulated within different theoretical frameworks. Characteristically they formed part of a much more radical critique of existing school procedures and, in some but not all cases, involved much more explicitly socio-political linkage. [. . .]

At School H two young teachers of sociology were attempting to develop alternatives to the 'liberal consensus' of the curriculum by providing courses designed to 'get kids to begin to construct their own knowledge; to view the world critically; to become socially aware and to become active in terms of changing their position if they want to'. Both saw such activity as a necessary and legitimate *countervailing influence* to the many conditions within their pupils' environment which tended towards the production of either social and political passivity, or the acceptance of conservative and even 'reactionary' views on a wide range of subjects.

The principle of *change of consciousness* was a central feature of such thinking about the curriculum and its possibilities were celebrated both at pupil and teacher level. Thus, in referring to her colleagues, one teacher observed:

I suppose the majority are middle-of-the-roaders. I wish they would all read the first part of Bowles and Gintis's *Schooling in Capitalist America* and that would certainly change their view. Schools *are* centres of cultural domination, they are custodial and repressive and they are reproducing the social relations for a capitalist mode of production, but in a subtle liberal way, so that it is not obvious to most of the teachers involved that this is what they are in fact doing.

Basically, I put my faith in the encounter with a critical literature as being a means of changing the consciousness of teachers (this reflects my own experience). Also as teachers get to work together more to discuss the *real issues* of the curriculum and of teaching (without petty subject status divisions), that would be the beginning of a new form of consciousness and solidarity.

Those inner-city teachers who saw themselves as developing alternative educational experiences for their pupils in the ways described, were united in their rejection of what they took to be the principles of *schooling* for an urban working-class population and in their advocacy of what they took to be the necessary principles of *education*. In their view, *principles of schooling were essentially concerned with hierarchy, individualism, passivity and acceptance. The necessary principles of education on the other hand, were concerned with fraternity, understanding, criticism and changing the world.* Urban schools (and all schools) had to be changed; such change to be in the direction of a greater collective realization of the intellectual and political power of 'ordinary people'. Such a revolution had hardly begun.

Reference

BERNSTEIN, B. (1977) *Class, Codes and Control, Vol. 3: Towards a theory of educational transmission* (2nd edn). London: Routledge and Kegan Paul.

1.7   The Curricular Transaction

Gabriel Chanan

Present confusion about the aims of schooling makes it increasingly clear that there is a need for a model of the curriculum which can serve as a general declaration of intent from the education service to society at large.

Any attempt to create such a model must immediately acknowledge severe limits. Schools cannot, any more than society, have a single overall aim. To pursue some ideal of *the* educated man is to engender interminable tasks of definition where no final definition is possible. A model of aims which tries to reach too far down into the objectives of specific school courses would be a model for minimizing the main resources of education – the teachers' judgements.

[. . .] If the overall aim is education for democracy – and what else can it rationally be where the society whose education system we are discussing is, or aspires to be, a democracy? – schools must be seen not simply as transmitters of established [. . .] knowledge, but as a meeting point of established and innovating knowledge, national and local consciousness, formal and informal culture.

But the principal meeting point is not the lesson itself. Coherence is the outstanding need in lessons, and coherence implies at least a provisional resolution of the questions raised by the confrontation of established and innovating knowledge. The principal meeting point is the minds of the teachers when they discuss, plan, and create new courses. The greatest single impediment to genuine modernization of schools is failure to recognize that this, collaborative teacher planning, and not the isolated classroom on the one hand or educational research and administrative policy on the other, is the key creative point for educational change.

[. . .] How far should teachers prescribe what pupils ought to know and think? Must prescription result in social subordination or could it contribute to social liberation? And how far should the education system prescribe to its teachers what they should prescribe to the pupils?

The traditional justification for prescription is that the education system exists to transmit a culture to the new generation. In order to examine the plausibility of this claim, we must get some workable idea of what a culture is.

A culture is the accumulated [. . .] mental resources of a society as it faces its [. . .] predicament, generation by generation. There is no such thing as ingesting or transmitting a culture whole. Education, both the formal education of school and the informal education of home and environment, selects and evaluates within the culture in the very act of transmitting it. If education is cultural transmission it is also, inescapably, cultural criticism.

Source: CHANAN, G. in KING, E. (ed.) (1977) *Reorganizing Education*. London: Sage.

What are the criteria for criticism and selection? Partly they lie in the momentum of the culture itself – in inherited conflicts of value. But partly too, and particularly in times of dynamic development, the criteria by which the accumulated resources of culture are revalued arise [. . .] from the special predicament of the generation in question.

Accumulated [. . .] culture is never enough of a guide to [. . .] the new predicament. As Kierkegaard said [. . .] life must be understood backwards but lived forwards. [. . .] Reality does not develop only in accordance with the schemata furnished by well-digested experiences of former times. New reality impinges on us and is perceived by us in fragments long before we integrate these fragments (if we ever do) into a schema or theory.

It is an occupational hazard of theoreticians, particularly Marxist-inclined ones, to see consciousness as being entirely composed of theories. All theories and disciplines of thought are refinements from ordinary language, the surpassing virtue of which is that it is *not* systematic in content (only in grammar); that it is [. . .] flexible and piecemeal, allowing us to formulate perceptions *ad hoc* and with no definite compulsion to reconcile them. Thus the newest elements in our predicament do register with us, but exist for a long time culturally undigested. It is therefore possible to speak of a common predicament, widely perceived, but not provided for in the established cultural resources.

[. . .] The curricular problem is: how shall we co-ordinate the established resources with the informal, piecemeal resources which consist in our awareness of the contemporary predicament? [. . .]

To understand both the value and the limitations of knowledge, we must [. . .] maintain a firm theoretical distinction between knowledge and reality. We may define reality as whatever it is that knowledge is knowledge *of* – plus a great deal more. The certainty that reality is always more than we know is embodied in all commonsense treatment of knowledge. A solipsist [. . .] will say 'Only what I know to exist, exists' or 'It only exists because I know it exists'. But the solipsist contradicts himself all the time in his daily [. . .] living. To ask a question, to read a paper, merely to watch out for an unexpected car as you cross the road, is to acknowledge that reality is always changing and always extends beyond what we know.

We must avoid, at the other extreme, the idea that objective reality totally determines consciousness. Each (particular) mind is a freeplay area for the creation of experimental meanings. If reality determined the whole content of consciousness, we would only be able to think what was true. Even the reality of a cultural environment does not determine consciousness, otherwise we would only be able to think what was conventionally established. Rather, consciousness, stimulated by reality and culture, continually creates structures of *possible* meaning and launches them into the world of discourse, where they are either confirmed and reinforced by the judgement of others or else modified, refuted or ignored.

Certainly it takes an exceptional effort to think against the stream of convention but it is possible otherwise convention itself would never change.

To be sure, this process of engagement with the consciousness of others has an all-but-irresistible psychological force, and through it some notions become part of the common definition of reality while others are destroyed. But it would be quite wrong to simplify this process into the formula 'reality determines consciousness', for that would obliterate from sight the marvellous raggedness of the process, whereby many contending notions and sensibilities can exist for a time in the same universe of discourse, with the continual possibility of new modifications or cross-fertilizations – so long as there is a healthy democratic respect for this natural process.

Established knowledge, as distinct from the informal universe of discourse, is knowledge which, for whatever reasons, has been thought worthy of special protection and systematic dissemination. Its roots are in ordinary discourse, and in the last resort it too remains experimental. Its authority rests on the extent of corroboration, interest and reaffirmation which it has accumulated. But, once established, it will also have attracted the attention of those who wish to feed off its reputation without ever applying to it the test of their own sense of reality. It thereby becomes a fetish and may be stultified by the weight of vested interest depending on it, which conceals its experimental, permanently provisional, nature.

It is in reaction against this stultifying institutionalization of knowledge that many progressives have sought to reaffirm the fluid nature of knowledge and to deny any special value or validity to the established disciplines. However it is not knowledge but reality that is a 'seamless cloak'. Knowledge is *representation* of reality, and it is always a very limited representation. Without boundaries it would have no coherence at all. This does not mean that the boundaries necessarily correspond to boundaries in reality. They may correspond only to the limitations of the human mind. But that, precisely, shows that they are indispensable. Without their help we are inherently incapable of reconstructing aspects of reality within the manipulable territory of our own heads.

The less we confuse knowledge with reality, and the more we realize that there must be many other means of access to reality than merely the established routes, the less imperative we will feel it to deny all value to intricate and complex structures of knowledge inherited from past thinkers. We can move among those intricacies without being enslaved by them.

The ultimate authority then is neither the teacher nor knowledge – but reality. The reality of a particular matter, however, is only established gradually, by the process of discourse. Meanwhile, in the school situation there are four different points of access to reality which may usefully be distinguished and which are all likely to be drawn on as the curricular transaction proceeds: formal traditions of knowledge, contemporary informal culture, the teacher's perceptions and life-experience and the pupil's perceptions and life-experience. [. . .] There is a broad band of contemporary culture which probably has equal impact on teacher and pupil. This consists of the continual processes of representation by which the present world is mediated to us. By applying special mental frameworks (such as, perhaps, a sophisticated historical sense) the teacher [should] be able to assimilate [. . .] these impressions better than the pupil, relate them to some kind of perspective. On the other hand, by the freshness of his response the pupil may be able to grasp some of the newer ideas more quickly and [. . .] respond to them more fully.

Other elements of contemporary culture, though in principle equally accessible to both parties, will be differently absorbed by teacher and pupil due to different expectations and taste. [. . .] The teacher will have a [. . .] longer memory of phases of contemporary culture. He [should be] less at the mercy of those who organize the distribution of mass culture. He [should] cultivate awareness of [alternative currents of thought].

On the other hand again, the pupil may receive currents from cultural circuits of which the teacher knows little, such as industrial skills, trade union life, local and family history.

In relation to contemporary culture, therefore, as well as in relation to personal perception and experience, teacher and pupil are on [a complementary footing].

What the teacher brings to the classroom encounter that is extra to these sources is, first his specialist knowledge of some aspect of formal culture, and secondly, his talent and training as a facilitator of on-the-spot cultural activity (that is, learning) – everything from conversation to the making of works of art. The teacher's special knowledge can never obliterate the fact that the pupil always has independent avenues of access to reality. The teacher's justification (his inescapable responsibility, in fact) for injecting aspects of formal knowledge into school life is the special contribution which formal knowledge makes to the total cultural mix.

There are two ultimates in the learning situation: the child's subjectivity, and the reality of the world – the *whole* world. That there will be some stress in the course of the encounter – the unending encounter – between these two will always be true, whether or not there are schools, and whatever schools decide to do. Schools, however, exist to make the best of this encounter. It is essential for them to give maximum access to the reality of the world and at the same time to display maximum respect for the reality of the student's subjectivity. In other words it is a question of balance. To stick out for a condition in which there will be no stress between these poles of reality will merely ensure that we never agree on any concrete plan.

But let me clarify: the subjectivity of an individual is in no way less real than the world. On the contrary, the world consists principally of the unimaginable abundance of individual subjectivities. But we are speaking of the encounter of each single individuality with all the rest, living and dead, and with all they have done and created. However reluctantly, however ineffectively, the older generation is responsible to the younger for this reality. If we have reached a point where the older generation truly understands as little about this reality as the younger, we have reached the end of [civilization – of any political hue].

Cultural activity is the cultivation of a shared understanding of the world.

At its most intimate and diffuse, this means ordinary conversation. At its most public and concentrated it means art and theory. Conversation is both the ground and the model for all culture. Culture, then, is something of which the roots are universal, spontaneous and anonymous – a vast social murmur into and out of which each person moves in the course of his daily commerce. In the fundamental cultural activity of face-to-face conversation, it is each puny individual who does the major work of 'constructing' reality.

This does not mean that all cultural activity is 'equal'. It does not mean that the school is mistaken in prescribing certain collections of knowledge as more valuable than others.

The education system is that part of the total culture which is most susceptible to conscious [social] direction. One of its functions must therefore be to complement those parts of the culture that are spontaneous and undirected. Ordinary conversation is local and transitory, and the harrying pressures of everyday survival rarely allow it to develop to its fuller potential.

The function of complementing informal culture is not to be achieved by putting a boundary between formal and informal culture. It is to be achieved on the one hand by making provision for the much fuller development of informal culture, and on the other by injecting into this congenial cultural space a digestible maximum of courses designed to add the kinds of knowledge which tend not to be encompassed informally: the highly structured symbol systems of art and science, theory and imagination.

A coherent world view is not achieved without the deliberate cultivation of perspective, recall of wide ranges of fact and event, the seeking and testing out of principles which can explain large numbers of such particulars, and the comparison of evidence and impressions from different sources and eras. All this can only be achieved by elaborate systems for recording and retrieving knowledge, by the division of knowledge into areas and aspects and the sustaining of expertise in the various areas. It is not done in casual conversation, nor in the work of the mass media.

The failure of the traditional curriculum when confronted with the task of universal education is explainable first by the fact of division – the fact that most pupils were simply not admitted to its intellectual benefits such as they were – and secondly by the following ten characteristics of its fully developed version (as in the British grammar school):

1 Certain important subjects were not usually available at all (for example psychology, philosophy, world history, law, sociology, technology, politics, economics).

2 It was not acknowledged and explained that each subject encompassed many possible styles of interpretation, some in conflict with others – that revaluations continually take place *within* the subjects.

3 Connections were not made between the subjects and pupils' experience and existing preoccupations.

4 The relation *between* subjects was not taught.

5 Material *within* subjects may have been given disproportionate priority

(for example, at the crudest level, the history of kings and queens, to the exclusion of social history).

6 The wrong *treatment* within subjects often prevailed (for example, the history of imperialism taught solely from the point of view of the imperialists).

7 It was not acknowledged that pupils had areas of knowledge and experience *not* covered by subject expertise.

8 Certain important skills or criteria of judgement which ought to enter into all or most subjects were wrongly regarded as the responsibility of one or none (morality, imagination, social implications, mastery of language, expression and communication).

9 Connections were not made between the prescribed subject matter and the current predicament of the world.

10 Knowledge was not presented as *permanently provisional*, open to re-interpretation and new evidence, some of which might come from the pupils themselves.

By thus breaking down our objections to traditional education into fairly specific indictments, we avoid the self-defeating effect of rejecting all features and elements of the traditional curriculum *in toto*. There are certain features which it will be necessary to salvage from the old system if a truly universal system is to be created.

[. . .] Traditional knowledge must be subject to reinterpretation, by both teacher and pupil. But reinterpretation implies access in the first place. The distance between a pupil's spontaneous awareness of a problem and the best resources of the disciplines which can help to throw light on it, is far too great for the route of 'discovery' alone. [. . .]

To insist that in every stage of learning there must be a demonstrable connection between the pupil's experience and the knowledge being introduced is virtually to rule out of court two vital educational objectives: first the attainment of a reasonably complex view of the whole world predicament; secondly the appreciation of otherness – of the validity and importance of experiential centres of gravity outside, sometimes far outside, one's own.

Progressive educational thought has been too one-sidedly concerned with the pupil, especially the working-class pupil, as victim, too little with him as instrument for his own *and others'* liberation. When it has thought of liberation it has often thought of it in terms of liberation to do as one likes, not often enough of liberation to help influence the collective destiny. At bottom this has been only superficially radical, an echo of the conventional view of liberation as getting away from it all. A genuinely radical programme must be concerned with getting to grips with it all. It must be concerned with how tomorrow's world is going to be run. This is why it must reappropriate the very best of intellectual resources, not throw them out with the bathwater of exploitative society.

The appreciation of otherness is necessary not only intellectually – there can obviously be no very elaborate grasp of reality without it – but emotionally. It goes hand-in-hand with achieving a belief in the reality of one's own moods other than the present one, and so of becoming whole. Both forms of appreciation of otherness are related to the ability to attach value to life before, after and outside the moment. It is only by grasping that which is very different from us that we come to a rounded understanding of ourselves. At the same time, every such grasp extends us.

But if the creative nature of the teaching task is understood, there is no necessity to be transmitting anti-social attitudes no matter what the source of the material being presented. We must ask where the impetus comes from that prompts our legitimate criticism of cultural material, and demand that the teacher be responsive to that impetus. The kinds of implicit message which we would object to are racist, sexist, militarist, anti-working class, inhumanly idealist, egocentric, ethnocentric, consumerist-fetishistic [. . .]. Where does the impetus come from that prompts this sort of judgement of elements in the cultural heritage? It comes from (a) currents of criticism *within* the formal heritage, that is one historian's criticism of another, one artist's implicit criticism of another, one scientist's overturning of another's theory; (b) from the contemporary struggle for equality; (c) from avant-garde art; (d) from introspection into one's own predicament; (e) from awareness of the predicament of others with whom one comes face to face, including one's pupils; and (f) from awareness of the predicament of the world as a whole. It is the teacher's job to be aware of and responsive to all these sources of judgement; and, at any one time, to co-ordinate them into a judgement determining his selection and treatment of material and his identification of present objectives. He is, in other words, a critic acting at the frontier of cultural revaluation.

A selection and treatment of historical, philosophical, literary, religious or other material that is carried out in this way is itself a contribution to the reinvigoration of the culture. An eschewing of this kind of responsibility in favour of a more completely child-centred approach may easily turn into an indulgence not so much of children's own perceptions, not so much even of volatile peer group subcultures, but of the systematically superficial preoccupations furnished by other highly centralized agencies which are far more crudely prescriptive with far less sense of responsibility than the education system – the advertising, marketing, public relations, consumer-journalism, exploitative entertainment industries.

[. . .] Pupils' creative and critical abilities [. . .] are the very frontier of informal culture, [but] creativity is not exercised in a void. It is the expression of the inner person, but the inner person is a consciousness trying to cope with all sorts of outer currents. The [character] of the locality, the currency of particular subcultures, the nature of local industries, variations in family culture, trends in mass-culture – these are the immediate reality with which pupils' imaginations have to wrestle. [. . .] The strongest of these currents – peer-group subcultures and the mass media – are the most volatile. School cannot compete with them in vividness. They cannot compete with school, however, in cultivating sustained focus on chosen areas of knowledge, without which intellectual development is not possible.

The mass media at their best are abundantly informative and stimulating. But they have three properties which make it almost impossible for them to generate real values on their own: first the transitoriness of their focus on any one topic; secondly their imperviousness to the [reaction] of the audience; and thirdly their overall formlessness – the way individual programmes are swallowed up in the endless succession of programmes. As a never-ending serial, the presentation of news, in particular, belies the sense of importance which it seems to claim. Last week's famine is annihilated by this week's plane crash, and this week's plane crash by next week's trade figures. We become aware of one society after another only at their moment of catastrophe. As soon as the most dramatic peaks of upheaval are over, we lose sight of them again as before. The mass media create an inescapable environment of intense, transitory fragments of reality. It remains for schools to create some kind of perspective in which to see them, and so to make the application of values to them possible. Only in the school, too, do discussion, questioning, gradual assimilation and the making of connections become possible. What we call creativity is essentially the assimilation of these outer images of reality to inner currents of emotion.

A serious idea of creativity, or indeed of culture in general, is not compatible with the belief that there are fixed limits to pupils' innate abilities. To create something new is to become something new, not merely to articulate a pre-existing attribute of oneself. This is true at whatever level, whether we are talking about sophisticated art or ordinary conversation. The artist becomes what he is by working at his art. Not until the artefact is complete has his mind actually reached the state expressed in the work. To work at his art is to work at his mind. The whole notion of 'ability' on which our present educational ideology draws so heavily is a misnomer. Ability can only be known in retrospect. Education is not the fulfilment of pre-existing abilities but the reaching out of minds to points which they have never previously occupied. The very phenomenon of culture cannot be understood unless we grasp that it generates mental attainments in all of us that could not possibly have been predicted from our 'abilities'. Culture extends us. [. . .] This function of creativity is not remotely comprehended in the use of the term 'creativity' in social science and educational research. The majority of differences in attainment which are now explained by differences in ability could be far better explained by differences in *continuity of cultural cues*.

As a means of access to formal culture, school must first extend its representation of formal culture to include the neglected areas, primarily philosophy, psychology, politics, law and sociology. [. . .] It is a mere prejudice to think that these new areas would not be of interest to adolescents when history, literature and science are. Of course, one has to think of their concrete subject-matter, not their academic image. Nothing is of wider popular interest than such questions as how we know that reality is real, what significance can be attached to dreams, who has power, what the law of the land is, and what the work and leisure habits of different strata of the population are.

But in soliciting their influence, schools must also be aware of the danger that these subjects could arrive in school stamped with a rarified academic interpretation. Philosophy and psychology, in particular, as presently understood in most British universities, are not in one of their most fertile or humane periods. Somehow, by drawing on a historical perspective in each field, by introducing comparative elements from continental traditions and by including avant-garde criticism of prevalent practice, a liberating spectrum of ideas should be attainable.

If it is unimaginable that teachers could engender such programmes on their own, it is to the universities themselves that we should be looking for the necessary help. A change in the norms of schooling demands some change in the function of universities. Why should academic research be synonymous with specialization? Has not this convention been responsible for as much atomization of knowledge as accumulation of it? To produce the necessary complementary breadth, the new synthesis, is just as challenging an intellectual problem as to add a brick to the palace of knowledge.

[. . .] Both the arts and sciences in schools are conceived on a watered down academic model and neglect [. . .] our major point of contact with the world, namely the man-made environment. The questions that occur to us naturally through our interaction with the world around us are mostly how and why questions about man-made things. This means first the realm of technology (which is by no means the same thing as the realm of science): why houses are built in this or that way, why the roads are laid out in such a way, how buses and cars and planes and radios and telephones work, and so on. It means also the intangible but very real man-made world consisting of symbolic exchanges – the circulation of money, information and ideas; the definitions of jobs and social roles; the distribution of culture. It is because these objects of spontaneous inquiry are missing from the traditional curriculum that teachers have to make such superhuman efforts to 'interest' pupils in 'subjects' which appear as discrete additions to the world, having no easily demonstrable connection with the things that inescapably bother us in our daily work of living.

How could the man-made realm enter more fully and directly into the curriculum? The problem is not so much the content of the formal disciplines, for this content has very deep connections with the man-made world, but the form: the fact that, as structured and presented, the subjects appear self-contained and follow an internal logic. The coherence of that internal logic is, indeed, their main virtue, which would be lost by simply dissolving them into loose multi-disciplinary courses and improvised foci of study. What we are looking for is not something to take the place of the disciplines, but something leading towards them which arises more visibly out of the momentum of living.

The missing connection, I suggest, is an explicit orientation to adult [life] – not just [to] paid work but [to] all [activities] that contribute to the sustaining of life. The traditional relationship of school to work is very indirect, and very mechanical in conception: adult work is defined as paid labour, paid labour is obtained by proof of possession of skills, skills are accredited by paper qualifications, qualifications are obtained by passing exams, and exams define the syllabuses that guide the curriculum.

Since this concept of the relation between work and school has long prevailed, it is not surprising that large numbers of teachers should see 'preparation for work' as a narrow and inadequate goal for education.

If, however, we re-examine what we mean by 'work' in an ecological perspective, we will find that work redefines itself in a way that has far-reaching implications for the curriculum. We should be preparing pupils not merely to do a job but to survive in that job, to think out the meaning of that job for society as a whole, and possibly to exert influence to change it; for the work of keeping a home going, the work of bringing up children, the work of sustaining local community life, the work of influencing public affairs, the work of material self-sufficiency in all sorts of possible ways from growing vegetables and organizing co-operative food-buying schemes to mending cars and making clothes. Pupils should learn to see their identity as not being wholly dependent on the authenticity provided by paid work. All productive labour done small scale outside the national market economy reduces reliance on the national market economy and so increases autonomy. This includes the making of entertainment and cultural artefacts as well as the material accomplishments. It includes also skills of participation in public affairs. [. . .] All these are ways of helping to sustain life, and should be regarded as needing to be anticipated educationally both in deciding what skills are to be learnt and in preparing expectations.

Obviously the way to do this is not to define a new set of subjects but to make school into a kind of supervised cultural centre where many of the above forms of work are facilitated, with direct benefit to the immediate community. To some extent the logic of this development is already inherent in progressive educational practice, and what is being suggested here is merely an extrapolation from the best innovations of recent years.

Learning would still remain a priority distinct from 'living', which means that the school should not merge completely with the community. Some kind of boundary should remain to prevent the pressures of production and consumption from pressing too powerfully on the learning environment.

For this reason as well as for good ecological reasons, none of the productive work done in schools should be fed into the ordinary market economy. It should run a much smaller circuit between production and consumption, being used to satisfy the needs of those who have actually done the work, or to barter with other neighbouring schools or social centres. This is a world away from what is normally meant by 'work experience', in which the young person gets a foretaste of what it is like to be a cog in a vast, impersonal machine over which he has no influence whatever.

Comprehensive schooling should mean not simply that the children of working-class families mix with the children of middle-class families, but that middle-class work and working-class work, verbal work and manual work, mix in the experience of all pupils. Of course there must be some specialization. There is nothing intrinsically anti-social or inegalitarian about specialization. It is the superimposed roles, rewards and mentality of exclusion attached to particular specializations which is objectionable.

But the manual work of a manual worker is only part of his life-sustaining activity; he also participates in public affairs, he also teaches his children to think, he also defends himself across the negotiating table. The verbal or numerical work of a lawyer, accountant, journalist, or teacher is only part of *his* life-sustaining activity. He also cooks, grows vegetables, mends the roof, washes clothes. And if a society is to develop a sustainable life-style, the importance of these 'fringe' activities is in both cases going to grow, taking more of the work of living back out of the market economy and into the realm of personal and local initiative. Large-scale industry will settle into a certain ecologically defensible limit. It will obviously always occupy a huge role in productivity, but not, in already industrialized countries, a permanently growing one. The manual worker will spend a greater proportion of his productive power in production for his own use, outside the factory. Most important of all for education, this will include more time devoted to the 'middle class' pursuit of monitoring and influencing social and political change.

[. . .] My argument has led to a curricular model in which the school houses two very different types of activity; on the one hand a range of practical and cultural activities having close connections with the immediate community, hence rather fluid in framework and open to continual influences from outside the school; on the other a range of intellectual skills, starting with basic studies and continuing to a point of intensive specialization, highly structured, highly teacher-prepared and therefore unavoidably highly teacher-directed.

Despite the objections that could be upheld against this grafting of seemingly polarized educational styles, there seems no a priori reason why this solution should not commend itself to teachers and pupils. To assume that one principle, either 'progressive' or 'traditional', either formal or fluid, must govern all curricular transactions, is quite arbitrary. What is being suggested is not two mutually isolated, insulated modes, but two different types of focus, each with its own reserved space and time, which will generate [. . .] cross-currents.

If the understanding of teachers' work outlined in this paper seems to imply an intensely demanding role, one can only answer that it can succeed if the education system and the community as a whole revises its idea of the kind of support it should give to teachers; not so much in terms of salaries but in terms of reorganization of existing resources, responsibilities and methods of working. The most committed teachers seem to feel impelled in the direction of a creative, culturally pioneering role. Because the education system is so little geared to support of it, because so many entrenched assumptions, defensive self-images and moribund role-sets are threatened by it, the best talents are sooner or later worn down by having to struggle against the grain. And yet it is what the best talents *want* to do, and I would not have had the temerity to propose it as a general rationale for the teaching task had I not seen teachers struggling to be enabled to do it.

1.8   The Dark Continent of Technology: the Power to Leap

Daniel Boorstin

The conduct of daily life for Americans in the later twentieth century would not follow the rules which had governed experience at the time of our nation's founding. Technology would tend to neutralize or destroy some peculiar American opportunities. For those had arisen out of the special situation of the North American continent in space, and the special situation of the birth of the United States in time. In our later age the therapy of distance, the shock of visible beginnings, the very meaning and potency of history would be diluted or dissipated.

The meaning of physical distance was transformed. The new technology was the conscious product of imaginative and energetic individual men and women, and of potent new institutions. But its consequences extended beyond the ken of the inventors. These seeping, pervasive, interstitial, unexpected consequences would become the daily problems and opportunities of twentieth-century Americans and eventually might become those of all mankind.

The distant no longer remote

Back in 1748, the pioneer French sociologist Baron de Montesquieu whose works were well known to the authors of the Declaration of Independence, had argued that a republic could endure only if confined to a small territory. Only then, he said, would the public interest be simple enough to be comprehended by the people. Many of the Founding Fathers of the American republic agreed. When Patrick Henry argued against ratifying the federal constitution in the Virginia Convention, on 9 June 1788, he challenged the Federalists to produce 'a single example' of a great extent of country governed by one Congress. 'One government,' he insisted, 'cannot reign over so extensive a country as this is, without absolute despotism.' The War for American Independence had been fought against government-at-a-distance from abroad. Would government-at-a-distance on the American continent be any more tolerable?

Even those, like James Madison, who championed the new Constitution, noted dangers in the large reach of the new confederacy. But in *The Federalist* they argued that American geography could provide a built-in safeguard against the threat of centralized government. That safeguard was the variety of interests to be found in the wide extent of the American colonies. If a large

Source: *Exploring spirit: America and the world experience* (1975). London: BBC.

nation would offer the danger of government-at-a-distance, it might also offer the salutary checks and balances of a heterogeneous continent. Thomas Jefferson made precisely this point after his party won the election of 1800. 'Had our territory been even a third of what it is,' he observed, 'we were gone. But while frenzy and delusion like an epidemic, gained certain parts, the residue remained sound and untouched and held on till their brethren could recover from the temporary delusion; and that circumstance has given me great comfort.'

The importance of sheer distance in shaping American political thought appeared again and again and in obvious ways. This federal republic assigned all the 'police powers' – the lion's share of legislation and administration – to the political unit which was closer to the citizen. For a citizen's concern and his knowledge of affairs were supposed to be directly proportionate to his closeness to the problem. The Constitution therefore gave to the central government only certain specified powers, and left all the rest to the States. In foreign policy, too, the force of distance became an axiom that was soon translated into policy. In 1823, the Monroe Doctrine declared the American determination to preserve the oceans as a moat-protective, to enforce quarantine from the many ills 'on that side of the Atlantic'.

By the twentieth century, technology in the United States had done much to destroy the power of distance. Of course, the twin technologies of transportation and communication played the largest role. The most influential American successes in these areas have been (for transportation) the automobile and the airplane, and (for communication) the radio and television. Nothing was more obvious. But some of the indirect consequences of the American conquest of distance were less obvious. Perhaps the most important social by-product was a fantastic increase in man's Power to Leap.

To understand this we must recall how, five centuries earlier, seafaring Europeans had first acquired a Power to Leap. In the Age of the Sea the progress of technology and of geographic, astronomic, and scientific knowledge – man's newly amplified Power to Leap – had made possible the 'discovery' and then the settlement of America. By the early sixteenth century Europeans had developed the means to carry communities through the cultural vacuum of thousands of ocean-miles, by-passing everything in between. These communities arrived on American shores uninfluenced and unadulterated by all the ages and stages between the North American Indian and the post-Renaissance European.

Five centuries later, in the Age of the Air, the twentieth-century Americans' Power to Leap was still more unprecedented. Aeronautics and electronics extended the reach of man's leap all over the earth and into the heavens. The time required to send a message across the planet was abbreviated until it became practically instantaneous. This was a quantum jump in technological progress.

Aeronautics and electronics obviously brought Americans much closer to the moon, but not any closer to their next-door neighbors. In surprising ways, the Power to Leap now tended to isolate and segregate each citizen from those nearby. This is an example of what I would call the Law of Inverted Distance: *Advancing technology tends to have a proportionately much greater effect on large quantities than on small.* The longer the distance to be covered, the greater the power of technology to reduce the required time. This means that within the short distances circumscribing man's everyday community, the distances that measure his neighborhood, the powers of this technology are negligible. [. . .]

By-products

This power to conquer distance tended to revise or abolish the circumstances on which Franklin and Jefferson and Madison had based their political wisdom. The conditions which had supported the Founding Fathers' hopes for the future of the Republic were transformed.

Technology homogenizes. The very same forces which abridged the continental distances also tended to dissolve the continental variety. As people all over the United States came closer to one another, they became less different from one another. When businessmen and labor leaders flew halfway across the continent for a few hours' conference and returned home the same day, the whole nation's ways of doing business were assimilated. National advertising and national television programming brought the same sales slogans and the same entertainment celebrities simultaneously to everybody. Powerful homogenizing forces produced new reasons to share Thoreau's mid-nineteenth-century doubts. 'We are in great haste,' he noted in *Walden* in 1854, 'to construct a magnetic telegraph from Maine to Texas; but Maine and Texas, it may be, have nothing important to communicate.' The more alike became the economy, the standard of living, the spoken language, the folklore, the music, and the literary culture of the nation's distant parts, the less was added to any American's experience by bringing him words and music and images from remote parts of the nation. What had happened to the variety in which Jefferson had such confidence, and which gave him such comfort – that 'while frenzy and delusion like an epidemic, gained certain parts, the residue remained sound and untouched'? Was any part of the nation still immune to these powerful homogenizers?

Technology centralizes. The new technology required great investments of capital and new kinds of specialized know-how. The high cost and the homogenizing reach of the media put a premium on the celebrity-everything – the celebrity product, the celebrity entertainer, the celebrity newscaster. The celebrity was a person who was well known for his well-knownness. To judge political candidates or commercial products by the 'recognition factor' meant that candidates, products, and broadcasters would be valued quantitatively. The cost of commercial advertising announcements and the salaries of television entertainers and newscasters depended on how many people they reached and how many they managed to keep listening. These high costs could be borne only by high-powered, centralized institutions, the best-financed political candidates, and the most widely used soaps and soups and automobiles and deodorants. Every advance in technology seemed to increase the power of the broadcasting networks. The three great networks headquartered in New York employed the best technology and the best talent. An incumbent President who could command them all at will had a new advantage. News now tended to become afferent and efferent – no longer mostly dispersed near where it was gathered but attracted to centers from which it was dispersed everywhere.

Technology isolates. When Alexander Graham Bell exhibited his telephone in 1876, the popular imagination was excited by its fantastic possibilities. The author of a popular song, 'The Wondrous Telephone,' then unwittingly forecast the consequences of radio and television:

> You stay at home and listen
> To the lecture in the hall,
> And hear the strains of music
> From a fascinating ball!

In the following century, every new advance of electronic technology – from the telephone to the radio to television – tended increasingly to isolate individual Americans and keep them at home. This was perhaps the most momentous unpredicted consequence of the new Power to Leap. The telephone made it possible to have a conversation with a person without seeing his face or being in his physical presence. Television finally made it possible to join others in experiencing almost anything while remaining physically separated from them. [. . .]

Television became a form of transportation. In fact, it was better than any earlier form of transportation. For it brought preselected, well-focused, telephoto versions of the most interesting aspects of any experience instantaneously from everywhere. The old technology took the person to the experience; the new technology brought the experience to the person.

No longer was it necessary to go out into the presence of numerous of your fellow men to witness the most costly performances. Formerly the lavish extravaganzas brought out the biggest crowds, and even *had* to bring out the crowds to support the events. Now these were the very programs most likely to go direct to the greatest number of individuals, each at his receiver, each witnessing the performance in privacy. The biggest and best events tended to be witnessed-at-a-distance. The bigger and better the event, the greater the distance!

Television, then, produced a new segregation. And every advance in technology, every reduction in the cost of sets, every improvement in the quality of reception tended to increase the physical segregation of the individuals who shared an experience.

A similar tendency to isolation came along with the advancing technology of transportation. The Pilgrim Fathers on their voyage across the ocean had been packaged together in a shipboard community, and as they lived in forced intimacy for weeks, they grew into a seagoing village. Contrast this with the experience of the twentieth-century transatlantic traveler, who is urged to keep his seat belt constantly fastened. He is saved from the need to converse with fellow passengers by the headset which brings him a private concert or a humorous monologuist. For most of that few hours' voyage he need not see his fellow passengers, since the lights are dimmed for better viewing of the motion-picture screen.

Even before the airplane, the automobile had a similar atomizing effect. Traveling by train had been a social experience. In the nineteenth century, the characteristic open design of American railroad cars – unlike the closed compartments of the British or the continental cars – developed out of the Americans' desire to move about and mix with fellow passengers. The Pullman smoking room became a fertile source of American folklore. Those Americans who still commuted by train continued to have the friendly experience of waiting with their neighbors on the station platform, of conversing or playing cards, or even drinking a cocktail en route.

But the automobile was isolating and encapsulating. The American traveling to work by car was apt to be traveling alone, probably listening to his radio for music or news from some distant center. Car pools made little headway even in an age of gas shortages. The improved American highway system still further isolated the American-in-transit. On his speedway – identified only by a highway number, graded, landscaped, and fenced, with not so much as a stoplight to interrupt his passage – he had no contact with the towns which he by-passed. If he stopped for food or gas, he was served no local fare or local fuel, but had one of Howard Johnson's nationally branded ice cream flavors, and so many gallons of Exxon. This vast ocean of super-highways was nearly as free of culture as the sea traversed by the *Mayflower* Pilgrims. Just as television now tended to keep every man by himself at home, the automobile meant every man for himself on the road.

Meanwhile, technology tended to clog the short-distance channels. Americans found it difficult to accommodate traditional neighborhoods to the needs of the new machines. The automobile, which had the capacity to cruise at sixty miles an hour, seemed at first to give man a new Power to Leap on land. But around cities, where short-distance transportation was crucial, automobile passengers were often confined in traffic jams where they could not even progress at a walking pace. The shorter the distance, the larger the Parking Problem. In fact, parking began to rank with the dilemmas of sex and politics, death and taxes as the common lot of humankind – the most modern symbol of the Fall of Man. The automobile proved to be an effective time-saver only for longer distances, where it did not block the channels of its own passage.

Distance loses its force

In this curious upside-down world, men could leap the long distances in speed and comfort, yet they were more than ever cursed by the perils and congestions of short distances. What did this do to the therapy of remoteness? In the founding era, many of the special opportunities of American civilization had arisen from the fact that the long distances – betwen the Old World and the New, between one end of the colonies and the other, between one side of the continent and the other – were still intractable and still appeared unconquerable by any speedy means. This helped explain why Americans who were so far from the British Isles had established self-government, while the inhabitants of nearby Ireland had not, and why London monopolists could not enforce their privileges across the Atlantic. Simple remoteness explained countless American opportunities.

But those twentieth-century successes of American technology which brought people all over the United States closer to one another also made them less different from one another. New problems and new confusions came along with new benefits and opportunities. The tendency of modern industry to congregate workers in ever-larger factories had long been noted. In the early nineteenth century, Karl Marx shrewdly predicted that this fact might give a new self-consciousness, a new sense of community, and a new power to those who worked together. What Marx could not foresee (and what few Americans in the twentieth century noted) was that the ever-wider diffusion of the products of American factories tended toward the increasing isolation of consumers from one another. It was not just that Rebecca no longer went to the village well for her water – and her gossip. She no longer needed to go outside her kitchenette apartment to have her hot and cold running water, her hot and cold running entertainment. Even her garbage no longer had to be carried out, for the waste food went into the Disposall, while papers, cans, and bottles went into the trash compactor.

Part Two Structuring the Public Curriculum

The public curriculum, defined as the embodiment of the education system's shared assumptions about the main things pupils should do and learn, implies two needs. First, it requires some measure of consent among various interest groups and second the adoption of fairly common approaches towards teaching and learning within schools and colleges. The implications here are far-reaching. The achievement of an established curriculum would possibly restrict the diversity of curricular form currently sustained in formal institutions and hence the variety of ideological premises underlying practice. As yet, how the public curriculum should be derived is itself hotly debated. Nevertheless attempts to provide some framework have been pursued by agencies such as Her Majesty's Inspectorate and the Schools Council.

In the first article in this section, Tony Becher and Stuart Maclure examine several of the competing agencies seeking to make their influence felt. In particular they note the rejection of the committee of inquiry approach and emphasize the significance of the enlarged role of HM Inspectorate which they see as 'central to the development of a more activist Department of Education and Science'. The attitudes and beliefs held by the Inspectorate concerning the purpose of education may be seen in its advocacy of a common curriculum in secondary education and the report of their inquiry into primary education, conducted for the Plowden Committee.

One of the most detailed 'official' proposals for a public curriculum has emerged from the Curriculum Development Centre in Canberra, where Malcolm Skilbeck was a former director. Its current status in Australian education remains uncertain, but as an attempt to find national agreement about approaches to curriculum planning it warrants particular attention. Its stress on cultural analysis underlines Skilbeck's approach to curriculum, represented by his article in the first part of this collection (1.1).

William Taylor's contribution anticipates some of the problems associated with growth and innovation which are examined in the Part Three. Taylor challenges the assumption that all improvements in education are necessarily dependent on incremental increases in the finance available within education. In so doing, he challenges professionals to undertake new appraisals of their work. This suggests that a public curriculum, if and when established, need not necessarily bend to each and every prevailing economic wind.

2.1 Agents of Change

Tony Becher and Stuart Maclure

National objectives

Curriculum development can only take place within a framework of public education policy, however tenuously linked to this policy and to the public system of education the developer may be. How then are national objectives formulated? The method (or non-method) prevailing in England and Wales and the practice adopted by a centralized and self-consciously systematic European neighbour, Sweden, illustrate contrasting approaches.

Speaking to the Society of Education Officers in London in 1973, Mr Edward Heath, then Prime Minister, said:

> We try as a society to indicate to the professionals the human values, the social attitudes, the cultural traditions, the range of skills we wish them to foster in the young people we entrust to their charge. Thereafter we leave it to their professional responsibility and expertise to decide how to translate our wishes into courses and syllabuses and methods of teaching and learning designed as far as possible to meet the needs of each individual.

The impression intended and conveyed by this polite rhetoric was that it was up to the education officers to get on with the job of running the schools and that as a politician Mr Heath would defend their right to exercise their professional autonomy in doing so. What he actually said, however, exposed the vacuum in English curriculum development: very little is done by our society, in any formal way, 'to indicate to the profession the human values, the social attitudes, the cultural traditions, the range of skills we wish them to foster in the young . . .'

It seems a safe guess that most of the influential people in English education over the past quarter of a century have believed that the larger national educational objectives and the procedures to carry them out are inextricably linked; in other words, the dichotomy which Mr Heath assumed is a false one. And if it is false – if there is no profound or useful way in which one set of people (the politicians) can reach conclusions about objectives, and pass these on to another subordinate group (the educators) to translate into school programmes – then the consequences of any practical attempt to take Mr Heath's doctrine seriously would be unsatisfactory in the extreme. Either everyone would soon tire of the whole process and wilt under the weight of empty generalization, or else the politicians and administrators would feel obliged to go beyond objectives to much more specific discussion of the procedures by which these objectives might be attained. Professional

Source: BECHER, T. and MACLURE, S. (1980) *The Politics of Curriculum Change*. London: Hutchinson.

prerogatives would then be invaded by the politicians and their administrative aides, and the separation of functions would be swept away.

It may be argued that, in educational terms, a pluralism of method and
interpretation intensifies the difficulty of defining goals precisely, and that
diverse and possibly contradictory activities could and would be justified on
the grounds that they were intended to yield the same end result. The larger
the aim, the more difficult the evaluation and the harder it must be to pin
precise educational consequences on particular educational practices.

This characteristically English response to talk about goals and objectives
in education is not, however, the only possible response. To find a country
where a serious attempt has been made to establish national educational
goals and to offer these, ready-made, to the professional educators as the
basis of curriculum planning, it is necessary to go no further than
Sweden.

In the Western world Sweden has made some of the most conscientious
efforts to ensure that what happens in school is consistent with the larger aims
of society – a society, incidentally, whose homogeneous character is reflected
in the dominance of the Social Democrats as the party of government from the
early 1930s until the 1976 election. This strong political consensus carries with
it a commitment to the democratic ideal, and to what has been called the
'democratic value premise' that 'privileges in any field that cannot be justified
on rational grounds should not be allowed to continue'.

An OECD document which states these ideals goes on to quote five general
goals.

Objective 1
All Swedes of school age should enjoy equal right to public education, without regard to
income, social origin, sex, or place of residence. And since all individuals are 'born
equal' and are endowed with talents and personality potentials that differ but are in all
cases capable of development:
   (a) the aim of the school system should be to meet the differentiated needs of various
groups of students, and
   (b) no one branch of education should in itself be considered more worthy of esteem
than any other, the entire school system constituting a coordinated whole.
Objective 2
The school should aim at safeguarding and strengthening the democratic system. It
follows . . . that:
   . . . there should be a considerable common core of learning, particularly in the
comprehensive, but also in the upper secondary school;
   . . . provision should be made for frequent group work and discussion to strengthen
cooperation and tolerance among the pupils;
   . . . particular attention should be given to fostering an understanding of the
functions of the Swedish and other social systems;
   . . . critical and independent thinking should be encouraged . . .
Objective 3
Educational policy should contribute to general economic development, e.g. by
producing the required types and amounts of qualified manpower. However, this goal
is often subordinate to the first two . . .

Objective 4
The educational system should be made more flexible to fit the shifting talents, interests and plans of the pupils . . . as well as a continuously changing labour market. This . . . requires flexibility in administrative procedure and in planning ('rolling planning') as well as a continuous or 'rolling' reform throughout the educational system. Such flexibility is necessary in order to enable the system:
   . . . to change itself in response to the changing structure of demand . . . by individual members of the society as well as the equally dynamic requirements of the economy;
   . . . to provide sufficient breadth . . . to allow for changes in students' school careers . . . thus eliminating 'dead ends' in the system.
Objective 5
The educational system should make efficient use of limited human and real resources.

It requires a considerable effort of the imagination to see, in these paragraphs, objectives which represent the prior considerations on which subsequent development could be founded – still less to which it could be linked by rigorous deductive and analytical processes. It may be more illuminating to look at them as one striking reflection of the ideological context of the later 1960s, when the systems approach was in its heyday as an instrument of curriculum and educational planning. But in so far as objectives were written down at all, they were the subsequent rationalization of objectives already deemed to be implicit within the system – a justification for on-going activities rather than a fundamental attempt by the community (acting at an early state of the development process) to determine educational goals *de novo*.

The various committees which prepared the curricular instructions sent out to schools by the Swedish National Board of Education, however, enabled large numbers of people drawn from many different sections of the community to express what they perceived to be the educational consequences of national social policy.

It is important also to recognize that these community representatives have not confined themselves to statements of general goals. They have been drawn (thus confirming orthodox English expectations) right into the detailed discussion of content and methods as well – and in so doing have tacitly acknowledged that it is only in terms of process that many of the more specific and functional objectives can be stated.

The use of advisory councils

In England and Wales lack of systematic provision for public discussion of educational ends and means has meant that responsibility for such matters has been absorbed into the private domain of the large body of teachers, administrators, academics and laymen who collectively form the educational establishment. This gives significance to the most public form of traditional curriculum development conducted at national level in England and Wales –

the major commissions of inquiry, including the Board of Education's Consultative Committee and its successors, the Central Advisory Councils. In the inter-war period two of the consultative committee's reports – *The Education of the Adolescent* in 1926 and the 1931 Report on *Primary Education* – can be seen as major contributions to curriculum development, as later were such documents as the Crowther, Newsom and Plowden Reports.

The full-scale inquiry technique requires more or less eminent men and women, most of them involved in one way or another with making the existing system work, to consider the current practice of the schools and the directions in which development should move. They ponder the evidence submitted by political and professional pressure groups, as well as that provided by surveys and impressionistic studies carried out on the committee's behalf – and increasingly use commissioned research, though always as a supplement to more traditional methods of finding out which way the professional and administrative wind is blowing, and speculating on which way it ought to blow in the future. They present their reflections on this evidence in a report which is expected to include relevant sections on subjects within the curriculum as well as about the organized relationship of the different activities which make up the whole. [. . .]

The Plowden Report was the most self-conscious attempt to look at the curriculum of the primary school since the Hadow study of 1931 and perhaps marked the peak of traditional curriculum development. It appeared in 1967, just as the new heuristic approach to curriculum development was coming to first fruition in England and Wales. It made extensive use of research studies and of the services of the Inspectorate for the collection of information – including the appraisal of individual schools and the teaching methods they used, on the basis of the subjective, though practised, judgement of individual observers. And it developed a clear and optimistic point of view which gave force to its recommendations.

Chapter 15 of the Plowden Report contained a series of passages which sought to weave into a reasonably coherent pattern the threads of modern primary education, threads which could be traced clearly to the same skein of material from which the consultative committee's Report of 1931 had come. The committee rejected any attempt at a comprehensive definition of the aims of primary education on the traditional English ground that this could only lead to meaningless platitudes, but wrote three famous paragraphs at the end of the chapter which summed up what they thought good primary schools were about.

A school is not merely a teaching shop, it must transmit values and attitudes. It is a community in which children learn to live first and foremost as children and not as future adults. In family life children learn to live with people of all ages. The school sets out deliberately to devise the right environment for children, to allow them to be themselves and to develop in the way and at the pace appropriate to them. It tries to equalise opportunities and to compensate for handicaps. It lays special stress on individual discovery, on first-hand experience and on opportunities for creative work. It insists that knowledge does not fall into neatly separate compartments and that work and play are not opposite but complementary. A child brought up on such an atmosphere at all stages of his education has some hope of becoming a balanced and mature adult and of being able to live in, to contribute to, and to look critically at the society of which he forms a part. Not all primary schools correspond to this picture, but it does represent a general and quickening trend.

Some people, while conceding that children are happier under the modern regime and perhaps more versatile, question whether they are being fitted to grapple with the world which they will enter when they leave school. This view is worth examining because it is quite widely held, but we think it rests on a misconception. It isolates the long-term objective, that of living in and serving society, and regards education as being at all stages recognisably and specifically a preparation for this. It fails to understand that the best preparation for being a happy and useful man or woman is to live fully as a child. Finally, it assumes, quite wrongly, that the older virtues, as they are usually called, of neatness, accuracy, care and perseverance, and the sheer knowledge which is an essential of being educated, will decline: these are genuine virtues and an education which does not foster them is faulty.

Society is right to expect that importance will be attached to these virtues in all schools. Children need them and need knowledge, if they are to gain satisfaction from their education. What we repudiate is the view that they were automatically fostered by the old kind of elementary education. Patently they were not, for enormous numbers of the products of that education do not possess them. Still more we repudiate the fear that the modern primary approach leads to their neglect. On the contrary it can, and, when properly understood, does lay a much firmer foundation for their development and it is more in the interests of the children. But those interests are complex. Children need to be themselves, to live with other children and with grown-ups, to learn from their environment, to enjoy the present, to get ready for the future, to create and to love, to learn to face adversity, to behave responsibly, in a word, to be human beings. Decisions about the influences and situations that ought to be contrived to these ends must be left to individual schools, teachers and parents. What must be ensured is that the decisions taken in schools spring from the best available knowledge and are not simply dictated by habit or convention.

These paragraphs (505–7) have been dissected with much severity by Professor Richard Peters and others, who complain about the mixture of rhetoric and ideology which they present. But if they never came to grips with the objectives of primary school education in a manner rigorous enough to satisfy the philosophers, the Plowden committee gave their backing to one particular tendency in primary education: that combination of informal methods which cannot be defined or described with any precision but goes – abroad, if not at home – by the name of open education or 'the British primary school'.

If the report of an advisory council or consultative committee is the most obvious product of its deliberation, it is by no means the only one. Before specific recommendations which may lead to government actions are produced, the long-drawn-out process of consultation and argument has its own impact. One hundred and thirteen organizations and one hundred and seventy-seven individuals submitted written papers to Plowden. Thirty organizations sent delegates to engage in oral discussion with the committee; sixty-seven individuals, as well as twenty-seven HMIs and ex-HMIs and twenty other officials of the Department of Education and Science, also gave evidence. Such an inquiry focuses attention wonderfully. Immediately pervasive effects are apparent in the educational press and in the topics of discussion at the educational conferences which reflect the dominant concerns of the profession from year to year.

The committee of inquiry approach, though usually weak on research, is strong on consultation and the collection of opinions within the system. While specific proposals may be made directly to the government, the local authorities and the teachers the final results seldom comprise the kind of recommendations which a Secretary of State can accept or reject *in toto*, unless by chance there are a few clear-cut issues. Dissemination depends on the capacity of large numbers of individual teachers and administrators to absorb and internalize changes of emphasis which together point the way towards modest, incremental change. Curricular recommendations in conventional subject terms are fed into the system of blurred responsibilities and shared assumptions – a system which produces both the limited autonomy of teachers and the network of constraints which impose a measure of orthodoxy on secondary education and, to a lesser extent, on primary education too.

The weakness of the major educational inquiry as the English use it is obvious enough. Only a narrow range of non-professional opinion is tapped and the great majority of the participants, being themselves pillars of the system, often seem intent on extending the educational imperium over questions of value – about which the community as well as the professionals might seem entitled, as Mr Heath observed, to have views.

During the late 1960s and early 1970s the committee of inquiry system came into increasing disfavour with the Department of Education and Science and the politicians who then headed it, for three reasons. First, it was held that large-scale reviews of aspects and sections of the education service invariably gave rise to expensive proposals for development; second, the traditional method of filling places on such committees from within the system usually led them to produce a set of recommendations for 'more of the same' rather than to undertake any more fundamental appraisal; and third, such committees usually took about three years to report, and held up policy-making in the meantime. Section 4 of the 1944 Education Act laid down that there should be two Central Advisory Councils, one for England and one for Wales; that the Secretary of State should appoint the members and the chairman, together with a secretary who is to be a member of the Department; that members should be drawn from both the public and independent systems of education; and that, while the Secretary of State should make appointments for set periods of time and regulate the arrangements for meetings, the Council could largely determine its own procedure. But the Act does not, it seems, actually oblige the Secretary of State to keep a Council in being at any time to carry out its statutory duty of offering advice; and indeed from 1968 – when the Welsh Central Advisory Council completed its inquiry into primary education – until the time of writing, the Department of Education has kept the Council in abeyance.

Admittedly, politicians have continued to use the committee technique (or, when in opposition, to promise inquiries, thus demonstrating their reforming zeal). In recent years there have been formal inquiries by departmental committees into, among other things, adult education, reading and the education of handicapped children. After the 1970 general election Mrs Margaret Thatcher attempted to initiate a new technique by setting up a smaller group of full- and part-time members, led by Lord James, to review the education of teachers. The hope was that skilled analysis would thus be produced more quickly, and the planning staff of the Department of Education and Science would be more closely involved. The committee did indeed report in less than a year, as compared with the three years or so which the traditional inquiry might have been expected to take, but the method suffered from the defects of its virtues. Its very speed foreclosed the process of educating those who submitted evidence, and its small membership reduced its value as a kind of jury for the establishment.

The influence of HM Inspectors

The central government agency to whom most responsibility for traditional curriculum development has fallen hitherto has been the Inspectorate – the men and women known as Her Majesty's Inspectors (HMIs) who serve as the professional advisers and the eyes and ears of the Education Department. Now less than 500 strong, they have always enjoyed a measure of professional autonomy, as their title implies: but they are in fact appointed by the Secretary of State rather than by the Crown, and it is well established that they may receive direct instructions from him as to their duties. The Senior Chief Inspector is ranked with the Deputy Secretaries within the hierarchy of the Department.

The Inspectorate was first formed to oversee and evaluate the spending of public money by the teacher-training institutions and schools which received grants from the state, but an advisory function always existed alongside the judgemental. In recent years, as the formal inspection has become much less important, so the advisory role has taken pride of place. The methods they have used have been those of traditional curriculum development.

The Inspectorate's role is central to the development of a more activist Department of Education and Science, and even before the Prime Minister's intervention the Senior Chief Inspector had set in hand changes aimed at increasing the effectiveness of the Inspectorate. A series of studies of different aspects of the primary and secondary examination curriculum had been put in hand, leading to what can be seen as the resumption of the policy of publishing critical pamphlets. (For example, the review of *Modern Languages in Comprehensive Schools*, published by HMSO at the time of the regional conferences held in the winter of 1976–7, helped to focus attention on controversial issues such as mixed ability teaching.)

It is important to distinguish between the curriculum development function of the Inspectorate in primary and secondary schools – where the advisory role has overtaken regulating duties – from those of the Further Education Inspectorate. The latter retained a direct responsibility for the approval of courses until the mid-1970s. Their work married important curricular discretion with administrative obligations, and so produced in the colleges of further education a degree of control over the curriculum unlike any exercised by the central government over primary and secondary education. Although their object was to prevent the growth of uneconomic courses and to promote the efficient use of resources, they could not pursue this object without impinging on the curriculum.

The role of local authorities

Like the Department of Education and Science, each Local Education Authority is constantly engaged in policy-making and administration, with a consequent impact upon the curriculum. For example, the LEA is involved with the central government in establishing priorities for school building. It controls the capitation allowances which are available for books, stationery and materials, and the supply or denial of extra funds to finance extra teaching materials for certain kinds of subject-based curriculum development. Ideas like 'positive discrimination' increase the interventionist role of the LEA, and hence the LEA's potential influence in curriculum development.

For much of this century the semi-autonomy allowed to education committees by the county and county borough councils of which they were subsidiary institutions has been reinforced by the financial mechanisms chosen by the central government. Thus the personality and educational philosophy of individual Chief Education Officers has had a powerful effect on traditional curriculum development. Men such as Sir Alec Clegg (West Riding of Yorkshire, 1947–74), Stewart C. Mason (Leicestershire, 1947–71) and A. R. Chorlton (Oxfordshire, 1945–70) were able to initiate development in the directions of their choice. By the same token, other CEOs could move in other directions, or decide to mark time where they were.

But the ending (in 1958) of percentage grants as the means of providing Exchequer support for education spending by local authorities – that is, the payment by the state of a fixed proportion of all approved expenditure by authorities – initiated the move to bring education more fully into line with other local government services. This move culminated with the reorganization of local government areas and functions in the Local Government Act of 1972, and the application of the corporate management techniques associated with it. Corporate management has not yet had time to be put fully to the test, but it must be expected to rely less on individual dynamism and to bring to the fore a different, less charismatic leadership. In theory, too, it must be expected to be more eager to evaluate the claims of the educators.

Many a Chief Education Officer has been able to influence appointments so as to build up a cadre of staff in whom he has confidence – placing his chosen candidates in key posts in the schools and the advisory services. As local authority inspectors, organizers and advisers – the terms vary more often than the functions – share with the HMIs the agency for promoting traditional development at local level, this influence is highly important. Clearly, it has its dangers. But English and Welsh LEAs, in practice, have not simply steered people into jobs to promote a single point of view or direction of innovation. Most reformist aims have lacked careful definition, and therefore a valued characteristic of the traditional development process has been to preserve a variety of points of view – to go, if such an ideal is possible, for something as elusive as 'quality' at the expense of unanimity, and to make a virtue of the ensuing pluralism.

This pluralism has also been reinforced from another direction. As we have noted, the philosophy behind the open primary school movement has served to emphasize the professional autonomy and responsibility of the individual teacher. The leading exponents of this distinctively English curriculum development have insisted that, if head teachers, so, too, the Chief Education Officers and their advisory staff must respect the independent professional judgement of the heads. [. . .]

From traditional to heuristic

Much traditional curriculum development has gone unrecognized as such, because it falls outside the limits of the narrowly conceived definition of 'the curriculum'. [. . .] A wider perception of the nature of curriculum change had already begun to develop in England before the much publicized advent of new methods in North America in the late 1950s. The twin exigencies of the rapidly rising birth rate and the virtual moratorium on school building during and just after the war meant that a large school building programme was needed in a hurry and costs had to be balanced against the educational functions of the new schools. [. . .]

The spectacular success of Russian space technology in launching the first sputnik in 1957 dramatized the issue of technical achievement in a form which opened up the flow of public funds for development. But already the progressive 'life adjustment' education movement in the United States was in retreat and exponents of 'discipline-centred' education, many of them leading university scientists, had begun to mount their challenge to the secondary school curriculum. With a new urgency went a new strategy which drew heavily on the technologies which had been developed in the defence and aerospace industries. The essence of the approach was its rational, problem-solving basis. It assumed that clear-headed scrutiny of present practice would reveal what was good and what was bad. There was the hope that a recognizably 'best' way of organizing learning could be discovered and then applied. It was assumed that national shortcomings in scientific achievement could be traced to specific shortcomings in the school curriculum. Likewise, it was assumed that the curriculum could be remodelled to remedy perceived weaknesses by drawing on the best-available expertise inside the·schools – and, even more, outside them.

The optimism of the North American new-style curriculum developers was infectious. By the early 1960s the science curricula in secondary schools were also being questioned on this side of the Atlantic. The moving spirits in England and Wales were the Science Masters' Association and the Association of Women Science Teachers (later joined to form one of the strongest of the subject teachers' groups, the Association for Science Education). Soon after the launching of the American Physical Science Study Committee (PSSC) programme financed by the National Science Foundation under the leadership of Professor Jerrold Zacharias, the associations mounted a series of conferences from which they produced new O-Level science examination syllabuses for discussion. Their work engaged the interest of scientists in industry, of the Royal Society, and of the Advisory Council on Scientific Policy, whose chairman, Lord Todd, happened also to be a trustee of the Nuffield Foundation. A major outcome was the science curriculum programme sponsored in 1962 by the Nuffield Foundation. Instead of just promoting new O-Level syllabuses and thus seeking by the traditional method to change practice, the Nuffield trustees decided that a full-scale development project should be launched. This would necessarily involve revised O-Level examinations, but the important change of emphasis was that the new examination would follow a reappraisal of the curriculum, not precede it.

Significantly, the Nuffield approach, unlike the North American example, recognized that an English curriculum project needed to draw heavily on the expertise of the best practising teachers. University specialists might help in particular ways, but no⸀, as in the United States, as the presiding geniuses and moving spirits. The Nuffield Foundation went on to sponsor a number of other projects on similar lines (in mathematics, modern languages and classics) and continued to play an active part in the school curriculum till the late 1960s. In due course, however, the Schools Council emerged as the major institution engaged in heuristic forms of development.

The Council's predominant concern (like that of the Nuffield Foundation) with subject-based development had certain direct consequences. First, because in-service training (an important element in traditional curriculum development) was outside the Council's remit, no fully satisfactory links between development and this essential part of the dissemination process have yet been made. The finance of in-service training is the responsibility of the DES on the one hand and the local authorities on the other. A sharp dichotomy between the traditional and heuristic forms of curriculum development was ensured, and thus the implication of the wider definition of the curriculum has been lost.

Secondly, a belated attempt to take account of system-wide considerations exposed the limitations of subject-based development. The Schools Council had no over-arching theory of the whole curriculum – indeed there is none in the context of the English education system of the 1960s and 1970s. Nor will it emerge from the pursuit of innovation in one separate subject area after another. When the Council has sought to complement this piecemeal approach by setting up projects on 'the curriculum as a whole' the resort has been not to heuristic developmental methods, but to the old familiar working party or discussion group, with predictably marshmallow results.

2.2 The Case for a Common Curriculum in Secondary Education to 16

Her Majesty's Inspectorate

Recent history

The last twelve years have seen massive changes in secondary education, most obviously and notably as a consequence of reorganisation. [. . .] By far the majority of pupils now attend comprehensive schools. [. . .] There has been necessary change, too, in the work that goes on inside them. [. . .] Teachers have found themselves needing to think through the curricular implications of reorganisation, together with the implications of the raising of the school-leaving age, even while the institutional changes are still being completed.

Our society meanwhile has become noticeably more complex, and in many cases blurred in its perceptions of important issues. More and more responsibilities have been accepted by schools, particularly in matters of the personal and social welfare of pupils. During these same years a host of projects, schemes, proposals and suggestions about the curriculum has appeared. It is difficult to ascertain who has been influenced by what, and how; but teachers have been subject to a confusing series of propositions about what should or should not be done.

Acceptable and unacceptable variety

It is hardly surprising, therefore, that, in matters of the curriculum especially, variety is the order of the day. Such variety can reflect a healthy environment and vigorous and purposeful development in response to local need and opportunity; but equally it can be associated with an inadequate sense of direction and of priorities, with too little coordination both within and between schools, and with a reluctance to evaluate the curriculum offered as a whole. Undoubtedly, too, a major obstacle to coherent development is the sense of 'autonomy' of the individual school, and often of the individual teacher in the classroom, and a deep reluctance to face the implications of partnership in curriculum planning. They nevertheless must be faced – and shared responsibility must be accepted.

It is doubtful if the country can afford – educationally as well as financially – the wasted effort, experiments embarked upon and left unfinished or unexamined, unnecessary repetitions, and most of all, the apparent lack of agreement on fundamental objectives. Indeed, all this is

Source: DEPARTMENT OF EDUCATION AND SCIENCE (1977) *Curriculum 11–16* (Section 1). London: HMSO.

freely acknowledged in discussions all over the country by heads, teachers and administrators. Schools and administrators alike are anxious to do a good job, and there is concern about the bewildering diversity of practice, the problems of lack of balance within the curriculum, and the possibly adverse impact on pupils when unacceptable differences in the quality and range of educational experience offered result. The risks are recognised of inefficient use of resources, unnecessary fragmentation and lack of coordination. Some common framework of assumptions is needed which assists coherence without inhibiting enterprise.

Current practice: 11–16 curriculum

Given this greater willingness to look critically at our schools, we suggest that the general arrangements for the first five years of secondary education need particular scrutiny. In the typical curricular patterns which have emerged in comprehensive schools, there is generally a clear distinction between what is provided in the first three years for pupils aged 11–14, on the one hand, and in the fourth and fifth years for pupils aged 14–16 on the other. Most secondary schools now have a broad common curriculum in the first three years which is followed by all their pupils, with some exceptions in the case of those with need of remedial attention or with other marked learning difficulties.

Options

It is in the fourth and fifth years, however, that the pattern of a broad generally balanced curriculum common to all pupils gives way in the great majority of comprehensive schools to a structure in which they offer pupils a greater or lesser number of compulsory subjects – generally referred to as the 'common core' – together with a greater or lesser number of optional subjects – often only English, mathematics, religious education and physical activities – together with a large number of options arranged in blocks, from each of which a pupil has to choose one subject.

From such groupings a variety of broadly balanced curricula which match pupils' aspirations and keep open their career options can easily be chosen; but it is equally evident that a pupil allowed free choice from the subjects offered in each block could construct for himself a quite arbitrary and incoherent programme. There is a growing recognition that in such or similar circumstances continuity and progression in knowledge and understanding may be cut off or impaired, that decisions may be made prematurely, without any possible adequate basis of knowledge or foresight. Some pupils drop studies simply because they do not interest them or they are not making evident progress, but we all know that pupils are not well placed at 13 or 14 to foresee what skills and what knowledge they will need at 16, still less later on, and that they may subsequently continue to regret for many years the limitations of the programme they chose to follow.

What the school intends

Schools exist above all else to carry out a curriculum. This is the term commonly used to refer to the formal programme of courses organised by a school. In secondary schools, these are what is timetabled, with teachers and accommodation allocated to groups of pupils on a regular basis. Most of these courses are identified by subject labels, and in syllabus statements tend to be described in terms of 'content areas'. There is an implied assumption that we know what the individual subjects involve, and that such courses are designed to bring about learning of value to the pupils both for their own sakes and in their future lives as citizens and workers. [. . .]

The curriculum [. . .] is that which the school intends as its educational policy, and is the public expression of its educational thinking. We repeat that it is not the intention to advocate a standard curriculum for all secondary schools to the age of 16, not least because that would be educationally naive. One of the greatest assets of our educational arrangements is the freedom of schools to respond to differing circumstances in their localities, and to encourage the enterprise and strengths of their teachers. [. . .]

The 'core curriculum'

[. . .] It is not particularly difficult to advocate and indeed to implement, given the apppropriate resources, the notion of English, mathematics and science as a compulsory core for all pupils to 16. This, however, merely begins an educational discussion and does not provide a programme. What English? What mathematics? What science? If these are on the one hand compulsory, but on the other hand appropriately diversified in their objectives, content and methods of teaching, what exactly has been gained? Is this common enough? Or, indeed, is it a large enough common core to meet contemporary needs? We wish to put forward here for consideration a much broader curriculum for all pupils in secondary schools which would inevitably claim a substantial proportion of their time. [. . .]

Common needs

Since the majority of pupils leave school at the statutory leaving age, the nature and purposes of the curriculum up to this point must be determined by what we believe 16-year-olds should know, be able to do, and be able to do better at 16 than they could do at 11. Pupils and their particular needs and circumstances differ but we believe there are general goals appropriate for all pupils, which have to be translated into curricular objectives in terms of subjects/disciplines/areas of learning activity. If our view is right and more agreement could be reached nationally about these objectives, then the consequences of the diversity of schemes of secondary reorganisation and of school population mobility could be mitigated, though clearly not removed.

Towards a common curriculum

What have pupils a reasonable right to expect, given that they are obliged to be in school until they are 16? In the first place, without any doubt they have the right to expect to be enabled to take their place in society and in work, and this means that schools must scrutinise their curricula most carefully to see what is being done, by deliberate policies, to meet these expectations. Insofar as pupils may marry at 16, vote at 18, and become involved in legal responsibilities, what has the curriculum – the schools' deliberate educational policy – done to help them in these matters of fundamental importance to adult life? More than this, even though it may sound somewhat grandly put, pupils are members of a complicated civilisation and culture, and it is reasonable to argue that they have nothing less than a right to be introduced to a selection of its essential elements. Options systems may well prevent this from happening; the freedom to stop studying history, or art, or music, or biology at 14 means that pupils are not being given the introduction to their own cultural inheritance to which we believe they have a right. No one disputes the irrefutable case for basic skills and techniques; equally there is a case for cultural experiences and an introduction to values. There is also just as strong a case – less often acknowledged for the formation of attitudes: to each other, to work, to obligations in society and not least to themselves. For themselves, pupils will need competence and an increasing sense of self-reliance, and the means whereby to develop a sense of integrity in the inevitably changing circumstances that await them.

It is for these reasons that our definition of a common curriculum is broad and makes substantial claims on time. We see that common curriculum as a body of skills, concepts, attitudes and knowledge, to be pursued, to a depth appropriate to their ability, by all pupils in the compulsory years of secondary education for a substantial part of their time, perhaps as much as two-thirds or three-quarters of the total time available. The remainder would be used either to deepen understanding of studies already in hand, or to undertake new activities, or both.

Constructing a common curriculum

It is at this point that we come to the heart of our thesis. We see the curriculum to be concerned with introducing pupils during the period of compulsory schooling to certain essential 'areas of experience.' They are listed below in alphabetical order so that no other order of importance may be inferred: in our view, they are equally important.

Checklist

Areas of experience

The aesthetic and creative
The ethical
The linguistic
The mathematical
The physical
The scientific
The social and political
The spiritual

The list is not, or should not be, surprising; but the existing curricula of many pupils might well not measure up to it very satisfactorily. It does not in itself constitute an actual curricular programme. It is a checklist, one of many possible ones, for curricular analysis and construction. An advantage of such an approach is that many teachers would be rethinking what they know and do already, rather than beginning as novices in a new field. It does not in itself demand any one way of teaching or model of timetabling or pattern of internal school organisation. Given time for preliminary thinking and planning and the assembling and distribution of resources, it could be realised through a familiar-looking programme of single subjects, or through forms of interdisciplinary work, or with a combination of both; or it could lead to novel groupings and titles of studies. It does, of course, by enlarging the notion of a common 'core' to a curriculum that occupies the greater part of all pupils' time, put into question some types of 'option' scheme, though it does not deny the possibility of proper exercise of choice. The essential point to retain, in our view, is that any curriculum provided for pupils up to the age of 16 should be capable of demonstrating that it offers properly thought out and progressive experience in all these areas. Only so, we believe, can pupils' common curricular rights and society's needs be met.

None of the areas listed should be simply equated with a subject or a group of subjects, although obviously in some cases, for example the mathematical, a particular subject is recognisably the major contributor and means to learning. There is nothing essentially new in recognising that certain forms of learning experience, skills and concepts may be sought in a variety of curricular contexts: the Bullock report, *A language for life,* emphasised the importance of, but did not create, 'language across the curriculum' or the essential role of language in learning; the place of the aesthetic in mathematics or of the mathematical in music or geography has long been a familiar idea. Ethics does not normally appear as a separate and identifiable school course but it has a place in many sectors of the curriculum, wherever serious ethical questions need to be considered. Similarly, the spiritual aspects of human experience can be explored, for example, through art, music and drama as well as in say, history, literature and religion: but those planning the exploration need to know where they are going, and those engaged in it need to be helped to recognise what they have discovered. [. . .] It is not proposed that schools should plan and construct a common curriculum in terms of subject labels only: that would be to risk becoming trapped in discussions about the relative importance of this subject or that. Rather, it is necessary to look through the subject or discipline to the areas of experience and knowledge to which it may provide access, and to the skills and attitudes which it may assist to develop.

Using the check list

If the checklist is to be used as the basis of curriculum construction or of reshaping and refining existing curricula, it will be necessary for each faculty or subject department to examine what knowledge, skills, forms of understanding and modes of learning it can offer to the education of every pupil, and for all departments together to consider how their various and complementary roles combine in the pupils' developing experience. Once matters have been clarified thus far, planning can be taken a stage further by looking at the curriculum in a three-dimensional framework. The first dimension will consist of the essential areas of experience; the second of the subjects, groups of studies or courses within which the learning is to be organised; and the third will be the progression that is planned for over five years. Within such a framework can be considered also the more effective utilisation of time over the whole span of secondary education: the balance of emphasis between activities may shift from one stage to the next, as best suits the developing skills and maturing interests of the pupils, and new elements of knowledge or experience may need to find a place, but the balance over all can be kept in steady perspective. [. . .] Given these three dimensions of the curriculum, it should be easier to identify gaps in the sum of the parts.

2.3   Judging Quality in Primary Education

From the Plowden Report

Assessments of primary education

267. So far this chapter has been confined to the organisation of education on which definite statements can be made and comparisons drawn. Although this is more difficult when judgements of quality are concerned, we think that the attempt should be made. First, however, we should remind ourselves of a comment made by the Hadow Committee on aspects of the later stages of primary education:

> It can, however, hardly be denied that there are places in our educational system where the curriculum is distorted and the teaching warped from its proper character by the supposed needs of meeting the requirements of a later educational stage. . . . The schools whose first intention was to teach children how to read have thus been compelled to broaden their aims until it might be said that they have now to teach children how to live. This profound change in purpose has been accepted with a certain unconscious reluctance, and a consequent slowness of adaptation. The schools, feeling that what they can do best is the old familiar business of imparting knowledge, have reached a high level of technique in that part of their functions, but have not clearly grasped its proper relation to the whole. In short, while there is plenty of teaching which is good in the abstract, there is too little which helps children directly to strengthen and enlarge their instinctive hold on the conditions of life . . . [Consultative Committee on the Primary School, 1931, paragraph 22.]

268. We visited as many schools as possible, received much written and oral evidence and had many informal conversations. But we could not possibly claim that we had in this way obtained anything like a complete picture of the state of primary education throughout the country. We felt the need for an assessment covering all the primary schools. Since H.M. Inspectors were in the best position to undertake a comprehensive survey we asked them to do so.
269. All the 20,664 primary schools in England were included in the survey, apart from 676 which were either too new to be assessed or for some other reason could not be classified. The whole body of H. M. Inspectors responsible for the inspection of primary schools took part. It is probable that misjudgments which must have occurred in particular cases cancelled each other out. The survey was planned to ensure that the various categories into which the schools were placed were exhaustive and did not overlap, to eliminate as far as possible the idiosyncrasies of personal judgment and to make certain that the identity of individual schools could not be discovered.
270. In the first category were placed schools described as 'In most respects a school of outstanding quality'. These are schools which are outstanding in

---

Source: CENTRAL ADVISORY COUNCIL FOR EDUCATION (England) (1963) *Children and their Primary Schools* (The Plowden Report). London: HMSO, Volume 1, pp. 100–6.

their work, personal relationships and awareness of current thinking on children's educational needs. They are the pacemakers and leaders of educational advance. This category contained 109 schools in which there were about 29,000 children, representing one per cent of the total primary school population. The second category, 'A good school with some outstanding features', indicated schools of high quality, far above the average, but lacking the special touch of overall rare distinction needed to qualify for the first category. There were 1,538 of these schools educating nine per cent of the total number of primary school children. That ten per cent of the schools should fall into these two categories of excellence is highly satisfactory. 4,155 schools (23 per cent of the children) were in the third category: 'A good school in most respects without any special distinction'. These are schools marked by friendly relationships between staff and children, few or no problems of discipline, a balanced curriculum, good achievement and an unmistakable recognition of children's growth and needs as they are known. One third of the children in primary schools go to schools which are quite clearly good.

271. Category 9 was 'A bad school where children suffer from laziness, indifference, gross incompetence or unkindness on the part of the staff'. Into this category fell 28 schools with 4,333 children, or 0·1 per cent of the whole. We were at pains to discover not so much how such schools had come to be since in any large group of human beings or institutions there must always be a few complete failures, but what was done about them when they were identified. Each of the 28 schools was followed up by the local authorities and by H.M. Inspectors, and action taken. There may always be bad appointments of head teachers; and deterioration in health or character may explain schools such as these. We doubt whether any school in this category would be suffered to stay there long.

272. The number of schools in Category 8 – 'A school markedly out of touch with current practice and knowledge and with few compensating features' – is a little more disturbing. 1,309 schools with five per cent of the children were placed in this category. This is a small proportion, but large enough to cause concern. But the situation is not static, nor is it simply tolerated. The local authorities and H.M. Inspectorate do all they can to assist such schools to improve, but their weakness makes them less susceptible to constructive suggestion than better schools. We would like to see systematic efforts to provide special in-service training for teachers in these schools and to see they take advantage of it.

273. Category 6 is 'A decent school without enough merit to go in Category 3 and yet too solid for Category 8'. This is the largest single category. It contains 6,058 schools and 28 per cent of the children. These are 'run of the mill' schools. The fact that these schools, with Categories 8 and 9, considered above, contain only a third of the children gives some ground for satisfaction. Obviously all the schools in these groups are capable of improvement and ought to be improved, but the figures mean that the general distribution is quite markedly 'skewed' towards good quality. This is a cheering aspect of the assessment. It is reinforced when the remaining three categories are included.

These three were deliberately framed as 'odd-men out'. Category 4 is 'A school without many good features, but showing signs of life with seeds of growth in it'. This category contained 3,385 schools and 16 per cent of the children. It is really an offshoot of Category 6. The schools in it might well recently have been there, but all of them are on their way to Category 3. Some may not get there; some may go further; a few perhaps will drop back; but all are at present moving in the right direction and can reasonably be regarded as promising.

274. Category 5 is 'A school with too many weaknesses to go in Category 2 or 3, but distinguished by specially good personal relationships'. This was devised for schools in very poor areas, often with the large numbers of immigrant children, which cannot hope to match the achievements of the higher categories but which yet do splendid social work. Into this category the Inspectors put 1,384 schools with six per cent of the children. It is one to which any school so circumstanced might be proud to belong.

275. The remaining Category 7 ('Curate's egg school, with good and bad features') contained 2,022 schools (nine per cent of the children). It is likely to be an unstable one. The schools in it might drop into 8, move almost imperceptibly into 6 or 4, or rise to 3 or even further. The disparity is sometimes between the upper and lower part of the school in, for example, a full range primary school where infants may be taught more individually than the juniors, or where the work of the older children may be more interesting than that of the younger children.

276. There was no evidence in the survey that good or bad schools were characteristic of north or south, town or country. The various categories were far from being evenly spread over the areas of different authorities, but they were almost exactly balanced as between counties and county boroughs and the north of England and the south. We consider that it would be worthwhile to undertake similar surveys at intervals of ten years. They must always be based on subjective judgments and, in the absence of a fixed datum line, comparisons would have a limited value, but they would tell the Secretary of State and the people of the country something that they ought to know and be the means of revealing trends which would otherwise be only surmises.

Description of schools

277. Finally, we should like to accompany an imaginary visitor to three schools, run successfully on modern lines, which might fall into any of the first three categories. The pictures given are not imaginary, but the schools are composite.

278. The first is an infant school occupying a seventy year old building, three storeys high, near the station in a large city. The visitor, if he is a man, will attract a great deal of attention from the children, some of whom will try to 'make a corner in him'. He may even receive a proposal of marriage from one of the girls. This has nothing to do with his personal charms, but it is a sure

sign of a background of inadequate or absentee fathers. A number of children are coloured and some of the white children are poorly dressed. All, however, are clean. The children seem to be using every bit of the building (the top floor is sealed off) and its surroundings. They spread into the hall, the corridors and the playground. The nursery class has its own quarters and the children are playing with sand, water, paint, clay, dolls, rocking horses and big push toys under the supervision of their teacher. This is how they learn. There is serenity in the room, belying the belief that happy children are always noisy. The children make rather a mess of themselves and their room, but this, with a little help, they clear up themselves. A dispute between two little boys about who is to play with what is resolved by the teacher and a first lesson in taking turns is learned. Learning is going on all the time, but there is not much direct teaching.

279. Going out into the playground, the visitor finds a group of children, with their teacher, clustered round a large square box full of earth. The excitement is all about an earthworm, which none of the children had ever seen before. Their classroom door opens on to the playground and inside are the rest of the class, seated at tables disposed informally about the room, some reading books that they have themselves chosen from the copious shelves along the side of the room and some measuring the quantities of water that different vessels will hold. Soon the teacher and worm watchers return except for two children who have gone to the library to find a book on worms and the class begins to tidy up in preparation for lunch. The visitor's attention is attracted by the paintings on the wall and, as he looks at them, he is soon joined by a number of children who volunteer information about them. In a moment the preparations for lunch are interrupted as the children press forward with things they have painted, or written, or constructed to show them to the visitor. The teacher allows this for a minute or two and then tells the children that they must really now get ready for lunch 'and perhaps Mr. X. will come back afterwards and see what you have to show him'. This is immediately accepted and a promise made. On the way out two of the children invite the visitor to join them at lunch and he finds that there is no difficulty about this. The head teacher and staff invariably lunch with the children and an extra adult is easily accommodated.

280. Later in the day, the visitor finds a small group of six and seven year olds who are writing about the music they have enjoyed with the headmistress. He picks up a home-made book entitled 'My book of sounds' and reads the following, written on plain unlined paper:

> The mandolin is made with lovely soft smooth wood and it has a pattern like tortoise shell on it. It has pearl on it and it is called mother of pearl. It has eight strings and they are all together in twos and all the pairs make a different noise. The ones with the thickest strings make the lowest notes and the ones that have the thinnest strings make the highest notes. When I put the mandolin in my lap and I pulled the thickest string it kept on for a long time and I pulled the thinnest wire and it did not last so long and I stroked them all and they didn't go away for a long time.

281. Quite a number of these children write with equal fluency and expressiveness, and with concentration. The sound of music from the hall attracts the visitor and there he finds a class who are making up and performing a dance drama in which the forces of good are overcoming the forces of evil to the accompaniment of drums and tambourines.

282. As he leaves the school and turns from the playground into the grubby and unlovely street on which it abuts, the visitor passes a class who, seated on boxes in a quiet, sunny corner, are listening to their teacher telling them the story of Rumpelstiltskin.

283. The next school is a junior mixed school on the outskirts of the city in an area that was not long since one of fields and copses and which has been developed since 1950. The school building is light and spacious with ample grass and hard paved areas around it and one of the old copses along its borders. The children are well cared for and turned out and a high proportion of them go on to grammar schools. The visitor finds his way into a fourth year B class (the school is unstreamed in the first three years) and finds a teacher who is a radio enthusiast. The children, under his guidance, have made a lot of apparatus and have set up a transmitting station. They have been in touch with another school eighty miles away and sometimes talk to their teacher's friends who are driving about in their cars in various parts of England. While the visitor was present, part of the class disappeared into another classroom and there broadcast through a home-made microphone a number of poems chosen by themselves and all dealing with winter. 'In a drear-nighted December', 'When icicles hang by the wall' and 'This is the weather the shepherd shuns' were clearly and sensitively spoken and closely listened to. In another classroom the children had been asked to make models at home which showed how things could be moved without being touched. They had brought to school some extremely ingenious constructions, using springs, pulleys, electromagnets, elastic and levers and they came out before the class to demonstrate and explain them. When the visitor left they were preparing to describe their ideas in their notebooks. A random sample of these books showed that accuracy and careful presentation were as characteristic of the less able children as of the obvious grammar school candidates.

284. During break some of the children went into the hall and listened to the headmaster's wife playing the C major prelude. In another room the chess club was meeting and the visitor saw a Ruy Lopez and a King's Pawn opening and the school champion lose his Queen. In yet another room the natural history club was meeting to discuss its programme for the coming year, while outside the school football team was having a short practice. The library was filled with children. The visitor was interested to notice that there was no contrast between this rich and varied out of school life and the life in school hours which offered just as much choice and stimulus. The library, for instance, was in constant use throughout the day, and at many different points in the school were to be found examples of good glass, pottery, turnery and silver, all of a standard higher than would be found in most of the children's homes. With all the children the visitor found conversation easy. They had

much to tell him and many questions to ask him and they seemed to have every encouragement and no obstacles to learning.

285. The third school, a three teacher junior mixed and infant school, is in the country. It was built in 1878 by the squire and since 1951 it has been a Church of England voluntary controlled school. The church is a few yards away. The original building, with its high roof and window sills and its tiny infants' room, has been made over by the LEA, the infants' room being now a cloakroom and there is a big new infants' room at the back. This has encroached on the now very small playground, but there is a meadow just across the lane where the children play when it is dry enough. The village has grown and there are many commuters of varying social background who travel to the big country town nine miles away.

286. When the visitor arrived all the children in the first class were either on top of the church tower or standing in the churchyard and staring intently upwards. The headmaster appeared in the porch and explained what was happening. The children were making a study of the trees in the private park which lay 100 yards beyond the church. The tower party had taken up with them the seeds of various trees and were releasing these on the leeward side, and were measuring the wind speed with a home-made anemometer. The party down below had to watch each seed and measure the distance from the tower to the point where the seed landed. The children explained that ten of each kind were being released and that they would take the average distance and then compare the range of each species and calculate the actual distance travelled. When they had finished they went back to school to record their results, some in graph form, in the large folders which already contained many observations, photographs and sketches of the trees they were studying. The visitor was interested to notice a display of materials from which children were going to learn about their village, and social life generally, at the time the school was opened. They included photostats of pages in the parish registers, the school log book and a diary kept by the founder, as well as a collection of books and illustrations lent by the county library.

287. The second class of sevens to nines were rather numerous for their small room, but had spread out into the corridor and were engaged in a variety of occupations. One group was gathered round their teacher for some extra reading practice, another was at work on an extraordinary structure of wood and metal which they said was a sputnik, a third was collecting a number of objects and testing them to find out which could be picked up by a magnet and two boys were at work on an immense painting (six feet by four feet) of St Michael defeating Satan. They seemed to be working harmoniously according to an unfolding rather than a pre-conceived plan. Conversation about the work that the children were doing went on all the time.

288. In the large new infants' room, too, many different things were going on. Some children were reading quietly to themselves; some were using a recipe to make some buns, and were doubling the quantities since they wanted to make twice the number; a few older children were using commercial structural apparatus to consolidate their knowledge of number relationships; some of

the youngest children needed their teacher's help in adding words and phrases to the pictures they had painted. The teacher moved among individuals and groups doing these and other things, and strove to make sure that all were learning.

289. These descriptions illustrate a point perhaps not often enough stressed, that what goes on in primary schools cannot greatly differ from one school to another, since there is only a limited range of material within the capacity of primary school children. It is the approach, the motivation, the emphasis and the outcome that are different. In these schools, children's own interests direct their attention to many fields of knowledge and the teacher is alert to provide material, books or experience for the development of their ideas.

2.4 Core Curriculum for Australian Schools

Curriculum Development Centre, Canberra

Introduction

This paper is about core curriculum for Australian schools and students – all schools, primary and secondary, government and non-government and all students. It is designed to assist all who have responsibility for what schools teach and how they teach it – including teachers, teacher educators, administrators, parents and community groups. [. . .] In issuing this paper the Curriculum Development Centre aims to contribute to what it sees as a substantial and continuing program of inquiry, planning and action by Australian educators and the community.

By core curriculum, we mean that set of basic and essential learnings and experiences which can reasonably be expected of all students who pass through our schools. 'Basic' learnings are defined as those which provide a base or foundation necessary for other study and learning, and for continuing personal development. 'Essential' learnings and experiences are defined as those which are required by all for effective cultural, economic, political, group, family and interpersonal life in society. Examples of what we define as basic learning for children in school are initial reading skills or ability and willingness to work in groups with other pupils. Essential learnings include but go beyond basics; for example, knowledge of political processes, skill in interpreting simple scientific data, or understanding environmental issues.

The distinctions between basic and essential cannot always be made sharply but in using both terms we wish to emphasise that core curriculum relates to *fundamental* qualities of both personal development and social participation which need attention at *all stages* of schooling. However, we must not confuse these fundamental qualities with the full or total range of human qualities, social and individual needs with which educators must concern themselves. In order to provide for a full or total education we need, *in addition to the core curriculum*, a wide range of specialist, optional, technical and advanced studies. These additional studies, important though they be, are not the subject of the present paper. [. . .]

The core curriculum needs to be seen as a central and crucial part of general education for all Australians. In designing and teaching the core curriculum, schools and educational authorities must aim to meet the needs of society, to assist in its further evolution and development, and to help meet the personal needs of the individual. [. . .]

It is not for the Centre to determine detailed curriculum content and

Source: *Core Curriculum for Australian Schools* (1980). Canberra: Curriculum Development Centre.

teaching methods, or to prescribe syllabuses and texts. These are the responsibility of many different authorities and groups throughout the country, not least the teachers, parents and students in the schools. However, we believe that as a national body charged by the Commonwealth Parliament to devise and develop school curriculum, support curriculum development and undertake related research, there are sound reasons for us to suggest broad directions for Australian schools to follow in deciding on core curriculum.

The Centre has built close working relationships with State and Federal Departments and agencies, Catholic and other non-government school authorities, teachers and teacher educators, researchers, community groups and individual schools. We are in a good position both to assess the forces and factors influencing curriculum in Australian schools and to comment on what is needed to bring about further qualitative improvements in school learning. We believe that concerted discussion and review of core curriculum, followed by changes in practice, will assist in bringing about these improvements.

The core curriculum now?

(a) Social change

There are *significant changes and developments in our society to which schools must respond*. These changes include:

- increased demands for basic and essential skills, for example, in communication, human relationships, economic management and working life
- the multi-cultural composition and interests of our population
- our growing regional and broader international roles and interests
- the disturbance effect of rapid scientific and technological change
- increased mobility of families and individuals
- changing patterns of employment and the emergence of structural youth unemployment
- more open, flexible and varied ways of life or lifestyles
- the impact of powerful new and interacting forces in our culture such as television, the leisure industry and 'pop' culture, which affect children's tastes, values and interests.

Changes of these kinds permeate the whole society and require us to reassess the content, structure, methods and outcomes of school curricula whose main outlines were worked out at an earlier period in our history, in and for a very different social order. The school must do more than reflect these far-reaching social changes. Amongst other things, it must select those learnings and experiences which will best equip all students to understand and cope with these changes. A strong affirmation of core curriculum at this time is a useful and, many might say, *necessary* response to society's changing needs and expectations of our schools. But we would not claim that core curriculum is a *sufficient* response to these changes which impinge upon all aspects of curriculum and of school itself.

(b) Community concern with education

Despite a considerable measure of community satisfaction with schooling, as demonstrated in several recent research studies, there appears to be a *growing community and society concern about educational directions and standards.* In order to address this we believe a firm, clear and simple statement about basic and essential learnings and experiences for all Australians is needed. A wide measure of community agreement should be sought for this statement if we are, in the future, to find ways of achieving a national consensus about the purposes and roles of our schools.

(c) Education for all

Schooling is now for the whole population, not the select few for whom, until recent decades, secondary schools were reserved. The influence on schooling of the forces noted above, together with the declining influence of such traditional sources of authority and support as religion and family life require us to review the aims of schools. Are we endeavouring to teach all students what is most needed for contemporary life or are we limiting our horizons to an uneasy mixture: the legacy of the past combined with catering to current student interests? Schools cannot teach everything and they must seek to define which of the many and varied needs of students and society they should seek to satisfy. A statement of core curriculum is one important way of defining the role of schools in meeting the overall educational needs of children and youth.

(d) Innovations in education

Educational theory, research and teaching practice have thrown up a wide range of challenging innovations in recent years. These include open or progressive education, school-based curriculum development, inquiry or discovery-based learning and the introduction into the curriculum of a wide range and variety of new subjects, courses, topics and themes. These changes have been, very often, beneficial. Yet there is misunderstanding and misgiving in the community because of lack of clarity about assumptions and directions. We believe schools and the community at large would be helped by having clear guidelines for curriculum. These guidelines should incorporate a framework of basic, essential learnings for students and should specify some of the successful ways available for schools to organise learning and teach students.

(e) Limited educational resources

Financial and human resources for schooling are not unlimited. It is more than ever prudent, in a period of static or shrinking educational budgets, for us to define what we mean by basic and essential learnings and to concentrate on them more than we have been doing – although not to the exclusion of elective studies – and to seek all the human and financial resources schools need to provide these learnings.

(f) Outdated subject organisation

A redefinition of core curriculum is needed because *our traditional way of packaging knowledge into required subjects no longer satisfies either society or students.* The restructuring of the curriculum by introducing a wide and numerous array of electives, has met many requirements but is not proving to be quite the answer, either to individual student needs or society's expectations. We need to reestablish a balance between a comprehensive core of learnings which includes, but is not restricted to, established subject matter and a realistic set of elective studies.

(g) Looking ahead

Looking to the future, we need to consider how best to meet emerging social and individual needs whilst using our resources economically and to maximum effect. A nationwide concern by the community at large, educators and students for what is basic and essential in school learning would be, we believe, valuable and timely for Australian society. Our curriculum must be forward looking and geared to our hopes and expectations for the future. We need to consider a core for present and anticipated future needs and not to look back nostalgically to the past as many critics of schooling have tended to do.

The aims of schooling in Australia

We define schooling as a process whereby particular kinds of institutions, namely primary and secondary schools, provide organised and structured learning opportunities for both present and future life, guide and direct learning activities, assess and communicate the results of teaching and learning, and organise resources in support of learning. The business of the school is to provide – whether by formal or informal means – planned and intended, not haphazard learnings. Thus the school must have particular aims and purposes to guide its educational program.

Education is a much broader process than schooling. It may be, and indeed is, conducted in a very wide range of institutions and settings of which schools are only one part. *Educational processes* are defined and limited by certain criteria, standards and purposes to which we refer below. We normally assume that the aims and functions of schooling are educational, but it is worth remembering that schools may have other functions too, such as child-minding, alleviating youth unemployment or indoctrination. These functions may, at times, get in the way of, or even contradict, the schools' educational aims and functions.

For the purpose of this paper, in talking of the aims of schooling, we mean those distinctly educational aims which the community and educators seek to pursue through the establishment and conduct of schools. We mean to focus on both broad educational aims which are universal in character – and not a product of particular societies at given periods of time – and narrower ones which relate specifically to contemporary Australian society, its traditions, assumptions and needs.

Universal aims of education

Among the most fundamental universal aims of education are:

the nurturing and development of the powers of reasoning, reflective and critical thinking, imagining, feeling and communicating among and between persons

the maintenance, development and renewal (and not merely the preservation) of the culture; that is of our forms and systems of thought, meaning and expression – such as scientific knowledge, the arts, languages and technology

the maintenance, development and renewal (and not merely the preservation) of the social, economic and political order – including its underlying values, fundamental structures and institutions

the promotion of mental, physical, spiritual and emotional health in all people.

These universal aims of education must, of course, be interpreted within and for particular societies. Through education in general and the school system in particular, Australia aims to support, promote and strengthen the aspirations, ideals, basic values and interests of its own culture and society. This must not, however, be seen as a backward-looking, narrow or inward-looking concern, given our multicultural aspirations and our role in the international community. Since our aim is to educate, not brainwash, our children we should encourage and sustain free critical thought, foster concern for the needs and rights of others – including sub-groups in our society and other societies – promote the free exchange and sharing of experiences and teach for personal, interpersonal and social development.

Aims for Australian schools

There are a number of aims of schooling in contemporary Australia to which there appears to be wide assent. These aims, to be realistic, must acknowledge the context in which schools operate and the resources available to them.

When stated concretely, as in school reviews and policy statements, they can and should serve as benchmarks in curriculum planning.

We can advance a set of school aims, appropriate to contemporary life, and relate them to some of the main features of our society.

The statement of aims, below, is not intended as an exhaustive list but it does provide a basis from which core curriculum may be developed.

As we have pointed out, schools in addition to the core must provide an *extended* curriculum to meet a wide range of individual and specialised needs. These are no less important than the core. However, we emphasise that the effectiveness of the total curriculum is dependent on the effectiveness of the core and that schools and other educational authorities cannot expect to succeed in their overall curriculum planning if they do not squarely address the question of what is needed in core curriculum for contemporary Australian schools.

Curriculum responses in practice

From a situation only a few years ago where, on a state-by-state basis, there were prescribed syllabuses and texts, external examinations and an overall homogeneity of practice, schools have moved into a much more open curriculum environment. [. . .] No institution can be randomly open to all influences. We have suggested that schools ought to be open to change within the context of declared and agreed aims and a clear curriculum framework – they cannot and should not be expected to continually alter and expand curricula to meet what, in practice, are often conflicting pressures and demands from every interest group.

A commitment, by schools, to core curriculum is a commitment to a view about what is fundamental in every child's learning, what it is reasonable to be responsive to amongst the wide range of demands and requirements from outside the school, and what teaching and material resources are needed if the schools are to do their work adequately.

Aims for Australian schools

All individuals have the right to education freely, equally and with concern shown for their individuality and personality. School curricula, therefore, need to provide for and encourage the full and rounded development of *all* students for the *whole* period of schooling, for which there are, for all Australians, minimum legal entitlements and requirements.

Australia is a parliamentary democracy subscribing to basic human rights, the rule of law, full and active participation in civic and social life, and fundamental democratic values. Schools have an obligation to teach democratic values and promote an active democratic way of life, including participation in the parliamentary system.

Australian society sustains and promotes a way of life which values, *inter alia*:

- a sense of personal, group and national identity and unity in all its people
- free communication amongst and between individuals and groups
- responsible participation in community and civic affairs
- tolerance and concern for the rights and beliefs of others
- equality of access to and enjoyment of education, health, welfare and other community services
- self-reliance, initiative and enterprise
- personal and social achievement
- rights to the ownership and use of property including property in the form of personal labour
- productive and socially responsible work
- conservation and development of a shared and dynamic heritage
- a sense of individual and group identity
- membership of the international community.

The schools, therefore, should encourage students to understand, reflect upon and subscribe to these and other basic values of the culture.

Participation in our society requires the exercise of a responsible economic role. Just as society needs productive work from its citizens, all people are entitled to work and to economic satisfaction. The schools need to educate all students for effective and satisfying participation in the economy. Paid work is the most visible and obvious, but not the only means of ensuring this participation.

All individuals, to be educated, need to strive for mastery of basic learning tools and resources. These include:

- communicating in spoken and written language
- number skills, mathematical reasoning and spatial relationships
- scientific processes and their applications
- logical inquiry and analysis
- creative, imaginative and intuitive ways of thinking and experiencing
- the capacity to apply and use knowledge symbols, processes and skills
- perception, expression and appreciation through the arts and crafts
- manual and other physical skills
- management of bodily and mental health
- the personal articulation of experience and thinking into value and belief systems.

Schools, therefore, should sponsor and foster these basic learning tools and resources, not in isolation but in close working relationship with other social institutions and groups.

Core curriculum for Australian schools

Core learning experiences

[. . .] Since it is the students' learning experiences that ought to concern us – the curriculum as experienced by students – we must also give attention both to how students learn and the resources and situations they need. This cannot be stressed too strongly as the term 'core curriculum' is so often loosely used to refer to a set of required subjects.

Defining the core curriculum requires us to make selections from contemporary culture and organise them into programs of school learnings. In practice this is a very difficult undertaking. The range of meanings, values and processes to be found in any complex culture is both vast and elusive. Moreover, because in our thinking, planning and teaching we are attending to the core as experienced – that is, to the learning processes of students (for example, gathering evidence, reasoning, discussing, and so on) and to learning situations (for example, mixed ability groups, field work, and so on) – we can anticipate considerable diversity in practice.

Building a framework

How are we to proceed? It has been suggested above that we need to review general aims of education, educational aims for Australian society and defined social needs. We also need a firm sense of the general character and history of our society, sound understanding of pedagogical principles and recognition of what is practicable, given resources available to us and the capacity of our teachers. *In the last resort, we must deem certain kinds of learning to be basic and essential and bend our efforts towards them. Our membership of a unified Australian society and our commitment to common aims justifies us in doing this.*

A core curriculum framework has to satisfy a number of criteria. These criteria may be treated as the principles underlying core curriculum, in the context of the general aims of education discussed above.

The core comprises fundamental learnings for all students. It does not define *all* learnings in the *whole* curriculum. The core ought to:

- focus on general, universal elements in culture for present and future life – the common culture;
- acknowledge the plural, multi-cultural nature of our society and seek a form of cultural-social integration which values interaction and free communication amongst diverse groups and sub-cultures – the common multiculture;
- outline those areas of knowledge, understanding and experience which all students are to study – the common learnings;
- bring out in the subjects and themes studied, their bearing on contemporary social life, and their relevance to all human beings – the contemporary, relevant aspects of education;

● specify minimum desirable kinds of learnings for all students, instead of attempting to cover specialised, optional and additional learnings to meet particular student and social interests and needs – the basic, essential learnings;

● define long-term, well-sequenced and systematic learnings from the beginnings of primary to the end of school years – the structure of learning;

● provide opportunity for students of different levels of ability, background and interest to study together – the common learning situations;

● specify typical learning tasks and methods and ways of applying learning to life situations – the common applied learning tasks.

Assessing student learning in the core

Because individual schools have the responsibility and need to adjust curricula to local circumstances, community interests and the differing learning requirements and characteristics of students, *it would be a mistake to attempt to present the core as a set of required learnings which could be tested through a national or State testing program.* [. . .]

The Curriculum Development Centre believes that by training and supporting teachers as evaluators, extending the use of diagnostic tests and adjusting learning tasks accordingly, strengthening community participation in school policy making, bringing about closer working relations between schools and other social institutions and improving the two-way flow of information between school and home, we can create a more powerful and educationally valid form of assessment than any testing program can yield. [. . .]

Core learnings: processes

The core should incorporate many different kinds of learning which are available through different experiences and subject matter. Core learnings will include:

● learning and thinking techniques such as problem-solving, lateral thinking, organised study habits, systematic recording of information, memorisation and recall, reaching decisions and making judgments;

● ways of organising knowledge such as the use of themes and topics and ways of gathering and interpreting evidence, for example, in science and social studies;

● dispositions and values such as truth-telling, honesty, regard for others, and so on;

● skills or abilities such as those found in reading, speech, the conduct of scientific experiments, elementary statistics, the use of tools, and ways of organising and completing learning tasks in groups;

● forms of expression such as story-writing, music and film-making, movement, graphic communication, and so on;

- workshops, field excursions and other practical performances in both the mental and manual spheres;
- interpersonal and group relationships as in group work, field trips, and so on.

Since the core is that part or dimension of the curriculum in which we are striving for common learnings and experiences, we cannot, in the core itself, give undue emphasis to those levels and forms of intellectual, artistic, physical or other aptitude which only some gifted children have. Yet, we should aim in the core to enable all children to perform as well as they are able within their individual competency and to succeed. The full development and exact training of special aptitudes and talents and the quest for excellence in specialised areas belong to optional or elective parts of the curriculum.

In practice, distinctions between what belongs to the core and what properly lies outside it may be at times exceedingly difficult to draw, in the face of individual differences, the common practice of grouping children into ability levels and the fact that studies in the elective areas will often build on what is in the core. Yet it is not impossible – experience shows that determined efforts by teachers and administrators can be quite successful.

The arguments we have adduced lead us to think that our approach to a core curriculum framework within the total curriculum should acknowledge the reality of established school subjects and subject areas. We need to find ways of incorporating processes and experiences which have no unique dependence on particular subjects, but which should be approached in an interdisciplinary or nondisciplinary fashion. Even if we wished to do so, we cannot ignore the subject-based teaching of many of our schools or the strong arguments for a disciplinary basis of knowledge and understanding. On the other hand, neither changing social needs nor the diversity of interest and aptitude of our students is adequately served by a core of orthodox subjects. We approach the definition of core content, therefore, by acknowledging a variety of claims and seeking ways of defining sequences of well-structured, systematic studies for all students in all of the areas we nominate. Of course, different weightings and emphases will be given to the different components of the core at different stages of student development and by different schools in different parts of the country. Both the longer term learning sequences and the weightings will need to be specified by educators in refining and further developing the core.

Core learnings: areas of knowledge and experience

It cannot be stated too strongly or frequently, that it is a mistake to treat the core simply in terms of subject content. Although we are bound to some extent to use the language of content in describing areas of learning and experience in the core, we must in so doing keep in mind that the desirable emphasis is on learning process and kinds of experience. Thus we need to consider appropriate learning *experiences*, *situations* and *resources*. Content, moreover, cannot be thought of only in terms of bodies of *knowledge*. As we have seen above, such matters as *values education*, the development of *manual skills* and *reasoning processes* also enter into a consideration of the content of the core. Plainly, an outline summary can only draw attention to some of the main features of the core. For a clearer and fuller specification of the overall content, structures, organisation and teaching methodology, much more detailed studies and analyses are needed. This process will be assisted by delineating the areas from which the core should be drawn.

The Centre has nominated nine broad areas, each of which requires detailed justification. Generally, our selection is based on the arguments and ideas presented thus far in this paper. The areas as described below are not meant as our last word on the subject since we expect modification and elaboration through the debate and discussion we anticipate will follow publication of this paper. However, we believe that the structure we propose is sound and appropriate for schools and other educational bodies to use in their curriculum planning and decision-making.

These nine areas of knowledge and experience presented below are capable of being grouped and interrelated in many different ways. *How* they are organised for teaching is not our primary concern in this paper but will be of concern to all schools in their curriculum planning. [. . .].

1 Arts and Crafts. Arts and crafts cover a wide and diverse area including literature, music, visual arts, drama, wood, metal and plastic crafts, and many others. Whilst in some respect it is not satisfactory to group these together, in the school setting they have many features in common, especially in regard to the techniques and tools used and the approaches adopted towards the shaping and manipulation of materials. The neglect of particular art forms, divided opinions about the need for general aesthetic education as distinct from expression through the arts, and the uneven approach to basic craft teaching in many schools, suggest the need for a comprehensive review of these areas of the curriculum. We have yet to define essential elements of experience, understanding, appreciation and skill, and to select a manageable array of learnings for schools. Until this is done and strong rationales produced, there will be a tendency on the one hand to multiply options and on the other to treat the arts as dispensable in schooling when other pressures obtrude. In fact, they represent major, fundamental forms of human expression, understanding, appreciation and communication. Given the range and diversity of arts and crafts, further studies are needed on the selection, organisation and direction of a sequential core program through all the years of schooling.

2 Communication. Communication includes both verbal and non-verbal modes and relates equally to knowledge and feeling – and these frequently interact, as for example in face-to-face conversation. We must select for the core those which are basic and essential. Language studies are an indispensable tool in many areas of learning and are intimately related to student thinking and expression. They include listening, speaking, reading and writing, which should be kept in balance throughout the school years. Non-verbal communication is equally a fundamental part of social life. Visual learning directs students towards an understanding and appraisal of the mass media and visual competence is necessary in many school subjects. Body communication, apart from its significance in everyday life, has a central place in several of the arts. Should the core include languages other than English? Despite the persuasive arguments advanced for foreign and 'ethnic' languages, it would be difficult at present to justify these as part of a *practical* core for all students. What is indisputably essential is that all Australians should become competent users of the English language. How far the *core* should and could extend to include any language other than English is a question over which educators are divided and the Centre would wish to have more discussion – and evidence – on this point.

3 Health Education. Growing public concern over health standards of Australians, reflecting the economic and psychic costs of ill-health, and the introduction of extensive and costly community health programs, suggest a need for sustained effort in school education. Health education has an immediate value to and impact on students which are available to few other areas of the curriculum.

The core curriculum needs to give scope to physical, emotional, mental and community health studies, and to provide opportunity for practical applications. 'Health', in becoming a school subject, may run the risk of being perceived as yet another body of knowledge to be known about rather than directly experienced. The health area needs to be approached through a wide range of studies ranging from the sciences of human biology and nutrition to programs of sport and physical recreation, general health care and relaxation. As with arts and crafts, there is need for an overall review of the area, to produce a well-organised practical framework for teaching and to gain acceptance of the need for all students to become involved in self-help health education programs.

4 Environmental Studies. The central purpose of environmental studies within the core is awareness and understanding of both the physical and man-made environments and sensitivity to the forces that sustain or may destroy them. This requires both systematic knowledge drawn from such disciplines as biology, geography, landscape architecture, economics, and so on, and a readiness by schools to participate in environmental maintenance projects which give students practical experience in the field. As in other areas of the core, there is an emphasis on social action – environmental studies represents a blend of theory and practice which may be organised in many different ways. Within the core, what is important is not the particular kind of organisation, but the environmentalist approach or perspective. This is an amalgam of types of knowledge and understanding, and a disposition to sustain and protect the environment.

5 Work, Leisure and Lifestyle. The notion of educating for present and future life is of central importance in schooling. Whilst all other core areas should contribute to this, there remain a number of aspects of universal human experience which may not be touched upon at all unless some additional, umbrella-like area is included in the core curriculum. There is much debate about the extent to which school as distinct from other social agencies or indeed individuals themselves should shoulder responsibility for 'education for life'. The case is complex, and cannot be argued here. The Centre accepts that for many different reasons schools ought to incorporate into the core curriculum a progressive introduction to the working environment, to developing and changing human relationships, to leisure-time interests and pursuits, and to such universal requirements of our culture as the ability to drive a car, plan a budget, keep records, purchase goods wisely, and organise a household. Entire curricula have been built around such a 'life preparation' notion but the weakness of this approach has been shown to be a neglect of the fundamental forms of human knowledge and experience, and of the skills required to participate in them. It seems preferable, therefore, to build a life preparation element into the core, to plan it around a selection of requirements of everyday life, and teach it at the levels of knowledge, understanding and reflective practice rather than low-level skills and techniques.

6 Mathematical Skills and Reasoning and their Applications. In addition to an understanding of basic number processes and their application in individual and social life, the main role of mathematics within the core is as a form of symbolising and quantifying. Mathematics contributes a view of the world, not merely practical skills, and this view needs to be fostered through problem-solving approaches, a wide range of applications and the training of reasoning. Applied mathematics relates to several other subject areas, for example, sciences, social sciences and some aspects of craft and technology. The relevance of mathematics to contemporary life has become increasingly apparent through calculators, computers and other technical applications, of which students need at least a general understanding.

7 Scientific and Technological Ways of Knowing and their Social Applications. Science and technology are fundamental forms of human thought and powerful applications of organised problem-solving to practical situations in the everyday life of individuals, for whole societies and for the world order. They exemplify not only rational but also intuitive, imaginative and creative powers of the highest order. They are decisive forces in the transformation of social and economic life, belief systems and working life. Their study in the core requires an emphasis on forms of knowledge, synthesis, interpretation and extrapolation of data, problem-solving, decision-making, theory-practice relations and social action. They are a means of interpreting and modifying the environment. Thus, scientific and technological studies need to pay attention to social issues, interrelationships amongst science, technology and social trends and needs, and the historical conditions giving rise to scientific and technical change. Although choice of material for learning may vary widely, science and technology in the core should provide opportunity for a common set of skills, understandings and dispositions – scientific and technical thinking and their applications.

8 Social, Cultural and Civic Studies. The focus of social, cultural and civic studies is the understanding of what is required for effective participation in social life, including the major political, social and cultural institutions and processes of Australia as a democratic and economically advanced society. These studies include consideration of the place and significance of belief and value systems (religion, ideology) in our society. They have dimensions which are both historical (social/political/economic history) and contemporary (social issues and trends, the law, consumerism, social values, and so on). They may be taught separately as 'social sciences' (including history, economics, and so on) and 'cultural studies' (including religion and values education), or in an integrated fashion. The scope of these studies should include the diverse sub-cultures and common cultures within Australia (including ethnic and Aboriginal subcultures), and in other societies, and the ideas of an international or world order. Opportunity should be provided for students to appraise and assess the evolution, present status of and trends in the social and civic order and to undertake practical action projects. As prospective citizens, students have a part to play in deciding the future of their country and of the international order. For these studies to have practical relevance they must relate to the present life experiences and interests of the students.

9 Moral Reasoning and Action, Value and Belief Systems. The development of morality and the capacity to discriminate amongst values and beliefs is both a crucial part of the overall development of the rounded person and a civic necessity. Transformation of moral action from the level of habitual and routine behaviour in childhood to a mature stage of critical analysis and reflective action requires a systematic, continuing approach throughout the years of schooling. Values education relates to many aspects of life in addition to moral behaviour, but has close affinities with it. Whilst the teaching of morality and values, as such, readily lends itself to abuse through indoctrination, its neglect in the curriculum may be regarded as a serious deficiency in many schools. The teaching of morality and values need, and perhaps ought, not depend on a separate course, but may be incorporated in other areas – for example social, cultural and civic studies or the arts – and within established subjects and in a wide range of school relationships between students and teachers. Whilst the teaching of religious belief and practice cannot claim a place in a core, teaching *about* religion may be regarded as essential for all students in developing their understanding of the world in which they live.

2.5 Innovation without Growth

William Taylor

[. . .] It was during [the 1960s] that interest began to be shown in the phenomenon of innovation itself. National and international organizations arranged conferences and working parties, research workers by empirical enquiry tried to establish the conditions favourable and unfavourable to innovation, and whole books began to appear on the subject. In one of the best known, Matthew B. Miles's *Innovation in Education* (1964), the author had little doubt about what constituted the most significant causative factors – in his words, '. . . the sheer size and growth of the educational establishment itself is exerting perhaps the most profoundly innovative effect of all' (p. 9). Within the educational establishment, Miles argued, the higher schools were influencing the lower in the direction of innovation with (and again I quote), 'the apogee of influence turning out to be the graduate department in the university, which not only influences lower programs but also produces new knowledge, controls admission to itself, and trains related practitioners'.

The links between growth and innovation were not difficult to establish. Growth meant the recruitment of new teaching staff, many of them young, and the desire (which must sometimes be separated from the ability) of the young to innovate is supported both by commonsense observation and by evidence (Carlson, 1965; Miller, 1967).

Growth produces a regular increment of additional resources, which can be applied to new purposes without having to meet the political costs of reducing allocations to existing activities or ceasing to support on-going work. So people can be hired, departments and units established, equipment purchased, buildings erected, and programmes funded, without too much pain for those who do not wish to, or cannot, participate in the innovation. And if innovation is not as rapid as some of the providers and some of the customers and clients might wish, then growth also provides an alibi, a set of plausible reasons why in the face of continuing demands for taking on additional students, hiring inexperienced staff, commissioning new plant, it has proved impossible to undertake the fundamental modifications in programmes and technology that 'everyone' agrees are necessary and desirable.

Size, too, is also associated with diversification in student interests and ability, teaching practices, course options, and organizational forms. Such diversity, in breaking down the tight collegiality and control that often characterized the smaller, more self-contained institution, facilitates interaction of a kind directed to the achievement of particular objectives. Within large schools, departmental and other working groups sometimes achieve a commitment to co-operative action through sustained face-to-face contact in

Source: *Educational Administration*, 1976, *4*, 2, Spring.

lunch-time meetings, curriculum projects, planning sessions and so forth that goes beyond what could have been achieved in the less differentiated framework of the smaller school, where staff meetings were rare, teachers were isolated from one another's practice, and control, if benevolent, was often autocratic.

In colleges and universities, growth enabled new units and departments to be financed within traditional structures, and complete institutional frameworks of a non-traditional kind designed, without too much anxiety being generated about threats to the excellence of the main stream of university activity. Growth yields money to back projects and programmes and units in educational research and development, and to see that the results of their efforts are disseminated widely through print materials and the media, by innumerable conferences and meetings.

It is hardly surprising, therefore, that we have come to associate innovation with increases in the size and scale of educational operations. Such an association is part of the biographies of very many of those who now occupy major positions of influence and power within the educational system.

Nor is it surprising that growth in numbers of teachers and pupils, lecturers and students, courses and programmes, books and journals, conferences and meetings, and in all the processes that contribute to the rate of turnover within the system, have come to be causally associated with efforts to achieve planned change in the service of particular educational objectives.

Now that the great bonanza is at an end, now that the metaphors have changed, and educational discourse is strewn with references to steady state, zero growth, the beauties of smallness, the advantages of not having to spread one's net too widely, the need to assess priorities and to identify and protect the essentials of one's own particular activities, what will be the consequences for innovation and planned change in education? Is the association between growth and innovation accidental and historical, or is it intrinsic to the nature of the processes that these terms seek to describe?

The semantics of the business have their own interest. There has been an attempt in recent years to separate more clearly the meanings of 'innovation' and 'change', generally in the direction of stressing the purposeful nature of the former and the ubiquity of the latter. Thus, we have moved from definitions such as that of H. G. Barnett (1953): 'Innovation is any thought, behaviour or thing that is new because it is qualitatively different from existing forms', to the more precise, if somewhat laboured, definition of Richland (quoted in Huberman, 1974): 'Innovation is . . . the creative selection, organization and utilization of human and material resources in new and unique ways which will result in the attainment of a higher level of achievement of the defined goals and objectives.'

Although definitions of this kind limit the concept of innovation and make it more manageable, their stress upon the goal-directed nature of innovations may result in neglect of the situational and environmental influences that help to stimulate and shape the action of individuals and groups. I have to confess that I find it difficult to separate the concept of innovation from the notion of educational improvement, particularly since the latter already incorporates the normative element that has come to be assumed in recent usage of 'innovation'.

[. . .] If we stick to the 'growth promotes innovation' argument, we must believe that the absence of annual resource increments during the coming years will inevitably slow down the rate of planned change and strengthen resistances to innovation. The inability to recruit young staff; the absence of an undistributed margin to fund new developments; the fact that innovation will no longer pay in career terms as it might have done in a period when the proportion of specialist and promotion posts was increasing; the effect on morale and willingness to commit personal resources fully to organizations that may result from the absence of opportunities to do new and exciting things; the forms of consciousness associated with steady state (Berger *et al.*, 1974); less money for the research and development organizations, and thus for the activities they seek to stimulate; fear of an uncertain future, and a desire to hold on to what is proven and what works; less willingness to take on short-term risk-bearing appointments, given the greater difficulty of breaking back into the main career stream – all these, and many other factors, could be adduced as likely to contribute to a downturn in innovative action, and a lengthening of the time scale that separates invention, development, large-scale adoption and institutionalization.

[. . .] Most efforts to relate innovation, size and growth over-emphasize economic factors and give insufficient place to the political, social and psychological conditions that govern the possibility of educational improvement.

The forces that produce educational innovation are complex. They include changes in the size and composition of the groups for which the educational system attempts to cater, changes in the occupational, social and political skills and types of knowledge deemed relevant and useful to life in a particular kind of society, changes in the bases of institutional legitimacy and the development of new technologies that have application to ways of teaching and learning. Innovations in ideas, technology and organization occur in society, in educational systems, and in schools. There are obvious connections between these types and levels of innovation. The invention of semi-conductors has affected the technology of the classroom, the political emphasis on equality combined with the liberal value of respect of persons has encouraged mixed-ability teaching. But equally there have been and there remain discontinuities. The reorganization of secondary education has gone on almost without reference to changes in classroom technology and pedagogical ideas which we can *now* see as essential to its success. In turn, innovations in technology have been slow to influence organization at school or system level. Despite all that we now do by way of distance teaching, through television, VTR, radio, sound tape, visual projection, computers and the like, most children still spend most of their time learning and being taught by traditional methods within conventional classrooms.

By now I hope that it will be clear that in my view there is no *necessary* link between innovation (equated with improvement) and growth, although many of the conditions associated with growth do facilitate innovatory processes.

If innovation is to be stimulated without growth, what is increasingly needed is a willingness to spend time and energy on articulating the various elements that contribute to educational improvement, and this is more often than not a political and organizational rather than an economic or technological problem. Indeed, failures of articulation are characteristic of periods of rapid growth and change. The couple of hours that technology enables us to cut off transatlantic flight are spent in coping with the security checks that arise from breakdowns in the political fabric. Having delegitimized (and almost physically abolished) the kind of teacher training institution that sought to internalize commitments and values which enabled its graduates to be left free to practice without direct supervision, we now have to devise more sophisticated forms of control in the form of operational goal-setting and accountability.

Those who argue that we should declare a moratorium on research and development until everything that has been done in the past twenty years is evaluated, the good absorbed into the practice of the schools and the bad discarded, have a rather naive conception of what is involved in educational change. Whatever the merits of seeing social life in terms of a journey, it is not one that can be halted while we consult the map. But if what they mean is that the availability of a particular set of materials or a particular piece of equipment or knowledge of a particular organizational possibility or technique is seldom the principal condition of educational improvement, and conversely, that lack of availability of knowledge is seldom the prime reason for the absence of such educational improvement, then they have a point. Just as a man's busy-ness may help him to avoid confronting the existential emptiness that lies at the core of his life, so the kinds of expensive innovatory efforts that were facilitated by growth may have helped us to avoid facing up to the need for the development and exercise of those political, organizational, administrative and social skills on which the possibility of genuine educational improvement depends.

But what does all this amount to in terms of practical decision-making in school, system and society? We have to look at the models of innovation that we have created at different levels and see to what extent these remain viable without the annual increments of resources to which we have become accustomed. Is it true, for example, as critics have suggested, that in Britain the Schools Council operates in terms of centre-periphery assumptions that are suspect even in times of plenty, still more so in periods of shortage? We have to understand the dynamics of improvement much better than we do now, orienting our studies not so much to the failures of the system – the schools where order has broken down, the communities that have ceased to support their teachers – as to the successes. We need to know more than we do today about why and how many schools display an impressive capacity for improvement, enjoy the support of parents, are characterized by high teacher and pupil morale and satisfy a broad range of educational expectations. Why these and not the others? And then there is the business of stimulating a commitment to personal and professional improvement on the part of the individual teacher, and the kinds of mental habits that see the educative possibilities of everyday situations and familiar materials.

We have also to create conditions within our own schools, colleges and universities that will maintain and enhance capacity for innovation of staff and organization. Let me suggest some of the staffing and resource strategies that might, within the kind of academic framework with which I am most familiar, facilitate innovation at a time when there is unlikely to be any growth in real terms. The following list does not reflect any very systematic research, and will be far too prescriptive, programmatic and cryptic for those who believe that educationists should limit themselves to the careful statement of findings from carefully controlled empirical analyses.

1 Try to re-define growth in terms that owe more to the psychologists than to the economists. Admittedly, our psychological colleagues have produced a deal of windy rhetoric around this theme, and their suggestions are sometimes politically naive, but that is not to dismiss the central core of values and practices that they advocate as unworthy or unimportant.

2 Seek to identify that which is distinctive about the operations of one's own organization, and that which might, without too much difficulty, be performed in other people's space and time. This is particularly important in the face of real crisis if it comes, for then it may be necessary to act quickly in a climate unconducive to the cool appraisal of alternative strategies.

3 Avoid committing resources on a permanent basis to activities that have an uncertain future. In the University of London Institute of Education we are using the well-known device of creating 'Centres' (an unsatisfactory term) as the basis of a number of new inter-disciplinary initiatives, such as teaching and research in political education, to the work of which interested staff from a number of existing Departments will contribute under the Chairmanship of a convener. In so far as it proves possible to appoint staff to take major responsibility for the activities of a Centre, these people will also have their feet firmly in one of the subject departments. Then in five years' time, if the agenda has changed or something else has happened to make a Centre non-viable, it can be closed down without threatening the identity or the jobs of those concerned. Alternatively, if its work flourishes, and resources flow more freely, we can give consideration to establishing the group on a more permanent basis.

4 Give more attention to all the relationships and processes involved in what has come to be called 'staff development', including a more open approach to promotion procedures, and the possible development of intermediate statuses that will provide the ego-protection threatened by a loss of opportunities for professional mobility. This includes, for example, means whereby all staff who have not achieved promotion by a certain age can have their cases reviewed on a regular basis by a representative group, the membership of which is rotated completely every year.

Another aspect of this matter is the need to make provision for those senior members of staff who, nearing retirement or having had enough of high-pressure administration, wish to make way for younger men but are prevented from doing so because of loss of salary and status. It was commonplace a few years ago to read and to hear that, as society became wealthier, so individuals would choose to shorten their working lives in the interests of post-retirement leisure and the development of personal interests. Those who made these predictions did not reckon with the effects of inflation on capital and pension prospects. Given the age structure in many sectors of educational employment, attention to this problem is becoming a matter of urgency.

5 Maintain and enhance flexibility in the deployment of vacancies. Understandably, the trade unions do not like short-term appointments. Nonetheless, some may need to be made, especially in the face of doubtful institutional futures. In tertiary institutions, sums not large enough to support a full-time post can sometimes be used to establish short-term Fellowships for doctoral or post-doctoral candidates who are willing to teach for a few hours each week and to study and participate in research alongside a senior member of the department. Additional short-term help, which does not require a permanent financial commitment, can sometimes be obtained through secondment from elsewhere; there is a greater readiness on the part of colleges to second staff in this way during a period in which enrolments are tending to fluctuate somewhat unpredictably.

6 If you have any discretion in these matters, work out the respective costs and benefits of worsening conditions of service (student-staff ratios, secretarial help, sabbaticals, departmental budgets) in order to take on the maximum number of staff. There are some fine judgments to be made here. Is it better to maintain the morale and work conditions of existing staff, and to take the risk that the level of future funding might be influenced by a shortfall in student numbers, or to respond to buoyant demand and the needs of the system by worsening ratios? Such questions are likely to become more rather than less important if we move towards the kind of 'formulae funding' that is now well established in some other English-speaking countries.

7 Diversify staff incentives, and encourage a spread of personal invest-ments that minimizes the impact of career frustration and professional disappointment on morale. Just as we have so frequently measured the success of systems and of institutions by their rate of growth and overall size, so at lower levels we have accorded esteem and prestige to the head of department who is visibly successful in building up the numbers and size of his staff, the amount of his research grants, and the range and variety of courses and programmes in which he and his colleagues engage. The steady state organization will offer fewer incentives and rewards of this kind. In lieu of the manifest achievements of a consistently developing career, we may have to provide more opportunities to succeed in relation to the work of what have been called 'temporary systems', short-term activities, and initiatives which do not demand additional increments of resources. Those accounts that we

have of life in universities and the civil service before the Second World War suggest that the norm of overwork is a relatively recent introduction. In part, as Cohen and March (1974) have shown, overwork may be a response to increased uncertainty about the place of educational institutions within society, and the roles of those who work within them. Writing of the College Presidency, they claim that (p. 149):

Presidents feel misused. Most of the Presidents with whom we talked appeared to feel rather little control over their schedules. They felt themselves to be the victims of the pressures upon them and the limitations of time and their own energies. Too many people asking too much too often. Too many 'trivial' activities that had to be engaged in. No time for thinking or reading or initiating action.
[Presidents] . . . seem to believe that the presidential report card has two components: effort and performance. Performance is largely an Act of God or at least not clearly under the control of the President. If the President works hard, he may still face a financial, student or faculty catastrophe. But if he doesn't work hard, he will be treated as a failure in any event.

I do not think we shall rid ourselves easily of the ethic of hard work, nor do I think it would benefit us or our fellows to do so. Since most of our educational organizations will continue to be 'organized anarchies' in the sense defined by Cohen and March, whatever spurious appearance of system and order we may attempt to give by carefully-devised behavioural objectives and techniques of evaluation, then ambiguity is a condition of our lives and we may have to put up with the overwork syndrome that goes with it. But most of our schools and colleges and universities would be better places for the students that inhabit them if, as is already the case for a large number of our colleagues, staff had more rather than less developed tastes in literature, music, poetry, food and drink. Some semblance of taste in the quality of life and choice of leisure pursuits of academics is not necessarily correlated with a disregard for the unprivileged of our own society or of the world, or unconnected with the quality of education they help to provide.

8 Generate better and fuller data collection and information within the organization or system in order to maximize the useful deployment of resources. In recent years, schools and colleges have become much more sophisticated than in the past about the use of space and time. The latter is a major ingredient in innovation, and also one of the most expensive resources within the control of individuals and groups. As has recently been re-emphasized in Britain by the Department of Education and Science, in connection with the OECD review of national policies for education (OECD, 1975), some 70 per cent of all educational costs are in the form of academic salaries, and payments to non-academic staff account for nearly another 10 per cent.

'Cutting back' is nearly always conceived as trimming marginal expenditures, reducing spending on those items over which an individual or an organization has discretion – phone calls, transport, stationery, photo-copies, heating and magazines in Reception – as distinct from those items where little or no short-term discretion exists, such as tenured staff, buildings, and the implementation of current policies. Furthermore, 'cuts' are seen as abnormal, temporary measures to be cancelled as soon as more normal times return. But if outside the area of peripherals nothing can be done immediately to redirect patterns of spending, then at least we can ensure that the time of tenured staff is used to the maximum effect in whatever the organization is trying to do. Hours are still spent by teachers in primary or secondary schools on what are essentially stock-taking activities, where the expenditure of time is often considerably in excess of the value of the goods in the stock-book. In higher education a passion for democratization and the erosion of trust in the motives and decision-taking capabilities of senior staff sometimes result in unproductive wrangling that takes up many hours that would be better spent in teaching, private study and research.

9 Delegate as many decisions as possible in the utilization of scarce resources, in order to increase the chances of people being able to identify and satisfy their self-perceived needs and wants. For example, in a school, college or university that has faculties or some other kind of functional division, it makes sense to allocate a portion of the available replacements, additional appointments or re-allocations to each division to work out an internal distribution amongst the various subject groups or units. Apart from being a possibly more efficient way of using resources, this also avoids concentrating blame for shortages and misallocations upon one individual or committee, no bad thing at a time when the policies of institutional life are becoming more rather than less complicated.

10 Maintain an appropriate balance between, on the one hand, security and reward for seniority, and, on the other, early and rapid promotion for the ideas man, the productive cosmopolitan, and the innovator. Maintaining such a balance is by no means a new problem, but it takes on added emphasis at a time when lack of turnover and opportunities elsewhere may well affect staff morale. If people are going to have to spend longer in the one organization, then they need to have greater confidence in its willingness to recognize their contribution. Carried to excess, this could result in the type of career profile that has shown itself inimical to innovation in some school systems. There are no simple rules that govern such a balance. It can only be struck by vigilance, the availability of high-quality data and sensitivity to the nuances of inter-personal feeling and morale within the organization.

11 Finally – at least for the present purpose of illustrating strategies conducive to innovation – devise means for the management of the inept. In teaching, at all levels, as in every other occupation, there are different degrees of competence and performance. We do not know much about the variables involved, to what extent these are a function of personality or of situation. When criteria are obscure and diffuse it ill behoves us to be dogmatic. In teaching there are fewer manifest disaster criteria than in some other occupations. The numbers of people who believe that we should not put up with incompetence in teaching, and that means are necessary to terminate the appointments of those who fall below a certain standard, are growing.

Professor Maurice Kogan (1975) has been reported as saying: 'Teachers in all institutions, including those offering higher education, could well go on to five-year contracts to be renewed by decision of the employing authority and by the appointments board of the school.' Whatever attraction such an idea may possess in terms of added accountability, it runs counter to the consequences of much recent legislation affecting employment. Anyone who has had recent experience in negotiating a conditions of service agreement with a trade union, or interpreting the provisions of legislation in relation to the termination of contracts, or examining the implications of the Sex Discrimination Act for appointment and promotion procedures, might be somewhat less sanguine about the possibilities of such termination. It could be argued that spelled-out procedures and criteria for the satisfactory completion of probation, passing the efficiency bar, and achieving promotion strengthen the arm of the institution as much as that of the individual member of staff. But in practice nearly all the advantages accrue to the individual. And, whatever the humane and liberal intentions of those who drafted these bills, the consequent bureaucratization may well stimulate defensive strategies that will stultify rather than encourage innovation.

But, legislation apart, I have to confess myself unsympathetic to suggestions that we deal with our problems by passing them on to someone else. In a rapidly growing system this was often possible. In more static conditions it is much more difficult, and we must be more imaginative, inventive and patient in finding ways in which to employ the talents of everyone on the staff of a school or college, whatever his or her limitations and deficiencies. This is more than mere piety. Most institutions have their share of the incompetent, the intransigent and the inept. Increasingly, since they cannot or will not leave us, we shall have to learn to live with them. And, just possibly, those of us who make judgments about other people's work, whether heads, chief officers, vice-chancellors or even the proposed 'Appointments Boards' of schools, could sometimes be wrong, and individuals need protection against our errors.

I have tried to suggest some of the ways in which the absence of growth in many areas of educational provision will make innovation and improvement more difficult. I do not believe that we shall see any sharp downturn in the rate at which new ideas and practices and institutional forms and techniques appear, are tested, modified and incorporated into our schools and our systems, because despite our current problems many of the non-economic conditions that stimulate innovation are still likely to be with us. There is a lively debate about the distribution of educational opportunities that is reflected in problems of school and system organization. There are competitive pressures within the developed world that place a premium upon maintaining a high level of educational achievement. The institutions and roles that have been established during the past ten years to sponsor and to facilitate innovation are likely to continue in being with an added awareness of the need for support within their constituencies and for their work to satisfy more stringent criteria of usefulness. The pace of social change is unlikely to diminish, although its character may owe more to forces other than simple technical and economic expansion.

Such change will inevitably exert pressures upon the schools. Despite a new stress upon accountability, on the need to ensure that all children have access to a guaranteed minimum of curricular content, and on the dangers to the civil condition posed by the presence of Trotskyite teachers in the schools, it is likely that a very considerable measure of freedom will remain for the individual teacher and head to introduce innovations that find their way into the language and literature of our trade and into the practice of institutions other than those in which they originated.

For all these reasons we need not be too pessimistic about future prospects for innovation. Growth helped. But the absence of growth need be no bar to the development of those political, social and administrative skills without which the most advanced forms of technique are ineffective in making a contribution to educational improvement.

References

BARNETT, H. G. (1953) *Innovation: The Basis of Cultural Change*. New York: McGraw Hill.

BERGER, P., BERGER, B. and KELLMAN, T. (1974) *The Homeless Mind*. Harmondsworth: Penguin Books.

CARLSON, R. (ed.) (1965) *Change Processes in the Public School*. Eugene, Oregon: University of Oregon.

COHEN, M. A. and MARCH, J. G. (1974) *Leadership and Ambiguity: The American College President*. New York: McGraw-Hill.

HUBERMAN, A. M. (1974) *Understanding Change in Education: An Introduction*. Geneva: UNESCO International Bureau of Education.

KOGAN, M. (1975) *The Times Educational Supplement*, 17 October.

MILES, M. B. (1964) *Innovation in Education*. New York: Teachers College Press.

MILLER, R. (ed.) (1967) *Perspectives on Educational Change*. New York: Appleton Century Crofts.

OECD (1975) *Educational Development Strategy in England and Wales*. Paris: The Organization for Economic Cooperation and Development.

Part Three Reforming the Curriculum

Innovations are planned and implemented by people. They involve complex judgments about human motivations and organizational processes. To some extent such judgments will be unique to individual situations but studies of strategies and procedures used to effect change suggest that they may be grouped according to the underlying assumptions about motivations and organizational processes which the strategies contain. One of the best known formulations was developed by Chin and Benne (1967, second edn 1969) and provided the theoretical framework for a major international study undertaken by Per Dalin between 1970 and 1973. The first reading in this section is from that research: *Case Studies in Educational Innovation*. In it Dalin analyses three main strategies of innovation.

The second reading also has its origins in the 1960s. The decade was characterized by a high degree of optimism about people's capacity to bring about planned change and by a strong technological emphasis on the process of innovation. Progress and technology were equated and influenced innovation in medicine, agriculture, industry, education and other fields. Several hundred studies of innovation from this period were reviewed by Havelock. He focused on the dissemination and utilization of knowledge and concluded that there were three main models which could be used to describe the utilization process. His proposition, which has been widely used in subsequent analyses, constitutes the second reading.

The paper by Harlen presents an evaluation of the Schools Council Science 5–13 project in the course of which she illustrates how a central team research and develop materials and how they are modified. Harlen's evaluation notes additional questions on the dissemination process which need to be explored and importantly acknowledges that innovations may be introduced without the philosophy being accepted. It reminds us that innovations are not adopted, they are adapted by the users.

The next paper is concerned with theoretical issues. In it Bernstein distinguishes between two types of curricula – an 'integrated-type' and a 'collection-type'. He argues that these two types of curricula are related to a number of other organizational phenomena, for example, forms of management, pedagogy and assessment procedures and beyond educational institutions to the distribution of power and the principles of social control.

Bernstein's paper offers an opportunity to move from macro-level analysis to school-level analysis. This opportunity is taken by Hamilton in the next reading. The introduction of integrated science into two Scottish schools is examined using Bernstein's analytical framework. It emerges that innovation proved more difficult than anticipated and that schools though attempting the same innovation developed different social, intellectual and organizational priorities over time.

Richardson's study which follows similarly focuses on implementation rather than dissemination. Like Hamilton's the technique adopted is participant-observation. The particular innovation at Nailsea school was a change in the management structure. Written within a human relations perspective it reminds us that the implementation of innovation is a social process involving role changes which are problematic for many participants. It also underlines that an innovation in one part of a social system has effects on other parts of the system.

The final article is a reminder that the social system of the school is set within a larger social system. Values, preferred models and priorities in the two systems are not always congruent. But in order to function effectively the school must find ways to reduce or manage incipient conflict. Reid's article considers possible strategies.

3.1 Strategies of Innovation

Per Dalin

Empirical–rational strategies

The underlying assumption in these strategies, as defined by Bennis, Benne and Chin (1969), is that man is reasonable and will act in some rational way. The primary task of the innovator, therefore, is to demonstrate through the best known method the validity of a certain innovation in terms of the increased benefits to be gained from adopting it. An innovation is usually proposed by some person or group that knows the effect and also knows the person, group or organization that will be affected by the innovation.

Obviously this strategy is based on an optimistic view of human beings. It can be found throughout the whole Western world. It is the basis for liberal practice and empirical research as well as general education.

Some of the basic empirical – rational strategies as seen by Bennis, Benne and Chin are discussed below:

(i) *Basic research and dissemination of knowledge through general education*
This strategy of innovation is, of course, still the most common strategy in the Western world. The underlying assumption is that innovations will most probably occur through the actions of people and that people will innovate as soon as their basic understanding is altered.

(ii) *Personnel selection and replacement*
Very often the difficulty of ensuring innovation is looked upon as a personnel problem. The strategy of specially selecting personnel for a given task was given a scientific 'boost' by the development of scientific testing of potentialities and aptitudes.

This approach has often been used to maintain a system in accordance with the interests of the people in power rather than to change the system for the benefit of the individuals and groups involved. In many cases, also, focusing on the personnel problem has made it impossible to reveal difficulties inherent in the social and cultural system itself.

(iii) *Systems analysts and consultants*
An emerging strategy is the use of behavioural scientists as 'systems analysts'. This approach regards innovation as a wide-angled problem in which all the input and output features are considered. The application of educational technology to curriculum development comes closest to this school of thought. The approach is based upon an 'equilibrium model', transforming a system of some discomfort into a system 'in harmony'. Usually the question of redistribution of power in the system is not taken into account, and the continuance of present structure is taken for granted.

(iv) *Applied research and linkage systems for diffusion of research results*
The best known example of this approach is to be found in America in the land-grant university and the agricultural extension system. The idea was to link basic research

Source: DALIN, P. (1974) *Case Studies in Educational Innovation: IV*. Paris: OECD/CERI, pp. 44–51.

with applied research and with professional practitioners, very often through demonstration centres and field experiments. This system developed extension services, and county agents and practitioners were attached to the demonstration centres or the land-grant colleges; from this the idea of 'change agents' developed. Recently in education, similar attempts have been made in America (as well as in Europe) to link applied research activities with basic researchers on the one hand and with persons in action and practice settings on the other. This can be seen in particular in the creation of research development centres based in universities and the regional laboratories connected with State departments of education, colleges and universities in a geographical area, and with various consortia and institutes which tackle problems of innovation.

Bennis, Benne and Chin (1969) say about this approach: 'The questions of *how* to get a fair trial and *how* to instal an innovation in an already going and crowded school system are ordinarily not built centrally into the strategy.' The rationale behind this is that if an innovation can show that it can achieve what it is supposed to achieve, the consumer will adopt it . . .

(v) *Utopian thinking as a strategy of change*

In the last few years a number of projects have been set up to study the future of education; for example, the Eight-State Project and the Europe Year 2000. In both public and private organizations futurology seems to have emerged as one approach to innovation in education.

Basically this approach builds on present knowledge in an attempt to 'forecast' the future. It implies that the future (which commonly is presented as 'alternative futures') will be based on trends and tendencies which can be observed today.

The underlying assumption behind the empirical – rational strategies is that research is 'neutral' and 'objective'. This model of social science research is taken from the natural sciences. The model defines the researcher as an 'observer'. Philosophically it is idealistic and closely related to positivism and classical liberalism . . .

Since the strategy by definition excludes the question of values and ideologies and assumes an 'objective' position, the process of innovation can be defined as a 'knowledge utilization process'. If 'knowledge' were accepted and utilized in this simple and direct manner, it would have tremendous impact. We know, however, that *knowledge in the social sciences is not identical with power*, since we know much more than we are able to put into practice.

The definition of 'empirical – rational' which is implied in the discussion above would be regarded as a rather narrow definition by many researchers. Also, the approach seems to build on a 'consensus-model' which is not necessarily the only basis for empirical – rational strategies.

Normative – re-educative strategies

Normative – re-educative strategies of innovation develop from theories which can be traced back to work of Sigmund Freud, John Dewey, Kurt Lewin and others. Their basis is to regard as of central importance the question of how the client understands his problem. The problem of innovation is not a matter of supplying the appropriate technical information, but rather a matter of changing attitudes, skills, values and relationships. Change in attitudes is just as necessary as change in products. Acknowledging the client's value-system implies less manipulation from outside. Innovation is defined as activating forces *within* the system to alter it.

As we can see, these assumptions about human motivation differ from those underlying the rational – empirical strategies. Bennis, Benne and Chin say about this:

These strategies build upon assumptions about human motivation different from those underlying the first. The rationality and intelligence of men are not denied. Patterns of action and practice are supported by sociocultural norms and by commitments on the part of individuals to these norms. Sociocultural norms are supported by the attitude and value systems of individuals – normative outlooks which undergird their commitments. Change in a pattern of practice or action, according to this view, will occur only as the persons involved are brought to change their normative orientations to old patterns and develop commitments to new ones. And changes in normative orientations involve changes in attitudes, values, skills, and significant relationships, not just changes in knowledge, information or intellectual rationales for action and practice . . .

Intelligence is social, rather than narrowly individual. Men are guided in their actions by socially funded and communicated meanings, norms and institutions, in brief, by a normative culture. At the personal level, men are guided by internalised meanings, habits and values. Changes in patterns of action or practice are, therefore changes, not alone in the rational informational equipment of men but at the personal level, in habits and values, as well as at the sociocultural level, are alterations in normative structures and in institutionalised roles and relationships, as well as in cognitive and perceptual orientations.

In normative – re-educative strategies a change agent works *with* the client. He bases his work on the behavioural sciences and his main concern is to identify and bring out into the open and take into account the attitudes, values and opinions of the client. According to this school of thought, the change agent seeks to avoid manipulation of the client by bringing the values of the client, along with his own, into the open, and by working through value-conflicts responsively.

Bennis, Benne and Chin emphasize the involvement of the client in the innovation. It is assumed that the change agent must learn to operate collaboratively with the client in order to solve the client's problems. Non-conscious elements must be brought into consciousness, and the methods and concepts which are used are drawn from the behavioural sciences. Two groups of strategies are mentioned by the authors:

(i) *Improving the problem-solving capabilities of a system*
The stress here is on the potentiality of the client system to develop and institutionalise its own problem-solving structures and processes.
(ii) *Releasing and fostering growth in the persons who make up the system to be changed*
Here the emphasis is on the person as the basic unit of any social organization. It is believed that persons are capable of creative action if conditions are made favourable. Various methods have been designed to help people discover themselves as persons and commit themselves to continuing personal growth in the various relationships of their lives.

Emphasis has been placed recently on releasing creativity in persons, groups and organizations to cope with accelerated changes in modern living.

Both these approaches believe that creativity may rise within human systems and does not have to be imported from outside as, for example, assumed in the rational – empirical approaches.

Basically these strategies are not looked upon as a relationship between 'knowledge' and *something* (or someone) to be changed (as in the empirical – rational strategies). On the contrary, the process is looked upon as a *dialogue* involving a client and a 'change agent'.

The normative – re-educative strategies build on an idealistic understanding of human beings and an optimistic assumption of the possibilities for meaningful changes initiated by the individual and through the individual. The effectiveness of the strategies is among other things based on the following assumptions:

1 Changes start with the individual and his 'attitudes' *and not with the social structure in which he is living*. A danger may be that the client easily accepts the *status quo* of his environment, and that the type of innovations which occur are merely minor alterations within a certain framework (which is taken for granted).

2 A change agent can operate in a 'value vacuum'. There is a danger that he may play a 'social engineer' role. In some approaches, however, the values of the change agent are made explicit.

3 Changes can happen without any change in power or subsequently any change in power relationships between individuals and groups.

4 The basis for meaningful changes is consensus between different interest groups in the system.

Power–coercive strategies (Political–administrative strategies)

The imposition of power alters the conditions within which other people act by limiting the alternatives or by shaping the consequences of their acts. For the European tradition, at least, it is quite clear that power-coercive strategies, or maybe *political – administrative strategies*, are the best-known ways in which educational systems have been developed and regulated. To what extent these strategies have been taken for granted in an historical and social climate where authoritarian leadership was accepted as the only leadership style, cannot be judged. It may be suggested as a hypothesis that rational and empirical approaches and normative – re-educative approaches reflect mainly the value systems which are commonly shared in some parts of our culture today. Still, political – administrative strategies are very frequently used, both for control and for reshaping the educational systems.

About this approach Bennis, Benne and Chin say: 'It is not the use of power, in the sense of influence by one person upon another or by one group upon another, which distinguishes this family of strategies from those already discussed. Power is an ingredient of all human action.' They see the differences rather in the ingredients of power upon which the strategies of change depend, and the ways in which power is generated and applied in processes of effecting change.

As further emphasized by Bennis, Benne and Chin, the rational – empirical strategies also depend on power. Information or new knowledge is in itself potential power. The flow of information goes from men who know to men who don't know. Normative – re-educative strategies do not deny the importance of knowledge as a source of power. In general, however, the political – administrative strategies emphasize political, legal, administrative and economic power as the main source of overall power. Other coercive strategies emphasize the use of moral power, sentiment, guilt and shame as legitimate.

Educational systems have been accustomed to the use of political – administrative strategies in a variety of ways. Laws have been passed against certain activities or ensuring others, social interaction is controlled by school regulations, economic power is used towards certain ends, for example, as support to one part of a curriculum and not to another.

More specifically Bennis, Benne and Chin mention the following sub-strategies:

(i) *Strategies of non-violence*
This has been and still is one of the main strategies of minority groups for changing the conditions. Schools also have seen this strategy developed by students in recent years.

(ii) *Use of political institutions to achieve change*
Political power has played an important part in all institutional life and will probably continue to do so. In education this has been very much the case, in particular where majority votes have been used to introduce changes into the system.

Those educational systems which still rely on administrative and legal processes as the only basis for innovation, experience the difficulties of getting these actually working in the system. The process of re-educating persons who will have to behave in different ways if the innovation is to be effective, has to be undertaken. The innovation often requires new knowledge, new skills, new attitudes and new value orientations. It may require changes in norms, roles and relationships. These cannot be dealt with in a coercive way.

There are clear differences in the processes of *formulation, adoption* and *implementation* of innovations . . .

(iii) *Changing through the recomposition and manipulation of power elites*
Innovations, as seen by those using this strategy, cannot be achieved through consensus, but will always be achieved through conflicts and power redistribution.

(iv) *Political – administrative-related strategies*
In education coercive strategies have been used for a number of purposes. The use of selection procedures, both for teachers and students, can be looked upon partly as an administrative strategy. Reward and punishment systems for teachers as well as students is another variant of such a strategy. The use of grants as well as the re-allocation of resources has a power-coercive effect on behaviour and in the teaching – learning process.

There is one distinct difference between the political – administrative strategies and the others described above. The ideologies and value differences between interest groups are exposed by the open use of power. Real change is seen as a redistribution of power, and the subjective position of any viewpoint is not hidden.

We see two major problems in this position. Certainly there are differences of interests and in the use of power in education as in all other human institutions. However, concentration on the differences between interest groups in the struggle for alterations in power distribution *might* divert energy from other important problems. We take the position that differences in interests can best be understood as different relationships to the *material structure* in society and its reward system. Alterations in power *inside* the educational system will probably not alter the basic problems which are common to virtually all individuals working in this system.

The second problem which arises with the political – administrative strategies is the lack of coherence between intention and reality. The strategies indicate procedures for the *formulation and adoption* of innovation, but we are left with problems concerning the *implementation* of these policies . . .

As we have already indicated, a specific approach to innovation cannot be described as *either* empirical – rational *or* normative – re-educative, *or* political – administrative, but rather as more or less influenced by all three strategies, depending partly on *which stage of the process* we are discussing.

Reference

BENNIS, W. G., BENNE, K. D. and CHIN, R. (eds) (1969) *The Planning of Change.* New York: Holt, Rinehart and Winston. (2nd edn)

3.2 The Utilisation of Educational Research and Development

Ronald G. Havelock

[*Havelock looks at the confusion surrounding many new developments in education. Using three models of knowledge utilisation – the Research, Development and Diffusion Model, the Social Interaction Model and the Problem-Solving Model – he concludes that a strong link between source systems and user systems needs to be created and suggests a national system manned by 'change agents' to link research and practice.*]

The United States appears to be on the brink of an extraordinary educational revolution, but as one well-known educator said recently, the pieces of that revolution are lying around unassembled (Brown, 1970). There are indeed a lot of pieces: considering only what has happened in the last five or six years, we find five new 'R & D Centres', twenty new 'Regional Laboratories', private non-profit development organisations, private profit organisations' subsidiaries, a set of Educational Resource Information Centres (ERIC), over 1,000 locally-based innovation centres of every conceivable size, description and function, information systems and centres of various sorts, and new university programmes and centres for research, development, and dissemination on every aspect of curriculum, pedagogy, and administration. Largely financed by new federal legislation in the mid-1960s, these developments are rapidly changing the landscape in the educational research community (National Centre, 1970).

At the same time the schools are bursting their doors and are submerged in crisis from blacks and whites, striking teachers and rebellious taxpayers. Things are happening. The resources are blossoming and so are the needs. It is usually very hard to discern a clear pattern in all this. Sometimes it appears that we have only created chaos: a muddle of organisational forms with no cohesion, no joint purpose, no relationship to each other, and no relevance to real educational needs.

But in this paper I want to suggest some alternative perspectives that will help us make some sense out of these developments. I propose that all these forms and projects and programs that have been developing over the last five years are truly pieces of an educational revolution, a giant mechanism which has the potential of generating continuous educational reform and self-renewal based on scientific knowledge. The key words in arriving at this understanding are 'dissemination' and 'utilisation'.

Source: *British Journal of Educational Technology*, 1971, 2, 2, pp. 84–97.

Three models of knowledge utilisations

In 1966 I undertook a three-year review of literature to find out what scholars, researchers and practitioners had to say about dissemination and utilisation (Havelock). I looked at several hundred studies from a number of fields; not just from education but also from medicine, agriculture, industrial technology, and so forth. From this review I concluded that there are three main models or orientations which are used to describe the utilisation process. Each of these is valid in a different way but each represents a special perspective. I have labelled them as follows:

1 The RD and D Model
2 The Social Interaction Model
3 The Problem-Solving Model

First consider the *RD* and *D* (*Research Development and Diffusion*) *Model*, which is portrayed by Figure 1. The most systematic categorisation of processes related to educational innovation is that evolved first by Brickell (1961) and later by Clark and Guba (1965) under the headings 'Research, Development, and Diffusion'. This orientation is guided by at least five assumptions. First, it assumes that there should be a *rational sequence* in the evolution and application of an innovation. This sequence should include research, development, and packaging *before* mass dissemination takes place. Second, it assumes that there has to be *planning*, usually on a massive scale over a long time span. Third, it assumes that there has to be a *division and coordination of labour* to accord with the rational sequence and the planning. Fourth, it makes the assumption of a more or less *passive but rational consumer* who will accept and adopt the innovation if it is offered to him in the right place at the right time and in the right form. Fifth and finally, the proponents of this view point are willing to accept the fact of high initial development cost prior to any dissemination activity because of the anticipated long-term benefits in *efficiency* and *quality* of the innovation and its suitability for *mass audience dissemination*.

This RD and D model is presumed to be operational in the space and defence industries and in agriculture. Figure 1 provides an outline of its major components. In broad terms RD and D is a grand strategy for planned innovation. At its best, when it really works, R and D can be a process whereby ideas and tentative models of innovations are evaluated and systematically reshaped and packaged in a form that ensures benefit to users

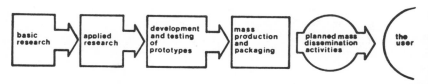

Figure 1 The Research, Development and Diffusion Model

and which eases diffusion and adoption. In this process most of the *adaptation* and *translation* problems of the user are anticipated and adjusted for. The final outcome is therefore 'user-proof', guaranteed to work for the most fumbling and incompetent receiver. To some degree the Regional Laboratories supported by the US Office of Education have been established to carry forward this strategy of high-performance product development (Boyan, 1968).

The second of the three models, the *Social Interaction Model* is depicted in Figure 2. Advocates of this approach place emphasis on the patterns by which innovations diffuse through a social system, and they are able to support what they say with a great deal of empirical research. The overwhelming body of this research tends to support five generalisations about the process of innovation diffusion; (1) that the individual user or adopter belongs to a network of social relations (Mort, 1964) which largely influences his adoption behaviour; (2) that his place in the network (centrality, peripherality, isolation) is a good predictor of his rate of acceptance of new ideas; (3) that informal personal contact is a vital part of the influence and adoption process; (4) that group membership and reference group identifications are major predictors of individual adoption; and (5) that the rate of diffusion through a social system follows a predictable S-curve pattern (very slow rate at the beginning, followed by a period of very rapid diffusion, followed in turn by a long late-adopter or 'laggard' period).

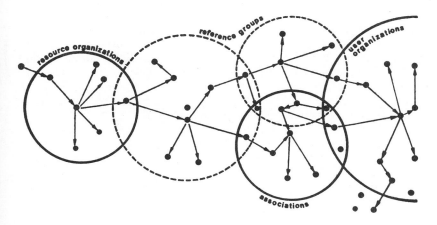

Figure 2 The Social Interaction Model

Although the bulk of the evidence comes from rural sociology, these five propositions have been demonstrated in a remarkably wide range of situations in every field of knowledge and using every conceivable adopter unit including individuals, business firms, school systems and states. Figure 2 suggests the types of variables usually considered by the social interactionists (for example characteristics of senders and receivers, social relationships, memberships, leadership and proximity). They have also looked at the relative effectiveness of different media and message forms. In education major advocates of the Social Interaction perspective have been Mort (1964), Ross (1958), and Carlson (1965).

Because of the strong empiricist orientation of this group it has generated relatively few explicit strategies or action alternatives. Social Interaction theorists generally prefer to observe and ponder the 'natural' process without meddling in it. Therefore, the relevance of their work for policy makers and practitioners has not become evident until very recently.

Most in favour with practitioners in education is the third model, which I call the *Problem-Solving Model*, and which is represented by Figure 3. This orientation rests on the primary assumption that innovation is a part of a problem-solving process which goes on inside the user or client system. This designated client system may be of any size and complexity, for example the school district, the school building, the classroom teacher or even the student.

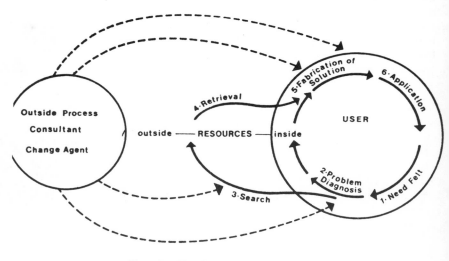

Figure 3 The Problem-Solving Model

Problem-solving is usually seen as a patterned sequence of activities beginning with a *need* which is sensed and articulated by the client system. This need must be translated into a *problem* statement and *diagnosis*. When he has thus formulated a problem statement, the client-user is able to conduct a meaningful *search and retrieval* of ideas and information which can be used in formulating or selecting the innovation. Finally, after a potential solution is identified, the user needs to concern himself with adapting the innovation, trying it out and evaluating its effectiveness in satisfying his original need. The focus of this orientation is the user, himself: *his* needs and what he does about satisfying his needs are paramount. The role of outsiders is therefore consultative or collaborative as suggested by the dotted lines in this figure. The outside change agent may assist the user either by providing new ideas and innovations specific to the diagnosis or by providing guidance on the process of problem-solving at any or all of these problem-solving stages.

At least five points are generally stressed by advocates of this orientation: (1) that user *need* is the paramount consideration; this, they say, is the only acceptable value-stance for the change agent, what the user needs and what the user thinks he needs are the primary concern of any would-be helper; (2) that *diagnosis* of need always has to be an integral part of the total process; (3) that the outside change agent should be *nondirective*, rarely, if ever, violating the integrity of the user by setting himself up as the 'expert'; (4) that *internal resources*, that is those resources already existing and easily accessible within the client system itself should always be fully utilised; and (5) that *self-initiated* and self-applied innovation will have the strongest user commitment and the best chances for long-term survival. A few of the major advocates of this orientation are Ronald Lippitt and his co-workers (1958), Goodwin Watson (1967), Charles Jung, and Herbert Thelen (1967). Most of those who belong to this school are social psychologists in the group dynamics human relations tradition.

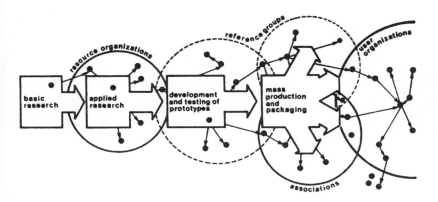

Figure 4 RD and D takes place in a social context

Although the various orientations to innovation discussed above are espoused by different authors and represent different and often competing schools of thought, the pragmatic change agent should see each of them as illustrating different but equally important aspects of a total process. Consider for example Figure 4 which shows the figures for RD and D and Social Interaction superimposed in one another. Here we see the flow of knowledge from research to practice, both as a logical sequence of steps and as a natural flow from person to person and group to group. This figure probably comes a little closer to what happens in real life. There *are* logical steps but there are human senders and receivers who behave more like social animals than like logical elements. Research is not merely a series of operations, it is also a community; and the same holds true for development and for practice. As separate communities they have boundaries and barriers to sending and receiving knowledge.

Now looking at this same array from closer range we see in Figure 5 that information is not merely passing from point to point but also from person to person, and inside each person there is an internal problem-solving process going on, determining in part whether or not information will flow in and through and out to others. Moreover, social interaction is not merely a matter of passively receiving from others; it is also a matter of give-and-take, of mutual influence and two-way communications.

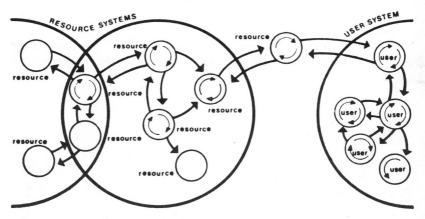

Figure 5 Users and resource persons are social interactors and problem solvers

To consider this two-way feature in more detail let us look at Figure 6 where one resource person and one user are in interaction with each other. On the right we have the user trying to help himself like a good independent problem-solver. He identifies a need, he decides on a potential solution; he tries out the solution, and if it works, his need is met. But let us not forget that there is a man on the left, too. Where does the man on the left fit into this picture? That is the number one linkage question: anybody who wants to be effective as a resource person, as a helper, or as a linker to resources has to know when, where and how he fits in. Therefore he needs to have information from the user, not just about what the user needs but also about how the user goes about solving problems. He has to be able to simulate the user's problem-solving process so that he can feed him solutions and solution ideas that are both relevant and timely.

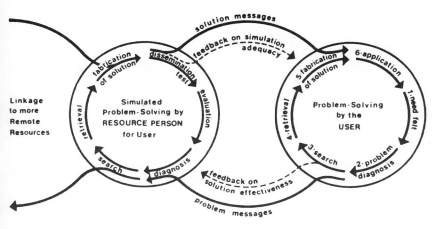

Figure 6 The Linkage Process

To co-ordinate helping activities with internal user problem-solving activities, the outside resource person must be able to recapitulate or simulate that internal process. Technically speaking, the resource person needs to develop a good 'model' of the user system in order to 'link' to him effectively. Clinically speaking, we could say that he needs to have empathy or understanding. At the same time, the user must have an adequate appreciation of how the resource system operates. In other words he must be able to understand and partially simulate such resource system activities as research, development and evaluation.

In order to build accurate models of each other, resource and user must provide reciprocal feedback and must provide signals to each other which are mutually reinforcing. This type of collaboration will not only make particular solutions more relevant and more effective but will also serve to build a lasting relationship of mutual trust and a perception by the user that the resource person is a truly concerned and competent helper. In the long run, then, initial collaborative relations build effective channels through which innovations can pass efficiently and effectively.

Linkage is not seen merely as a two-person process, however. The resource person, in turn, must be linked in a similar manner to more and more remote expert resources as indicated in previous diagrams. As the advocates of the RD and D approach hold, there must be an extensive and rational division of labour to accomplish the complex tasks of innovation building. However, each separate role-holder must have some idea of how other roles are performed and some idea of what the linkage system as a whole is trying to do. In particular, there is a need for some central agency, as shown in Figure 7, which has a primary task of 'modelling' the total innovation building and disseminating system and which acts as a facilitator and coordinator, seeing to it that the 'system' is truly a system, serving the needs of the user.

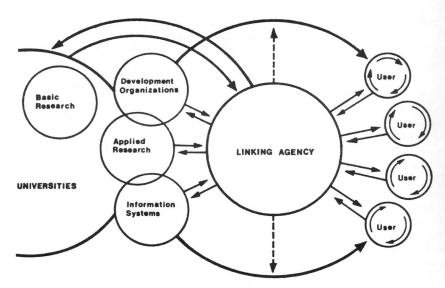

Figure 7 The Central Linkage Agency in the Macrosystem

This brings me to the main point I want to make in this paper: we need to build national systems which allow any school district to plug into the most sophisticated sources of information in such a way that they get knowledge and materials which are relevant and timely and truly cost beneficial.

As I view the landscape, trying to put pieces together, I usually find that there is one important missing piece. Many scholars have talked of the need for dissemination and utilisation of what we now know and many have talked of the need for a better problem-solving process in schools which would make adequate use of available resources, but we have not provided the institutional mechanisms that would allow these things to happen. We have research organisations, universities and R and D centres; we now have some impressive product development centres (for example, the regional labs) and a few privately-funded organisations which are similarly engaged, but what we do not have and what we need so badly is a network of regional centres which can serve as truly comprehensive resource centres and resource linking centres with the skills and the staff to be an effective mediating mechanism between R and D on the one hand and operating school districts on the other.

Though such a network does not presently exist, there are, nevertheless, isolated cases of successful linkage agencies, and I would like to describe one of these as an example of the type of agency which I feel is needed. There is an organisation in Albuquerque, New Mexico called the South-western Co-operative Educational Laboratory. This is one of the fifteen currently surviving laboratories set up by the US Office of Education in 1966 to carry out programmatic development work. This particular laboratory wanted to specialise in language arts programmes for preparing young children from Indian, Spanish-speaking and very poor families to participate in and take advantage of the established school system on a par with middle-class whites. This was a very ambitious goal, but they are very serious about it and very methodical about what will be achieved, when and at what cost. This laboratory started on this mission by adapting an 'oral language programme' for elementary school children who did not hear English spoken in the home. The programme had been sketched out by Dr Robert Wilson at the University of California at Los Angeles. The laboratory took Wilson's model and developed a prototype programme, evaluating and testing two or three advanced models with a large number of school districts throughout the southwest. They made certain that their oral language programme was producing results to specification before going on to each additional stage of development. Their prototype included complete teachers' manuals with behavioural objectives, materials and a complete in-service training package. The training package, itself, was also evaluated and improved from year to year. They have also gone beyond the teacher-training problem to look at the total question of *diffusion and installation* considering the kinds of institutional safeguards and conditions that have to be built-in to insure the programme's success in a given setting. They are currently working to develop a new kind of role in school settings which they call the 'Quality Assurance Specialist' someone who is trained to work at the school level to make sure that innovations such as the 'Oral Language Program' are used in the way they were designed to be used.

The key role of regional service centres

A very significant aspect of the Albuquerque Laboratory's programme is its growing relationship with a network of regional service centres in west Texas. These centres are assuming the installation function for the language arts programme in their region, leaving the laboratory to concentrate on its assigned mission which is 'development'. Now, in addition, the laboratory has a contractual relationship with New Mexico State University to train teachers in this programme, once again illustrating this budding-off process from development into viable continuous operations. From the University of California to the Laboratory to the teacher-training at New Mexico State University to the Texas service centres to the operating school districts there is a true knowledge chain based on genuine collaboration and two-way communication. In this chain the regional service centre was the key link to the educational consumer; without a national network of regional centres which operate in this manner, educational research, development, dissemination and utilisation cannot be coordinated as a system. Really significant improvement in education in the 1970s will depend largely on the emergence of these service centres as comprehensive resource linking agencies. They are the vital bridge between a very complex array of resource

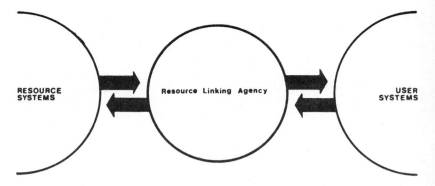

Figure 8 The Resource Linking Agency has two major linking tasks to perform

systems on the one hand and the operating school districts on the other.

The service agency therefore has two major tasks, as shown in Figure 8: first, to build and maintain adequate linkage to resource systems; and second, to build and maintain adequate linkage to the educational users in its region. Let us consider each of these tasks in turn.

1. Linking to resource systems

The task of building linkage to resource systems may be outlined in three steps. As a first step, shown in Figure 9, the agency develop a wide span of *awareness* of potential resource systems, who they are, where they are, which ones seem to be more relevant or less relevant, more accessible or less accessible. The array of resources identified in this diagram is, of course, only partial and sketchy. Figure 10 represents the second step, in which the agency

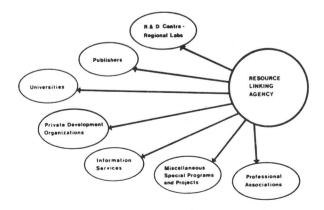

Figure 9 The Resource Awareness File

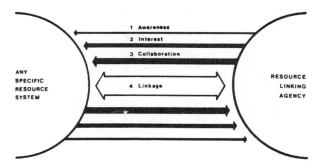

Figure 10 Building linkage to resources

begins to make contact with the most relevant and accessible resources, initiating two-way interchanges to promote mutual awareness and to learn about their potential resource-giving capacity. Finally, as a third step the agency begins to develop joint projects, testing out the *actual* resource giving capacity of outside agencies.

This process of building linkage to resource systems is exactly what took place between the west Texas centres and the Albuquerque Laboratory. What I describe in that case was an example of how the RD and D model works when it really works (which is far more rare than some of its advocates would have us believe). There are very few fully developed and fully evaluated innovations of such quality that are actually ready for installation. Most of the time the information is partial and it is scattered; it has to be retrieved from a number of sources, screened and pulled together in some sort of order before it can really be used by anybody. This pulling together can be a very complex and costly process which requires very sophisticated resource linkage. However, the successful linking agency knows how to enlist help from the above mentioned array of resource systems to do the job which it cannot do itself. Thus, it increases its linkage to resource systems and simultaneously increases its capacity to serve clients.

2. *Linkage to user systems*

Let us turn to the second side of a service centre's activities, linkage to and service to the school districts in its designated region. To approach its service function on a rational basis the regional centre must first conceive of itself and all of the client groups it serves as one system for utilising knowledge and upgrading educational practice. This system is shown in Figure 11. As with the inventory of potential resource systems, the agency needs to make a thorough accounting of the number of districts and schools it serves, their needs, their resources, and their current capacity and level of competence in problem-solving, resource retrieval, planning and so forth.

Once they have defined the systems they are trying to serve, the agency staff

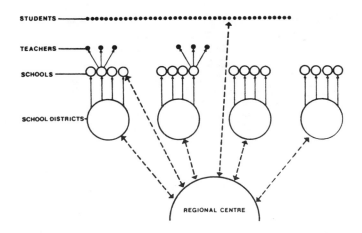

Figure 11 The Linking Agency and its users together are one system

can begin to develop a step-by-step programme for establishing a truly linking role; these steps are shown in Figure 12. The first step is creating awareness, letting the users know you exist, that you are there to help them as a general resource in their problem-solving efforts. The agency's staff create this awareness by visiting the clients, asking them what they see their needs to be, letting them see and feel the service centre as a real organisation. The centre should also have a newsletter which goes out to every key educator in the region: this can get to far more people than can be reached personally and it is a periodic reminder to them that the centre is a going concern, trying to do some things that are relevant to local educational needs in a helpful non-threatening way.

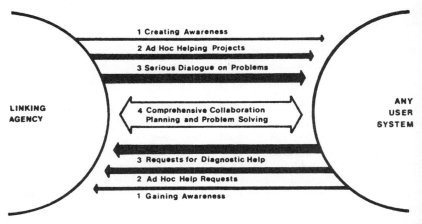

Figure 12 Building linkage to users

Beyond awareness the centre must start to become directly involved on a project-by-project basis. The Oral Language Program described previously in this paper is one good example of an *ad hoc* 'project' approach to linkage, a very visible co-operative activity on something that will be concretely helpful in some specific area. It does not have to be large but it must be *successful*. These specific successful projects, however small they are, are terribly important in building the utilisation chain because each project builds trust, builds interest, builds knowledge of each other, and builds competence and confidence on both sides. These are the beginnings of the linkage process I described earlier where resource and user understand each other's internal process, simulate one another, and thereby co-ordinate their behaviour for mutual gain.

As a third step, the centre begins to develop a serious dialogue with client systems on what their problems really are. This is very difficult to do in a systematic system-wide way, and there must be a basis of trust with the schools before one can really get very far with this. Once the schools are thinking about problems, then the service centre can start some major *ad hoc* problem-solving, using its capacity as a helper and linker to more remote resources.

It is only after the centre has started getting some success in *ad hoc* problem-solving that it can start to get schools and school districts to work in a more comprehensive way about planning, working out behavioural objectives and generating the kind of continuous monitoring and programmatic upgrading that the systems analysts tell us we need.

If this is how an ideal service centre would work, the next question is: How do we build a set of agencies which are real linking organisations? I suggest that this can be done through a systematic application of what we know about dissemination, utilisation and the planning of change. First we need to train and recruit a core staff of people who understand these processes, who understand the four models I described and can integrate them and incorporate and apply them in their daily thinking and their daily work. There are training programmes now under development which will start to provide many of the necessary skills and understanding (Havelock, 1971). There are manuals on the change process, written for change agents and administrators (Glaser, 1971; Havelock, 1970; Rogers and Svenning, 1969). There are also books and articles which cover every aspect of dissemination and utilisation and change planning (Bennis, Benne and Chin, 1969; Havelock; Rogers, 1971) and there are reports of the actual field experience of many educational change agents which can be drawn upon (Hearn, 1969).

So many problems seem to be crowding in on us in this last half of the twentieth century, and again and again we hear that the key to solving these problems is education. Well, the key probably *is* education, but what is the key to the key? What can we do to change education so that it can deliver? I propose that the key to the key must be national systems for coordinated research, development, dissemination and utilisation, systems which are simultaneously national, regional and local and in which there is a continuous chain of interdependence and two-way linkage from researcher to developer to practitioner to consumer. The pieces of the educational revolution are lying around unassembled; we need to build systems that would link the research world and the practice world to each other on a continuous basis for their mutual gain. We need to start putting these pieces together, finding out what pieces are still missing and fashioning those new pieces. From my work, I have come to believe that there is a need for a new type of agency right in the heart of this system, an agency manned by people – 'knowledge brokers', 'linkers', 'change agents', call them what you will – people who can work in the middle between research and practice. There is a set of skills in this area which can be taught and learned, but very, very few people have them today. This is a critical task for the 1970s.

References

BENNIS, WARREN G., BENNE, KENNETH D., and CHIN, ROBERT (eds) (1961, 1969) *The Planning of Change*. New York: Holt, Rinehart and Winston. (2nd edn)

BOYAN, NORMAN J. 'Problems and Issues of Knowledge Production and Utilization', in T. L. EIDELL and J. M. KITCHEL (eds) *Knowledge Production and Utilization in Educational Administration*, Centre for Advanced Study of Education Administration, University of Oregon, Eugene, 1968.

BROWN, B. FRANK (1970) Address to *Educational Press Association*, Atlantic City, New Jersey, 17 February.

CARLSON, RICHARD O. (1965) *Adoption of Educational Innovations*, University of Oregon, Eugene, 1965.

CLARK, DAVID L. and GUBA, EGON G. (1965) *An Examination of Potential Change Roles in Education*. Paper presented at the Symposium on Innovation in Planning School Curricula, Airlie House, Virginia, October.

GLASER, EDWARD M. and staff at the Human Interaction Research Institute, Los Angeles, California, are under contract with the National Institute of Mental Health to develop a manual on research utilization, which should be available in 1971.

HAVELOCK, RONALD G. (1970) *A Guide to Innovation in Education*, a handbook on the innovation process for change agents, Institute for Social Research, University of Michigan, Ann Arbor.

HAVELOCK, RONALD G. in collaboration with GUSKIN, ALAN *et al.*, Planning for Innovation through Dissemination and Utilization of Knowledge, Institute for Social Research, University of Michigan, Ann Arbor.

HAVELOCK, RONALD G. *et al.* (1971) *Designs for Change Agent Training in Education*. Report on the Conference on Educational Change Agent Training, High/Scope, Clinton, Michigan, May 1970. Sponsored by the Centre for Research on Utilization of Scientific Knowledge, University of Michigan. Available from the Institute of Social Research, Ann Arbor, Michigan.

HEARN, NORMAN F. (1969) *Innovative Education Programs: A Study of the Influence of Selected Variables upon their Continuation Following the Termination of Three-Year ESEA Title III Grants*. Dissertation for Doctor of Education Degree, Washington D.C., George Washington University, September 30.

JUNG, CHARLES, Research Utilizing Problem Solving: *An Instructional Program for School Personnel*, North-West Regional Educational Laboratory, Portland Oregon.

LIPPITT, RONALD, WATSON, JEANNE and WESTLEY, BRUCE (1958) *The Dynamics of Planned Change*. New York: Harcourt, Brace and Company, Inc.

MORT, PAUL R. (1964) 'Studies in Education Innovation from the Institute of Administrative Research' in MATHEW B. MILES (ed.) *Innovation in Education*, Bureau of Publications, Teachers College, Columbia University, New York.

NATIONAL CENTER FOR EDUCATIONAL RESEARCH AND DEVELOPMENT (1970) *Educational Research and Development in the United States*. Superintendent of Documents, Catalogue No. HE5.212.12049, US Government Printing Office, Washington D.C.

ROGERS, EVERETT M. with SHOEMAKER, F. FLOYD (1971) *Communication of Innovations: A Cross-Cultural Approach*. New York: Free Press of Glencoe.

ROGERS, EVERETT M. and SVENNING, LYNNE (1969) *Managing Change*, Operation PEP. San Mateo County Superintendent of Schools, San Mateo, California.

ROSS, DONALD H. (1958) *Administration for Adaptability: A Source Book Drawing Together the Results of More than 150 Individual Studies Related to the Question of Why and How Schools Improve*. Metropolitan School Study Council, New York.

THELEN, HERBERT A. (1967) 'Concepts for Collaborative Action-Inquiry', in *Concepts for Social Change*. Moran Printing Service. Published by N. T. L. National Education Association for COPED, Baltimore, March.

WATSON, GOODWIN (1967) 'Resistance to Change', in G. WATSON (ed.) *Concepts for Social Change*. Moran Printing Service. Published by N. T. L. (National Training Laboratories) National Education Association for COPED, Baltimore, March.

3.3 Evaluation of the Project: Past, Present and Future

Wynne Harlen

It is fitting that a project which endorses and promotes discovery learning should have provided opportunity for learning, through discovery, a great deal about the effectiveness of various approaches to the evaluation of its materials. Because Science 5–13 produced and tried out its units in separate sets it was possible to learn from experience the importance of gathering information of various kinds to suit the aims of the formative evaluation. Much was 'learned by doing' about the types of information which can be effectively used for particular purposes, and about ways of gathering them.

While it is not the intention to summarize here what has been said about the evaluation in earlier chapters [in *Science 5–13: a formative evaluation*], it seems relevant to point out some of the lessons which have been learned. Undoubtedly the most positive aid to revising the trial units came from the teachers' questionnaires; here were the reports of how far the suggestions could be put into practice, the accounts of how activities had begun and ended, reasons for parts of a unit being unsatisfactory, and suggestions for changes. No other source of information was so rich in detailed and definite indications of how the material could be made more helpful to teachers. Yet it must be said straight away that the value of this information would have been far less without the addition of data from observation of how the units were being used. Furthermore, the use of a computer programme to classify information from teachers and classroom observers added significantly to the usefulness of such data. Without this facility there would have been ambiguities in interpreting teachers' comments, arising from inability to relate them systematically to the background in which they had been made.

From the first set of trials it was learned that information coming from children's test results was tentative and not readily usable for guiding rewriting without being supplemented by other data. The results played a useful part in confirming that the general approach of the material was effective in promoting achievement of its stated objectives, and the development of tests also had side benefits for the production of units. But for indicating changes which would make the units more effective they were of much less use than information from other sources. The tests were also by far the most expensive item in the evaluation, both in direct cost and in man/woman hours. While it could not be said that the test information was without value for this project, it can be said that, where resources are limited and it is necessary to concentrate upon gathering information to give the greatest

Source: HARLEN, W. (1975) *Science 5–13: a formative evaluation*. Schools Council Research Studies. London: Macmillan Education, pp. 86–91.

return on money, time and human energy, then the choice would be for teachers' reports and direct observations in the classroom and not for tests of short term changes in children's behaviour.

Results for the second set of units largely confirmed this conclusion about the value of test results in relation to other data. In the evaluation of *Early Experiences* the additional information provided by using the Preferences Form indicated an important relationship between teachers' attitudes and satisfactory use of the unit. Teachers with a high score on attitude towards giving children freedom to learn through active exploration tended to be those who used the activities as intended, while the reverse was true for those with a low score. No significant change in attitude was detected during the trial period, a finding later confirmed from the more extensive use of the Preferences Form in the third trials.

The findings from earlier trials made it possible to learn about the content of the evaluation instruments as well as about sources of information. The questions asked in the teachers' forms used in the first two sets of trials were examined critically to discover if the answers had been used at all in making decisions about revising the unit. Some questions were eliminated as a result; for example, feedback from an item about the desirability of having a subject index and from another about the value of photographs in the unit had not been used because decisions about these things were based on other considerations. Questions of which answers had been used were examined for overlap and ambiguity; the results of the computer analysis were invaluable for this. After the reduction and modification of questions in the forms, which then became possible, new items were added to draw out information which the authors had felt lacking.

The results of the classification analysis were similarly used to reshape the team members' report form, used in the first and second trials, into the visitors' report form, used in the third and fourth trials. The purpose of these forms was to supply information about how the units were being used, so it was necessary for the forms to be efficient, to focus the observations on features and events which were particularly pertinent to the use of the units, and not to consume the observers' time in recording things common to most classrooms. Among the items most highly weighted in the groups from the analyses of earlier results were the few relating to contacts between teachers and children. It was felt there were not enough of these, so a new section was added to the Visitors' Form in an attempt to investigate more closely the interaction between teachers and children, and do this from the children's point of view. Findings from extensive use of the resulting form led to another discovery; information coming directly from talking to the children was extremely effective in describing how the material was used. Furthermore, looking at the way in which less able children were working was especially helpful in making discriminations according to the 'grasp and application of the project's ideas'.

Throughout the various trials the results underlined the value of gathering and combining information about different aspects of the use and effect of the units. Information from any one source was inadequate on its own, and really became useful only when supported by evidence from other sources. In describing the various formal evaluation instruments it should not be forgotten that information was also gathered informally by the team members in their contacts with teachers and visits to trial classes. In general the formal evaluation results gave substantial backing to the informal impressions gathered by the team members. This was important, for it would have been disquieting if one had led to a very different picture of the trial situation than the other. The formal results were used with greater confidence because they supported, and were supported by, what the team felt. Nevertheless the team's impressions were gathered from short and probably unrepresentative glimpses of the work, and the evaluation provided a more thorough account of what went on throughout the trials.

So much for the past, but what has been learned from the evaluation which is of present value? First, it is hardly necessary to state that the units in their final form are likely to be more helpful to more teachers because of the information provided by the evaluation. It is also possible that teachers may use the units with greater confidence, knowing that they were widely tried out and evaluated during their production.

A second point refers to application of what was found about the combination of circumstances associated with using the unit as intended. Repeatedly, in different trials, the same features were found to be present when the units were used with success and brought satisfaction to the teachers. Some of these features, such as those relating to the school environment and the past experience of the teacher and children, could not now be affected, but others – at least in theory – were susceptible to change. The latter provided detailed indications of the changes in classroom practice that might profitably be made. The adoption of conditions favourable to optimal use of the units was urged in the revised version of *With Objectives in Mind* and in the units, but it was also kept in mind as a major aim of courses preparing teachers for using the units.

Details of these favourable conditions were communicated to the area representatives [. . .] because these were the people responsible for running courses in various parts of the country, not only for the trials but also for the wider dissemination of the project's materials. It seems a reasonable conjecture, moreover, that taking part in gathering information on the Visitors' Form may have helped the area representatives to identify critical aspects of classroom practice relevant to successful use of the materials. Consequently they may have been able to direct help in courses to these aspects.

The project is making a more direct attempt to help teachers and course leaders when the project's materials are introduced for the first time. The unit *Understanding Science 5–13* is designed to help the understanding of the project's philosophy, its aims and objectives, the teacher's role in using the units, the interaction of objectives and activities and the application of all these ideas in the classroom. It consists of a guide in the form of a programmed book, supported by slides and tapes, and can be used in a number of ways, as material for a course or for self-instruction.

The impetus to produce this unit came largely from contrasting the way units were used by teachers who had been on a course, and those who used the units without the benefit of a course. The unit is an acknowledgement that the project's books do not on their own give as much help as many teachers need in starting children learning science actively for the first time. The evaluation findings confirmed, with objective measurement of teachers' attitudes, [. . .] that using the units did not significantly change teachers' willingness to adopt methods for enabling children to learn more active inquiry. Although increase in attitude score was associated with successful use of the units, these increases were among those who already had a favourable attitude. Here was further evidence that some action was needed to improve attitudes before the materials were used.

No further evaluation of Science 5–13 is planned at present. Nevertheless, it may be useful to review the outstanding problems and suggest what seem to be, at this time, the more important subjects for later evaluation and research.

At many points in this report shortage of time has been mentioned as a restraining factor; it has often determined limitations on how problems could be approached and even which problems could be tackled. In particular it prevented any long term study of the use of the material and any longitudinal survey of the effect of the material on the children. This is seen as a most important subject for future work. It may have value not only with respect to Science 5–13, however, since it could help to validate the evaluation strategy. In the third and fourth trials evaluation attention shifted from the outcomes of using the materials to the processes by which the outcomes were expected to be brought about. The changed strategy proved more effective for formative evaluation but involved the assumption that, if the children's learning is conducted in a certain way, then intended outcomes will follow. There needs to be some test of the truth of this assumption. Such an investigation might try to correlate long-term changes (over several years) in children's behaviour with various different approaches, one of which would be that of Science 5–13, to producing desired changes.

For the above investigation to be possible it is assumed that teachers will use Science 5–13 materials for some years to come and that at least some of them will use the material as intended. However, this assumption may not be true, and introduces another set of questions which should be systematically studied. Hopefully, by the end of the next three to five years there will be some teachers using Science 5–13 materials, some who took them up but dropped them, some who never heard about them, and some who heard about them but were not interested. To inquire about reasons for various patterns of usage or non-usage would be valuable in many ways. It could throw further light upon the problems of dissemination, on the success of various in-service courses, and provide extremely useful data for the next wave of curriculum development in science for five-to-thirteen year olds. It may be possible, for instance, to distinguish varying degrees in the application of the project's philosophy – from using the units as vehicles for putting the philosophy into practice to using the units as ideas for teaching in a way quite out of keeping with the philosophy. If failure to apply the philosophy is widespread, it may mean that it is unrealistic in the changing school situation, and new approaches may have to be developed. On the other hand, teachers may become more able to apply the philosophy as they become more confident in guiding the activities. We do not know which of these, or variations of them, will be the case; we should find out.

Further work is also required in relation to development of units. It may be useful to produce material for pre-school children, especially now that there will be more of them. Then there is the relation between mathematics and science activities for young children. Does it make sense to continue developing science and mathematics curriculum material separately?

At the top of the age range the remaining problems abound. [. . .] The trials and evaluation of Stage 3 units [were] in many respects unsatisfactory. There is especial need for long term study of the problems of providing suitable learning experiences in science for children between eleven and thirteen. What Science 5–13 has been able to do so far has only been a first step, made somewhat in the dark because of the distinct and widespread absence of detailed information about the way children in this age group learn. There is room for much research on this subject, but following the progress for several years of children whose teachers use Science 5–13 units might also make a significant contribution to knowledge about it.

It would not be useful to suggest that any of these problems have priority, since their relative importance will depend very much upon what happens to Science 5–13 materials in the next few years. This may in turn be strongly affected by whether some organization is maintained for servicing the project's materials when the team finally breaks up. However, it is not inappropriate to recommend that some future work should be done, if only because – to echo a remark at the beginning of this report – Science 5–13 was a major Schools Council project, and therefore an expensive undertaking. It will provide opportunity for exploring many of the long term problems involved in inducing curriculum changes which are relevant to other projects. It would make sense, educationally and financially, to take advantage of this opportunity.

3.4 On the Classification and Framing of Educational Knowledge

Basil Bernstein

Educational knowledge is a major regulator of the structure of experience. From this point of view, one can ask 'How are forms of experience, identity and relation evoked, maintained and changed by the formal transmission of educational knowledge and sensitivities?' Formal educational knowledge can be considered to be realized through three message systems: curriculum, pedagogy and evaluation. Curriculum defines what counts as valid knowledge, pedagogy defines what counts as a valid transmission of knowledge, and evaluation defines what counts as a valid realization of this knowledge on the part of the taught. The term, educational knowledge code, which will be introduced later, refers to the underlying principles which shape curriculum, pedagogy and evaluation. It will be argued that the form this code takes depends upon social principles which regulate the classification and framing of knowledge made public in educational institutions. Both Durkheim and Marx have shown us that the structure of society's classifications and frames reveals both the distribution of power and the principles of social control. I hope to show, *theoretically*, that educational codes provide excellent opportunities for the study of classification and frames through which experience is given a distinctive form. The paper is organized as follows:

1 I shall first distinguish between two types of curricula: collection and integrated.
2 I shall build upon the basis of this distinction in order to establish a more general set of concepts: classification and frame.
3 A typology of educational codes will then be derived.
4 Sociological aspects of two very different educational codes will then be explored.
5 This will lead on to a discussion of educational codes and problems of social control.
6 Finally, there will be a brief discussion of the reasons for a weakening of one code and a strengthening of the movement of the other.

Two types of curricula

Initially, I am going to talk about the curriculum in a very general way. In all educational institutions there is a formal punctuation of time into periods. These may vary from ten minutes to three hours or more. I am going to call each such formal period of time a 'unit'. I shall use the word 'content' to

Source: BERNSTEIN, B. (1975) *Class, Codes and Control*, Vol. 3. London: Routledge and Kegan Paul.

describe how the period of time is used. I shall define a curriculum initially in terms of the principle by which units of time and their contents are brought into a special relationship with each other. I now want to look more closely at the phrase 'special relationship'.

First, we can examine relationships between contents in terms of the amount of time accorded to a given content. Immediately, we can see that more time is devoted to some contents rather than others. Second, some of the contents may, from the point of view of the pupils, be compulsory or optional. We can now take a very crude measure of the relative status of a content in terms of the number of units given over to it, and whether it is compulsory or optional. This raises immediately the question of the relative status of a given content and its significance in a given educational career.

We can, however, consider the relationship between contents from another, perhaps more important, perspective. We can ask about any given content whether the boundary between it and another content is clear-cut or blurred. To what extent are the various contents well insulated from each other? If the various contents are well insulated from each other, I shall say that the contents stand in a *closed* relation to each other. If there is reduced insulation between contents, I shall say that the contents stand in an *open* relationship to each other. So far, then, I am suggesting that we can go into any educational institution and examine the organization of time in terms of the relative status of contents, and whether the contents stand in an open/ closed relationship to each other. I am deliberately using this very abstract language in order to emphasize that there is nothing intrinsic to the relative status of various contents, there is nothing intrinsic to the relationships between contents. Irrespective of the question of the intrinsic logic of the various forms of public thought, the *forms* of their transmission, that is their classification and framing, are social facts. There are a number of alternative means of access to the public forms of thought, and so to the various realities which they make possible. I am therefore emphasizing the social nature of the system of alternatives from which emerges a constellation called a curriculum. From this point of view, any curriculum entails a principle or principles whereby of all the possible contents of time, some contents are accorded differential status and enter into open or closed relation to each other.

I shall now distinguish between two broad types of curricula. If contents stand in a closed relation to each other, that is if the contents are clearly bounded and insulated from each other, I shall call such a curriculum a *collection* type. Here, the learner has to collect a group of favoured contents in order to satisfy some criteria of evaluation. There may of course be some underlying concept to a collection: the gentleman, the educated man, the skilled man, the non-vocational man.

Now I want to juxtapose against the collection type, a curriculum where the various contents do not go their own separate ways, but where the contents stand in an open relation to each other. I shall call such a curriculum an integrated type. Now we can have various types of collection, and various degrees and types of integration.

Classification and frame

I shall now introduce the concepts, classification and frame, which will be used to analyse the underlying structure of the three message systems, curriculum, pedagogy and evaluation, which are realizations of the educational knowledge code. The basic idea is embodied in the principle used to distinguish the two types of curricula: collection and integrated. Strong insulation between contents pointed to a collection type, whereas reduced insulation pointed to an integrated type. The principle here is the strength of the *boundary* between contents. This notion of boundary strength underlies the concepts of classification and frame.

Classification, here, does not refer to *what* is classified, but to the *relationships* between contents. Classification refers to the nature of the differentiation between contents. Where classification is strong, contents are well insulated from each other by strong boundaries. Where classification is weak, there is reduced insulation between contents, for the boundaries between contents are weak or blurred. *Classification thus refers to the degree of boundary maintenance between contents*. Classification focuses our attention upon boundary strength as the critical distinguishing feature of the division of labour of educational knowledge. It gives us, as I hope to show, the basic structure of the message system, curriculum.

The concept, frame, is used to determine the structure of the message system, pedagogy. Frame refers to the form of the *context* in which knowledge is transmitted and received. Frame refers to the specific pedagogical relationship of teacher and taught. In the same way as classification does not refer to contents, so frame does not refer to the contents of the pedagogy. Frame refers to the strength of the boundary between what may be transmitted and what may not be transmitted, in the pedagogical relationship. Where framing is strong, there is a sharp boundary, where framing is weak, a blurred boundary, between what may and may not be transmitted. Frame refers us to the range of options available to teacher and taught in the *control* of what is transmitted and received in the context of the pedagogical relationship. Strong framing entails reduced options; weak framing entails a range of options. *Thus frame refers to the degree of control teacher and pupil possess over the selection, organization, pacing and timing of the knowledge transmitted and received in the pedagogical relationship.*

There is another aspect of the boundary relationship between what may be taught and what may not be taught and, consequently, another aspect to framing. We can consider the relationship between the non-school everyday community knowledge of the teacher or taught, *and* the educational knowledge transmitted in the pedagogical relationship. We can raise the question of the strength of the boundary, the degree of insulation, between the everyday community knowledge of teacher and taught and educational knowledge. Thus, we can consider variations in the strength of frames as these refer to the strength of the boundary between educational knowledge and everyday community knowledge of teacher and taught.

From the perspective of this analysis, the basic structure of the message system, curriculum is given by variations in the strength of classification, and the basic structure of the message system pedagogy is given by variations in the strength of frames. It will be shown later that the structure of the message system, evaluation, is a function of the strength of classification and frames. It is important to realize that the strength of classification and the strength of frames can vary independently of each other. For example, it is possible to have weak classification and exceptionally strong framing. Consider programmed learning. Here the boundary between educational contents may be blurred (weak classification) but there is little control by the pupil (except for pacing) over *what* is learned (strong framing). This example also shows that frames may be examined at a number of levels and the strength can vary as between the levels of selection, organization, pacing and timing of the knowledge transmitted in the pedagogical relationship.

I should also like to bring out (this will be developed more fully later in the analysis) the power component of this analysis and what can be called the 'identity' component. Where classification is strong, the boundaries between the different contents are sharply drawn. If this is the case, then it pre-supposes strong boundary maintainers. Strong classification also creates a strong sense of membership in a particular class and so a specific identity. Strong frames reduce the power of the pupil over what, when and how he receives knowledge, and increases the teacher's power in the pedagogical relationship. However, strong *classification* reduces the power of the *teacher* over what he transmits, as he may not over-step the boundary between contents, *and* strong classification reduces the power of the teacher *vis-à-vis* the boundary maintainers.

It is now possible to make explicit the concept of educational knowledge codes. The code is fully given *at the most general level* by the relationship between classification and framing.

A typology of educational knowledge codes

In the light of the conceptual framework we have developed, I shall use the distinction between collection and integrated curricula in order to realize a typology of types and sub-types of educational codes. The *formal* basis of the typology is the strength of classification and frames. However, the sub-types will be distinguished, initially, in terms of substantive differences.

Any organization of educational knowledge which involves strong classification gives rise to what is here called a collection code. Any organization of educational knowledge which involves a marked attempt to reduce the strength of classification is here called an integrated code. Collection codes may give rise to a series of sub-types, each varying in the relative strength of their classification and frames. Integrated codes can also vary in terms of the strength of frames, as these refer to the *teacher/pupil/student* control over the knowledge that is transmitted.

Figure 1 sets out general features of the typology.

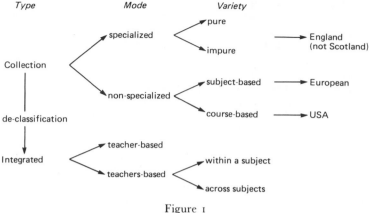

Figure 1

Collection codes

The first major distinction *within* collection codes is between specialized and non-specialized types. The extent of specialization can be measured in terms of the number of closed contents publicly examined at the end of the secondary educational stage. Thus in England, *although there is no formal limit*, the student usually sits for three A-level subjects, compared with the much greater range of subjects which make up the Abitur in Germany, the Baccalauréat in France, or the Studente Exam in Sweden.

Within the English specialized type, we can distinguish two varieties: a pure and an impure variety. The pure variety exists where A-level subjects are drawn from a common universe of knowledge, for example Chemistry, Physics, Mathematics. The impure variety exists where A-level subjects are drawn from different universes of knowledge, for example Religion, Physics, Economics. The latter combination, although formally possible, very rarely substantively exists, for pupils are not encouraged to offer – neither does timetabling usually permit – such a combination. It is a matter of interest that until very recently the pure variety at the university level received the higher status of an honours degree, whereas the impure variety tended to lead to the lower status of the general degree. One can detect the beginnings of a shift in England from the pure to the impure variety, which appears to be trying to work towards the non-specialized type of collection.

Within the non-specialized collection code, we can distinguish two varieties, according to whether a subject or course is the basic knowledge unit. Thus the standard European form of the collection code is non-specialized, *subject*-based. The USA form of the collection is non-specialized, course-based.

I have so far described sub-types and varieties of the collection code in simple descriptive terms; as a consequence it is not easy to see how their distinctive features can be translated into sociological concepts in order to realize a specific sociological problem. Clearly, the conceptual language here developed has built into it a specific perspective: that of power and social control. In the process of translating the descriptive features into the language of classification and frames, the question must arise as to whether the hypotheses about their relative strength fit a particular case.

Here are the hypotheses, given for purposes of illustration:

1 I suggest that the European, non-specialized, subject-based form of collection involves strong classification but *exceptionally* strong framing. That is, at levels *below* higher education, there are relatively few options available to teacher, and especially taught, over the transmission of knowledge. Curricula and syllabus are very explicit.

2 The English version, I suggest, involves *exceptionally* strong classification, but relatively weaker framing than the European type. The fact that it is specialized determines what contents (subjects) may be put together. There is very strong insulation between the 'pure' and the 'applied' knowledge. Curricula are graded for particular ability groups. There can be high insulation between a subject and a class of pupils. 'D' stream secondary pupils will not have access to certain subjects, and 'A' stream students will also not have access to certain subjects. However, I suggest that framing, relative to Europe, is weaker. This can be seen particularly at the primary level. There is also, *relative* to Europe, less *central* control over what is transmitted, although, clearly, the various requirements of the university level exert a strong control over the secondary level.[1] I suggest that, although again this is *relative*, there is a weaker frame in England between educational knowledge and the everyday community knowledge for certain classes of students: the so-called less able. Finally, relative to Europe, I suggest that there are more options available to the pupil within the pedagogical relationships. The frame as it refers to pupils is weaker. Thus, I suggest that framing as it relates to teachers and pupils is relatively weaker, but that classification is relatively much stronger in the English than in the European system. Scotland is nearer to the European version of the collection.

3 The course-based, non-specialized USA form of the collection, I suggest, has the weakest classification *and* framing of the collection code, especially at the secondary and university level. A far greater range of subjects can be taken at the secondary and university level, and are capable of combination; this indicates weak classification. The insulation between educational knowledge and everyday community knowledge is weaker, as can be evidenced by community control over school; this indicates weak frames. The range of options available to pupils within the pedagogical relationship is, I suggest, greater. I would guess, then, that classification and framing in the USA is the weakest of the collection codes.

Integrated codes

It is important to be clear about the term 'integrated'. Because one subject uses the theories of another subject, this type of intellectual inter-relationship does not constitute integration. Such intellectual inter-relation may well be part of a collection code at some point in the history of the development of knowledge. Integration, as it is used here, refers minimally to the *subordination* of previously insulated subjects *or* courses to some *relational* idea, which blurs the boundaries between the subjects. We can distinguish two types. The first type is *teacher*-based. Here the teacher, as in the infant school, has an extended block of time with often the same group of children. The teacher may operate with a collection code and keep the various subjects distinct and insulated, or he can blur the boundaries between the different subjects. This type of integrated code is easier to introduce than the second type, which is *teachers*-based. Here, integration involves relationships with other teachers. In this way, we can have degrees of integration in terms of the number of teachers involved.

We can further distinguish two varieties according to whether the integration refers to a group of teachers *within* a common subject, or the extent to which integration involves teachers of different subjects. Whilst integrated codes, by definition, have the weakest classification, they may vary as to framing. During the initiating period, the frames the teachers enter will be weak, but other factors will effect the final frame strength. It is also possible that the frames the *pupils* enter can vary in strength.

Thus integrated codes may be confined to one subject or they can cross subjects. We can talk of code strength in terms of the range of different subjects co-ordinated by the code, or if this criterion cannot be applied, code strength can be measured in terms of the *number* of teachers co-ordinated through the code. Integrated codes can also vary as to frame strength as this applies to teachers or pupils, or both.

Differences within, and between, educational knowledge codes from the perspective developed here, lie in variations in the strength and nature of the boundary maintaining procedures, as these are given by the classification and framing of the knowledge. It can be seen that the nature of classification and framing affects the authority/power structure which controls the dissemination of educational knowledge, and the *form* of the knowledge transmitted. In this way, principles of power and social control are realized through educational knowledge codes and, through the codes, enter into and shape consciousness. Thus, variations within and change of knowledge codes should be of critical concern to sociologists. The following problems arise out of this analysis:

1 What are the antecedents of variations in the strength of classification and frames?[2]
2 How does a given classification and framing structure perpetuate itself? What are the conditions of, and resistance to, change?
3 What are the different socializing experiences realized through variations in the strength of classifications and frames?

I shall limit the application of this analysis to the consideration of aspects of the last two questions. I feel I ought to apologize to the reader for this rather long and perhaps tedious conceptual journey, before he has been given any notion of the view to which it leads.

Application

I shall examine the patterns of social relationship and their socializing consequences which are realized through the European, particularly English, version of the collection code, and those which are *expected* to arise out of integrated codes, *particularly those which develop weak framing*. I shall suggest that there is some movement towards forms of the integrated code and I shall examine the nature of the resistance towards such a change. I shall suggest some reasons for this movement.

Classification and framing of the European form of the collection code

There will be some difficulty in this analysis, as I shall at times switch from secondary to university level. Although the English system has the distinguishing feature of specialization, it does share certain features of the European system. This may lead to some blurring in the analysis. As this is the beginning of a limited sociological theory which explores the social organization and structuring of educational knowledge, it follows that all statements, including those which have the character of descriptive statements, are hypothetical. The descriptive statements have been selectively patterned according to their significance for the theory.

One of the major differences between the European and English versions of the collection code is that, with the specialized English type, a membership category is established early in an educational career, in terms of an early choice between the pure and the applied, between the sciences and the arts, between having and not having a specific educational identity. A particular status in a given collection is made clear by streaming and/or a delicate system of grading. One nearly always knows the social significance of where one is and, in particular, *who* one is with each advance in the educational career. (Initially, I am doing science, or arts, pure or applied; or I am not doing anything; later I am becoming a physicist, economist, chemist, and so on.) *Subject loyalty* is then systematically developed in pupils and finally students, with each increase in the educational life, and then transmitted by them as teachers and lecturers. The system is self-perpetuating through this form of socialization. With the specialized form of the collection it is banal to say that as you get older you learn more and more about less and less. Another, more sociological, way of putting this is to say that as you get older, you become increasingly *different* from others. Clearly, this will happen at some point in any educational career, but, with specialization, this happens much earlier. Therefore, specialization very soon reveals *difference from* rather than communality with. It creates relatively quickly an educational identity which is clear-cut and bounded. The educational category or identity is *pure*. Specialized versions of the collection code tend to abhor mixed categories and blurred identities, for they represent a potential openness, an ambiguity, which makes the consequences of previous socialization problematic. Mixed categories such as bio-physicist, psycho-linguist, are only permitted to develop after long socialization into a subject loyalty. Indeed, in order to change an identity, a previous one has to be weakened and a new one created.

[. . .] Any attempt to weaken or *change* classification strength (or even frame strength) may be felt as a threat to one's identity and may be experienced as a pollution endangering the sacred. Here we have one source of the resistance to change of educational code.

The specialized version of the collection code will develop careful screening procedures to see who belongs and who does not belong, and once such screening has taken place, it is very difficult to change an educational identity. The various classes of knowledge are well insulated from each other. Selection and differentiation are early features of this particular code. Thus, the deep structure of the specialized type of collection code is *strong boundary maintenance creating control from within through the formation of specific identities.* An interesting aspect of the protestant spirit.

Strong boundary maintenance can be illustrated with reference to attempts to institutionalize new forms or attempts to change the strength of classification, within either the European or English type of collection. Because of the exceptional strength of classification in England, such difficulties may be greater here. Changes in classification strength and the institutionalizing of new forms of knowledge may become a matter of importance when there are changes in the structure of knowledge at the higher levels and/or changes in the economy. Critical problems arise with the question of new forms, as to their legitimacy, at what point they belong, when, where and by whom the form should be taught. I have referred to the 'sacred' in terms of an educational identity, but clearly there is the 'profane' aspect to knowledge. We can consider as the 'profane' the property aspect of knowledge. Any new form or weakening of classification clearly derives from past classifications. Such new forms or weakened classifications can be regarded as attempts to break or weaken existing monopolies.

So far, I have been considering the relationship between strong classification of knowledge, the concept of property and the creation of specific identities with particular reference to the specialized form of the collection code. I shall now move away from the classification of knowledge to its *framing* in the process of transmission.

Any collection code involves a hierarchical organization of knowledge, such that the ultimate mystery of the subject is revealed very late in the educational life. By the ultimate mystery of the subject, I mean its potential for creating new realities. It is also the case, and this is important, that the ultimate mystery of the subject is not coherence, but incoherence: not order, but disorder, not the known but the unknown. As this mystery, under collection codes, is revealed very late in the educational life – and then only to a select few who have shown the signs of successful socialization – then only the few *experience* in their bones the notion that knowledge is permeable, that its orderings are provisional, that the dialectic of knowledge is closure and openness. For the many, socialization into knowledge is socialization into order, the existing order, into the experience that the world's educational knowledge is impermeable. Do we have here another version of alienation?

Now, clearly, any history of any form of educational knowledge shows precisely the power of such knowledge to create endlessly new realities. However, socialization into the specific framing of knowledge in its transmission may make such a history experientially meaningless. The key concept of the European collection code is discipline. This means learning to work *within* a received frame. It means, in particular, *learning* what questions can be put at any particular time. Because of the hierarchical ordering of the knowledge in *time*, certain questions raised may not enter into a particular frame.

This is soon learned by both teachers and pupils. Discipline then means accepting a given selection, organization, pacing and timing of knowledge realized in the pedagogical frame. With increases in the educational life, there is a progressive weakening of the frame for both teacher and taught. Only the few who have shown the signs of successful socialization have access to these relaxed frames. For the mass of the population the framing is tight. In a sense, the European form of the collection code makes knowledge safe through the process of socialization into its frames. There is a tendency, which varies with the strength of specific frames, for the young to be socialized into assigned principles and routine operations and derivations. The evaluative system places an emphasis upon attaining *states* of knowledge rather than *ways* of knowing. A study of the examination questions and format, the symbolic structure of assessment, would be, from this point of view, a rewarding empirical study. Knowledge thus tends to be transmitted, particularly to élite pupils at the secondary level, through strong frames which control the selecting, organization, pacing and timing of the knowledge. The receipt of the knowledge is not so much a right as something to be won or earned. The stronger the classification and the framing, the more the educational relationship tends to be hierarchical and ritualized, the educand seen as ignorant, with little status and few rights. These are things which one earns, rather like spurs, and are used for the purpose of encouraging and sustaining the motivation of pupils. Depending upon the strength of frames, knowledge is transmitted in a context where the teacher has maximal control or surveillance, as in hierarchical secondary school relationships.

We can look at the question of the framing of knowledge in the pedagogical relationship from another point of view. In a sense, educational knowledge is uncommonsense knowledge. It is knowledge freed from the particular, the local, through the various languages of the sciences or forms of reflexiveness of the arts which make possible either the creation or the discovery of new realities. Now this immediately raises the question of the relationship between the uncommonsense knowledge of the school and the *commonsense* knowledge, everyday community knowledge, of the pupil, his family and his peer group. This formulation invites us to ask how strong are the frames of educational knowledge in relation to experiential, community-based non-school knowledge? I suggest that the frames of the collection code, very early in the child's life, socialize him into knowledge frames which discourage connections with everyday realities, or that there is a highly selective screening of the connection. Through such socialization, the pupil soon learns what of the outside may be brought into the pedagogical frame. Such framing also makes of educational knowledge something not ordinary or mundane, but something esoteric, which gives a special significance to those who possess it. I suggest that when this frame is relaxed to include everyday realities, it is often, and sometimes validly, not simply for the transmission of educational knowledge, but for purposes of social control of forms of deviancy. The weakening of this frame occurs usually with the less 'able' children whom we have given up educating.

In general, then, and depending upon the specific strength of classification and frames, the European form of the collection code is rigidly differentiating and hierarchical in character; highly resistant to change particularly at the secondary level. With the English version, this resistance to change is assisted by the discretion which is available to headmasters and principals. In England, within the constraints of the public examination system, the heads of schools and colleges have a relatively wide range of discretion over the organization and transmission of knowledge. Central control over the educational code is relatively weak in England, although clearly the schools are subject to inspection from both central and local government levels. However, the relationship between the inspectorate and the schools in England is very ambiguous. To produce widespread change in England would require the co-operation of hundreds of individual schools. Thus, rigidity in educational knowledge codes may arise out of highly centralized *or* weak central control over the knowledge codes. Weak central control does permit a series of changes which have, initially, limited consequences for the system as a whole. On the other hand, there is much stronger central control over the organizational style of the school. This can lead to a situation where there can be a change in the organizational style *without* there being *any* marked change in the educational knowledge code, particularly where the educational code itself creates specific identities. This raises the question, which cannot be developed here, of the relationships between organizational change and change of educational knowledge code, that is, change in the strength of classification and framing.

In general, then, the European and English form of the collection code may provide for those who go beyond the novitiate stage, order, identity and commitment. For those who do not pass beyond this stage, it can sometimes be wounding and seen as meaningless. What Bourdieu calls 'la violence symbolique'.

Integrated and collection codes

I shall now examine a form of the integrated code which is realized through very weak classification and frames. I shall, during this analysis, bring out further aspects of collection codes.

There are a number of attempts to institutionalize forms of the integrated code at different strengths, above the level of the infant school child. Nuffield Science is an attempt to do this with the physical sciences, and the Chelsea Centre for Science Education, Chelsea College of Technology, University of London, is concerned almost wholly in training students in this approach. Mrs Charity James, at Goldsmiths' College, University of London, is also producing training courses for forms of the integrated code. A number of comprehensive schools are experimenting with this approach at the middle school level. The SDS in Germany, and various radical student groups, are exploring this type of code in order to use the means of the university against the meaning. However, it is probably true to say that the code at the moment exists at the level of ideology and theory, with only a relatively small number of schools and educational agencies attempting to institutionalize it with any seriousness.

Now, as we said at the beginning of the paper, with the integrated code we have a shift from content closure to content openness, from strong to markedly reduced classification. Immediately, we can see that this disturbance in classification of knowledge will lead to a disturbance of existing authority structures, existing specific educational identities and concepts of property.

Where we have integration, the various contents are subordinate to some idea which reduces their isolation from each other. Thus integration reduces the authority of the separate contents, and this has implications for existing authority structures. Where we have collection, it does permit in principle considerable differences in pedagogy and evaluation, because of the high insulation between the different contents. However, the autonomy of the content is the other side of an authority structure which exerts jealous and zealous supervision. I suggest that the integrated code will not permit the variations in pedagogy and evaluation which are possible within collection codes. On the contrary, I suggest there will be a pronounced movement towards a common pedagogy and tendency towards a common system of evaluation. In other words, integrated codes will, at the level of the teachers, probably create homogeneity in teaching practice. Thus, collection codes increase the discretion of teachers (within, always, the limits of the existing classification and frames) whilst integrated codes will reduce the discretion of the teacher in direct relation to the strength of the integrated code (number of teachers – co-ordinated by the code). On the other hand, it is argued that the increased discretion of the teachers within collection codes is paralleled by *reduced* discretion of the pupils and that the reduced discretion of the teachers within integrated codes is paralleled by *increased* discretion of the pupils. In other words, there is a shift in the balance of power, in the pedagogical relationship between teacher and taught.

These points will now be developed. In order to accomplish any form of integration (as distinct from different subjects focusing upon a common problem, which gives rise to what could be called a *focused* curriculum) there must be some relational idea, a supra-content concept, which focuses upon general principles at a high level of abstraction. For example, if the relationships between sociology and biology are to be opened, then the relational idea (amongst many) might be the issue of problems of order and change examined through the concepts of genetic and cultural codes. Whatever the relational concepts are, they will act selectively upon the knowledge within each subject which is to be transmitted. The particulars of each subject are likely to have reduced significance. This will focus attention upon the *deep* structure of each subject, rather than upon its surface structure. I suggest this will lead to an emphasis upon, and the exploration of, *general* principles and the concepts through which these principles are obtained. In turn, this is likely to affect the orientation of the pedagogy, which will be less concerned to emphasize the need to acquire *states* of knowledge, but will be more concerned to emphasize *how* knowledge is created. In other words, the pedagogy of integrated codes is likely to emphasize various *ways* of knowing in the pedagogical relationships. With the collection code, the pedagogy tends to proceed from the surface structure of the knowledge to the deep structure, as we have seen, only the élite have access to the deep structure and therefore access to the realizing of new realities or access to the experiential knowledge that new realities are possible. *With integrated codes, the pedagogy is likely to proceed from the deep structure to the surface structure.* We can see this already at work in the new primary school mathematics. Thus, I suggest that integrated codes will make available from the beginning of the pupil's educational career, clearly in a way appropriate to a given age level, the deep structure of the knowledge, that is, the principles for the generating of new knowledge. Such emphasis upon various *ways* of knowing, rather than upon the attaining of *states* of knowledge, is likely to affect, not only the emphasis of the pedagogy, but the underlying theory of learning. The underlying theory of learning of collection codes is likely to be didactic, whilst the underlying theory of learning of integrated codes may well be more group or self-regulated. This arises out of a different concept of what counts as having knowledge, which in turn leads to a different concept of how the knowledge is to be acquired. These changes in emphasis and orientation of the pedagogy are initially responsible for the relaxed frames, which teacher and taught enter. Relaxed frames not only change the nature of the authority relationships by increasing the rights of the taught, they can also weaken or blur the boundary between what may or may not be taught, and so *more* of the teacher and taught is likely to enter this pedagogical frame. The inherent logic of the integrated code is likely to create a change in the structure of teaching groups, which are likely to exhibit considerable flexibility. The concept of relatively weak boundary maintenance which is the core principle of integrated codes is realized both in the structuring of educational knowledge *and* in the organization of the social relationships.

I shall now introduce some organizational consequences of collection and integrated codes which will make explicit the difference in the distribution of power and the principles of control which inhere in these educational codes.

Where knowledge is regulated through a collection code, the knowledge is organized and distributed through a series of well insulated subject hierarchies. Such a structure points to oligarchic control of the institution, through formal and informal meetings of heads of department with the head or principal of the institution. Thus, senior staff will have strong horizontal work relationships (that is, with their peers in other subject hierarchies) and strong vertical work relationships within their own department. However, junior staff are likely to have only vertical (within the subject hierarchy) allegiances and work relationships.

The allegiances of junior staff are vertical rather than horizontal for the following reasons. First, staff have been socialized into strong subject loyalty and through this into specific identities. These specific identities are continuously strengthened through social interactions *within* the department *and* through the insulation between departments. Second, the departments are often in a competitive relationship for strategic teaching resources. Third, preferment within the subject hierarchy often rests with its expansion. Horizontal relationships of junior staff (particularly where there is no *effective* participatory administrative structure) are likely to be limited to *non-task-based* contacts. There may well be discussion of control problems ('X of 3b is a —— How do you deal with him?' or 'I can't get X to write a paper'). Thus the collection code within the framework of oligarchic control creates for *senior* staff strong horizontal and vertical based relationships, whereas the work relationships of junior staff are likely to be vertical and the horizontal relationships limited to non-work-based contacts. This is a type of organizational system which encourages gossip, intrigue and a conspiracy theory of the workings of the organization, for *both* the *administration* and the *acts of teaching* are *invisible* to the majority of staff. (See Figure 2.)

Now the integrated code will require teachers of different subjects to enter into social relationships with each other which will arise not simply out of non-task areas, but out of a shared, co-operative educational task. The centre of gravity of the relationships between teachers will undergo a radical shift. Thus, instead of teachers and lecturers being divided and insulated by allegiances to subject hierarchies, the conditions for their unification exist through a common work situation. I suggest that this changed basis of the relationships, between teachers or between lecturers, may tend to weaken the separate hierarchies of collection. These new work-based horizontal relationships between teachers and between lecturers may alter both the structure and distribution of power regulated by the collection code. Further, the administration and specific acts of teaching are likely to shift from the relative invisibility to *visibility*.

We might expect similar developments at the level of students and even senior pupils. For pupils and students, with each increase in their educational life, are equally sub-divided and educationally insulated from each other. They are equally bound to subject hierarchies and, for similar reasons, to

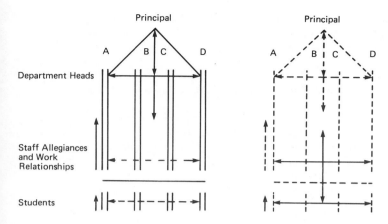

Key: Continuous lines represent strong boundaries, continuous arrows represent direction of strong relationships. Dotted lines represent weak boundaries. Dotted line arrows represent direction of weak relationships

Collection code type = Strong classification: strong frames
Integrated code type = Weak classification: weak frames

Figure 2

staff; their identities and their future is shaped by the department. Their vertical allegiances and work-based relationships are strong, whilst their horizontal relationships will tend to be limited to non-task areas (student/ pupil societies and sport) or peripheral non-task based administration. Here again, we can see another example of the strength of boundary maintenance of collection codes; this time between task and non-task areas. Integrated codes may well provide the conditions for strong horizontal relationships and allegiances in students and pupils, based upon a common work task (the receiving and offering of knowledge). In this situation, we might expect a weakening of the boundary between staff, especially junior staff, and students/ pupils.

Thus, a move from collection to integrated codes may well bring about a disturbance in the structure and distribution of power, in property relationships and in existing educational identities. This change of educational code involves a fundamental change in the nature and strength of boundaries. It involves a change in what counts as having knowledge, in what counts as a valid transmission of knowledge, in what counts as a valid realization of knowledge, *and* a change in the organizational context. At the cultural level, it involves a shift from the keeping of categories pure to the mixing of categories; whilst at the level of socialization the outcomes of integrated codes *could* be less predictable than the outcomes of collection codes. This change of code involves fundamental changes in the classification and framing of knowledge and so changes in the structure and distribution of power and in principles of control. It is no wonder that deep-felt resistances are called out by the issue of change in educational codes.

Collection, integrated codes and problems of order

[. . .] Order created by integrated codes may well be problematic. I suggest that if four conditions are not satisfied, then the openness of learning under integration may produce a culture in which neither staff nor pupils have a sense of time, place or purpose. I shall comment briefly on these four conditions as I give them.

1 There must be consensus about the integrating idea and it must be very explicit. (It is ironic that the movement towards integration is going on in those countries where there is a low level of moral consensus.) It may be that integrated codes will only work when there is a *high* level of ideological consensus among the staff. We have already seen that, in comparison with collection, integrated codes call for greater homogeneity in pedagogy and evaluation, and therefore reduce differences between teachers in the form of the transmission and assessment of knowledge. Whereas the teaching process under collection is likely to be invisible to other teachers, unless special conditions prevail, it is likely that the teaching process regulated through integrated codes may well become visible as a result of developments in the pedagogy in the direction of flexibility in the structure of teaching groups. It is also the case that the weak classification and relaxed frames of integrated codes permit greater expressions of differences between teachers, and possibly between pupils, in the selection of what is taught. The moral basis of educational choices is then likely to be explicit at the initial planning stage. Integrated codes also weaken specific identities. For the above reasons, integrated codes may require a high level of ideological consensus, and this may affect the recruitment of staff. Integrated codes at the surface level create weak or blurred boundaries, but at bottom they may rest upon closed explicit ideologies. Where such ideologies are not shared, the consequences will become visible and threaten the whole at every point.

2 The nature of the linkage between the integrating idea and the knowledge to be co-ordinated must also be coherently spelled out. It is this linkage which will be the basic element in bringing teachers *and* pupils into their working relationship. *The development of such a co-ordinating framework will be the process of socialization of teachers into the code. During this process, the teachers will internalize, as in all processes of socialization, the interpretative procedures of the code so that these become implicit guides which regulate and co-ordinate the behaviour of the individual teachers in the relaxed frames and weakened classification.* This brings us to a major distinction between collection and integrated codes. With a collection code, the period of socialization is facilitated by strong boundary mainten-ance both at the level of *role* and at the level of knowledge. Such socialization is likely to be continuous with the teacher's own educational socialization. With

integrated codes both the role and the form of the knowledge have to be *achieved* in relation to a range of different others, and this may involve re-socialization if the teacher's previous educational experience has been formed by the collection code. The collection code is capable of working when staffed by mediocre teachers, whereas integrated codes call for much greater powers of synthesis, analogy and for more ability to both tolerate and enjoy ambiguity at the level of knowledge *and* social relationships.

3 A committee system of staff may have to be set up to create a sensitive feed-back system and which will also provide a further agency of socialization into the code. It is likely that evaluative criteria are likely to be relatively weak, in the sense that the criteria are less likely to be as explicit and measurable as in the case of collection. As a result, it may be necessary to develop committees for both teachers, students, and, where appropriate, pupils, which will perform monitoring functions.

4 One of the major difficulties which inhere in integrated codes arises over what is to be assessed, and the form of assessment: also the place of specific competencies in such assessment. It is likely that integrated codes will give rise to multiple criteria of assessment compared with collection codes. In the case of collection codes, because the knowledge moves from the surface to the deep structure, then this progression creates ordered principles of evaluation in time. The form of temporal cohesion of the knowledge regulated through the integrated code has yet to be determined, and made explicit. Without clear criteria of evaluation, neither teacher nor taught have any means to consider the significance of what is learned, nor any means to judge the pedagogy. In the case of collection codes, evaluation at the secondary level often consists of the fit between a narrow range of specific competencies and states of knowledge, and previously established criteria (varying in explicitness) of what constitutes a right or appropriate or convincing answer. The previously established criteria together with the specific social context of assessment create a relatively objective procedure. I do not want to suggest that this necessarily gives rise to a form of assessment which entirely disregards distinctive and original features of the pupil's performance. In the case of the integrated code under discussion (weak frames for teacher and taught), this form of assessment may well be inappropriate. The weak frames enable a greater range of the student's behaviour to be made public, and they make possible considerable diversity (at least in principle) between students. It is possible that this might lead to a situation where assessment takes more into account 'inner' attributes of the student. Thus if he has the 'right' attitudes, then this will result later in the attainment of various specific competencies. The 'right' attitude may be assessed in terms of the fit between the pupil's attitudes and the current ideology. It is possible, then, that the evaluative criteria of integrated codes with weak frames may be weak as these refer to specific cognitive attributes but strong as these refer to dispositional attributes. If this is so, then a new range of pupil attributes become candidates for labels. It is also likely that the weakened classification and framing will encourage more of the pupil/student to be made public; more of his thoughts,

feelings and values. In this way more of the pupil is available for control. As a result the socialization could be more intensive and perhaps more penetrating. In the same way as pupils/students defend themselves against the wounds of collection, or distance themselves from its overt code, so they may produce new defences against the potential intrusiveness of the integrated code and its open learning contexts.

We can summarize this question of the problem of order as follows. Collection codes have explicit and strong boundary maintaining features and they rest upon a tacit ideological basis. Integrated codes have implicit and weak boundary maintaining features and they rest upon an explicit and closed ideological basis. The ideological basis of the collection code is a condensed symbolic system communicated through its explicit boundary maintaining features. Its covert structure is that of mechanical solidarity. The ideological basis of integrated codes is *not* a condensed symbolic system, it is verbally elaborated and explicit. It is an *overt* realization of organic solidarity and made substantive through weak forms of boundary maintenance (low insulations). Yet the covert structure of mechanical solidarity of collection codes creates through its specialized outputs *organic* solidarity. On the other hand the overt structure of organic solidarity of integrated codes creates through its *less* specialized outputs *mechanical* solidarity. And it will do this to the extent to which its ideology is explicit, elaborated and closed *and* effectively and *implicitly* transmitted through its low insulations. Inasmuch as integrated codes do not accomplish this, then order is highly problematic at the level of social organization and at the level of the person. Inasmuch as integrated codes do accomplish such socialization, then we have the covert deep closure of mechanical solidarity. This is the fundamental paradox which has to be faced and explored.

Change of educational code

I have tried to make explicit the relationships between educational codes and the structure of power and principles of social control. Attempts to change or modify educational codes will meet with resistance at a number of different levels, irrespective of the intrinsic educational merit of a particular code. I shall now briefly discuss some reasons for a movement towards the institutionalizing of integrated codes *of the weak classification and weak framing (teacher and taught) type*, above the level of the primary school.[3]

1 The growing differentiation of knowledge at the higher levels of thought, together with the integration of previously discrete areas, may set up requirements for a form of socialization appropriate to these changes in the structure of knowledge.
2 Changes in the division of labour are creating a different concept of skill. The in-built obsolescence of whole varieties of skills reduces the significance of context-tied operations and increases the significance of general

principles from which a range of diverse operations may be derived. In crude terms, it could be said that the nineteenth century required submissive and inflexible man, whereas the late twentieth century requires conforming but flexible man.

3 The less rigid social structure of the integrated code makes it a potential code for egalitarian education.

4 In advanced industrial societies which permit, within limits, a range of legitimizing beliefs and ideologies, there is a major problem of control. There is the problem of making sense of the differentiated, weakly co-ordinated and changing symbolic systems and the problem of inner regulation of the person. Integrated codes, with their stress on the underlying unity of knowledge, through their emphasis upon analogy and synthesis, could be seen as a response to the first problem of 'making sense'. The *inter-personal* rather than *inter-positional* control of the integrated code may set up a penetrating intrusive form of socialization under conditions of ambiguity in the system of beliefs and the moral order.

If these reasons operate, we could consider the movement towards integrated codes as stemming from a technological source. However, it is possible that there is another and deeper source of the movement away from collection. I suggest that the movement away from collection to integrated codes symbolizes that there is a crisis in society's basic classifications and frames, and therefore a crisis in its structures of power and principles of control. The movement from this point of view represents an attempt to de-classify and so alter power structures and principles of control; in so doing to unfreeze the structuring of knowledge and to change the boundaries of consciousness. From this point of view integrated codes are symptoms of a moral crisis rather than the terminal state of an educational system.

Notes

1 The content of public examinations between the secondary and the tertiary level is controlled by the tertiary level directly or indirectly, through control over the various syllabuses. Thus, if there is to be any major shift in secondary schools' syllabuses and curricula, then this will require changes in the tertiary level's policy, as this affects the acceptance of students. Such a change in policy would involve changes in the selection, organization, pacing and timing of knowledge at the tertiary level. Thus, the conditions for a major shift in the knowledge code at the secondary level is a major shift in the knowledge code at the tertiary level. Changes in the knowledge code at the secondary level are likely to be of a somewhat limited nature without similar changes at the tertiary level. There clearly are other interest groups (industry) which may affect a given curriculum and syllabus.

2 Such variations may well be linked to variations in the development of class structure.

3 It is a matter of interest that, in England, it is only in the infant school that there is relatively widespread introduction of this form of integrated code. This raises the

general question of how this level of the educational system was open to such change. Historically, the primary school developed distinct concepts of infant and junior stages, and distinct heads for these two stages. Given the relative autonomy over the transmission of knowledge which characterizes the British system of education, it was in principle possible to have change. Although only a ceiling may separate infant from junior departments, two quite distinct and often incompatible educational codes can develop. We can regard this as a necessary, but not sufficient, condition for the emergence of integrated codes at the infant school level. It was also the case, until very recently, that the selection function started in the junior department, because that department was the gateway to the grammar school. This left the infant school relatively free of control by levels higher than itself. The form of integration in the infant school, again until recently, was *teacher*-based, and therefore did not set up the problems which arise out of *teachers*-based integration. Finally, infant school teachers are not socialized into strong educational identities. Thus the English educational system, until recently, had two potential points of openness – the period between the ages of five to seven years, before selection began, and the period post-eighteen years of age, when selection is virtually completed. The major control on the structuring of knowledge at the secondary level is the structuring of knowledge at the tertiary level, specifically the university. Only if there is a major change in the structuring of knowledge at this level can there be effective code change at lower levels; although in any one school there may be a variety of knowledge codes.

3.5 Handling Innovation in the Classroom: Two Scottish Examples

David Hamilton

I

In 1964 a Scottish Education Department working party was set up to consider the development of science schemes for 'non-academic' pupils (that is, those not catered for by the 'alternative' schemes). In 1966, however, its remit was changed to take account of the (then) government's plans for universal comprehensive education. The revised remit was for the preparation of a so-called 'common core' science course for the first two years of secondary education, which in Scotland begins at age twelve. Full details of the Scottish Integrated Science Scheme were finally published in 1969. Compared to other novel science curricula developed in the 1960s, the most significant innovatory features of the integrated scheme were its unification of physics, chemistry and biology; its intention that the same teacher should take all the science lessons for any given class; and its suitability for '*all* pupils . . . whether streamed or unstreamed'.[1] According to a national survey, almost 90 per cent of Scottish secondary schools reported they would be following the scheme during the year 1971–2.

The official ideology of the integrated science scheme is contained in a Scottish Education Department report and an accompanying set of 144 worksheets. Curriculum Paper Seven – as the report is popularly known – contains not only a general discussion of the course but also a series of recommendations, a twenty-four page outline syllabus, and 210 specific educational objectives for the fifteen 'thematic' sections of the course. Although the worksheets cover the entire course, they are not intended to serve as its text, but merely as 'props' to support 'discovery methods'. Besides the features already outlined, the Integrated Science Scheme also intends that equal weight be given to biology, physics and chemistry within the unified whole; that the basis of the teaching be 'stage-managed' heurism (or 'discovery' learning); and that multiple choice exams be used for testing the stated objectives of the course.

In these formalised terms [. . .] integrated science is portrayed as a self-contained system or curriculum package: in this case containing a set of pedagogical assumptions, a new syllabus and details of techniques and equipment. Although for most purposes, this blueprint or catalogue description 'stands for' the scheme, it tends to gloss over the diversity of situations which become the focus of its implementation. It merely describes the essence

Source: REID, WILLIAM A. and WALKER, DECKER, F. (1975) *Case Studies in Curriculum Change, Great Britain and the United States*. London: Routledge and Kegan Paul.

of the Scottish scheme. As an idealised specification, then, it is rather like a genotype or an archetype. To use a term recently proposed, it is an 'instructional system'.[2]

Thus, a major concern of this account is the translation of such an instructional system into two real life settings. Central is the idea that when an instructional system is adopted, it undergoes modifications that are rarely trivial. Although it may remain a shared ideal, abstract model, slogan or shorthand, the instructional system assumes a different form in every situation. Its constituent elements are emphasised or de-emphasised, expanded or contracted as teachers, students and others interpret and reinterpret the instructional system for their particular setting. For example, even a cursory glance at the survey figures referred to above, shows that less than 60 per cent of the children described as following the integrated science scheme are, in fact, following a scheme where the biological, chemical and physical sections of the course are taught by the same teacher. Already, the original 'ideal' formulation has, in practice, been the subject of a redefinition process.

In a paper entitled 'On the classification and framing of educational knowledge'[3] Basil Bernstein returns to a theme sketched out in one of his earlier papers: 'Open schools, open society?' His discussion considers the relationship between the gross changes that are taking place in schools, and similar changes that are taking place elsewhere in society. To articulate certain of these ideas Bernstein makes a distinction between what he calls 'integrated-type' and 'collection-type' (that is, subject-specific) school curricula. This particular distinction – and Bernstein's treatment of it – do much to illuminate events at Simpson and Maxwell.

In Bernstein's terms collection curricula are characterised by a 'closed' compartmentalised relationship between the subjects; integrated curricula by an 'open' relationship. At the level of theory, the integrated idea is sustained by stressing the unity of a subject area, the collection idea by stressing its diversity. Furthermore, Bernstein goes on to argue that these two curriculum types can be linked to a range of distinct sociological and organisational phenomena. That collection types are associated with strong subject loyalties on the part of teachers; a range of different subject ideologies across the collection of subjects in the curriculum; didactic instruction; a hierarchical conception of valid knowledge ('facts' before 'principles'), and oligarchic control (vertical hierarchy of staff) within subjects. And that by contrast integrated types are associated with weak subject loyalties; a common pedagogy, practice and examining style; emphasis on self-regulatory instruction; early initiation into basic principles, and strong horizontal professional relationships among staff.

Much of Bernstein's characterisation of an integrated curriculum matches the intentions of Curriculum Paper Seven, namely:

Content openness   'Science . . . should be in the form of an integrated study of the various disciplines'

Self-regulatory instruction	The discovery method should be used wherever possible'
Common pedagogy, practice and examining style	This is implied by Curriculum Paper Seven's advocacy of worksheets and multiple choice examinations; and its presentation of the behavioural objectives for the course
Early initiation into deep structures (ways of knowing)	A much reduced emphasis on the retention of the factual content of the syllabus. Instead . . . pupils should be exposed . . . to many other aspects of the work of the scientist; . . . the experimental processes of thought by which he arrives at his conclusions and the language which he uses to communicate these conclusions to others'
Strong horizontal relationships among staff	'Science teachers in a school should all be free together at least once a week'

Despite these *prima facie* integrated characteristics of the Scottish Integrated Science Scheme, the Scottish secondary education system retains, overall, certain of the collection features described by Bernstein. All Scottish science teachers are necessarily university graduates. (This distinguishes them from their English counterparts.) After a year's obligatory subject-based, postgraduate training they are certificated not merely to teach (as in England) but to teach specified subjects. Throughout, therefore, there is strong subject loyalty induced and strong compartmentalisation of established subjects.

Besides a differentiation between subjects, there is also differentiation between categories of teachers. Although they may be doing identical work, 'honours' graduates receive higher salaries than 'ordinary' graduates. Another hierarchical distinction made between honours and ordinary graduates is that until recently ordinary graduates were precluded from holding principal teacher (head of department) positions in senior secondary schools. Thus, the vertical differences between honours and ordinary graduates within the same subject are widely reinforced and institutionalised.[4] This clash between the integrated basis of the Scottish Integrated Science Scheme and the overall collection characteristics of the system is important to the discussion that follows.

Bernstein's analysis is penetrating. It presents a theoretical basis for understanding the social, organisational and intellectual differences between subject-specific and integrated studies. Besides furnishing such an analysis, Bernstein also discusses a related problem of social order. He argues that by their very nature (clear boundaries, strong subject identities, hierarchical authority structure, and so on) the organisation of collection curricula, relative to integrated curricula, is more clearly defined and regulated; (given, of course, that those working within the 'collection' accept its value structure). In contrast, Bernstein suggests with respect to integrated curricula that 'if four conditions are not satisfied, then the openness of learning under integration may well produce a culture in which neither staff nor pupils will have a sense of time, place or purpose' What are these four conditions?

First, Bernstein declares that the integrated idea may only work when there is 'high ideological consensus among the staff'. For integration to become a reality rather than an ideal, he argues there should be widespread agreement on its aims and objectives.

Second, he maintains that 'the linkage between the integrating idea and the knowledge to be co-ordinated must also be coherently spelled out'. What is meant by this? With any integrated curriculum there is rarely a well-defined body of common knowledge (facts, principles, and so on) which can form a substantive basis for curriculum content (that is, the syllabus). Rather, to retain the idea of integration, the various contributing subjects must be linked at a higher conceptual or cognitive level. The first three sections of the Scottish scheme are concerned respectively with measurement (rather than, say, 'the metric system'), principles of taxonomy (rather than 'animals and plants'), and energy (rather than 'heat, light and sound'). Although, by and large, these sections are concerned with the same apparatus and experiments, their subject domains are more diffuse and their pedagogical intentions more elevating. They are, therefore, at one remove from the explication of 'mere facts'. In so far as the higher level concepts must emerge from the content of the course, then teachers working under integration should be under no illusion as to the particular high level concept(s) being endorsed.

Third, Bernstein suggests that as evaluation criteria are 'less likely to be as explicit and measurable as in the case of collection' there should be close face to face discussion and feed-back between staff and students.

Fourth, Bernstein points out that if confusion is to be avoided, clear criteria of evaluation (that is, what is to be assessed and the form of the assessment) should exist.

With regard to these last two *caveats* it is no doubt significant that hand in hand with the development of new curricula has gone a concern for new forms of evaluation and assessment. Curriculum Paper Seven is no exception. For example, its recommendations include the following (emphases added):

Tests should be designed to assess all aspects of teaching in science; they should not be limited to recall and simple comprehension exercises.
Tests should be used for *other purposes besides* ranking pupils.
Testing should have a limited place in education.
An investigation should be made of what should be tested in science.

In each case they reflect a change in the climate surrounding school assessment.

Throughout his paper, Bernstein treats integrated and collection curricula as ideal types; that is, in pure form as analytical constructs. Now I want to return to the murky reality of curriculum development and curriculum change.

II

The essential tension between science and its component parts has a long history in British science education. Throughout, the tension has derived from more than just pedagogic concern. In secondary education 'science' has been a low status subject, taught by poorly qualified 'generalists' in low status institutions to poorly endowed or very young pupils. After the Second World War, recognising the character of this ascription, secondary modern schools rejected 'general science'. Instead, they made considerable efforts to raise their status by presenting science in subject-specific form; that is, as was taught in high status grammar schools.[5] By the 1960s the expression 'general science' was one of the shibboleths of science teaching in Britain. It was scarcely mentioned, rarely advocated. The fact that current variants of general science are now called 'integrated science' or 'combined science' is thus perhaps understandable.

The science departments I studied at Simpson and Maxwell schools had an organisational structure that was essentially subject-specific; that is, each was organised separately for physics, chemistry and biology. When integrated science was introduced at Simpson it was grafted on to the pre-existing subject-specific organisation. At Maxwell – a new school – the two organisational forms were developed side by side.[6]

Simpson school is a large urban comprehensive school that serves an area of predominantly pre-war council housing. Observation took place at the Annexe one and a half miles from the main school. In effect the Annexe was an 'overflow' school which catered only for the first year children. Divided into thirty groups, the pupils (about 500) were taught science for five 35-minute periods per week. Each group contained from sixteen to twenty-one boys and girls drawn from the entire ability range. Up to five groups took science at any one time. (*N.B.* science is considered a 'craft' subject in Scotland and generally taught to half classes. Formally the class size should not exceed twenty pupils.)

There were four science laboratories at the Annexe, and a science hut across the tarmacadam playground. Each lab was similar in design, with rows of fixed teak benches arranged in front of a blackboard and a raised teacher's demonstration bench. In the two labs where observations were recorded, there were sinks and gas taps on the teachers' benches and two sinks on the benches that ran around the perimeter of the room. In one of the rooms there was only one electrical socket other than those on the teacher's bench.

My initial observations at Simpson did not match the picture of integrated science presented by Curriculum Paper Seven. Instead of support materials the worksheets had become *the* syllabus; and, as teacher demonstrations were often substituted for pupil practical work, class teaching had become the dominant activity. Further observation and discussion suggested reasons for this state of affairs.

Although there was only enough teaching for four full-timers, ten people taught science at the Annexe, but only one of them full-time. Most of the remaining teachers commuted from the separate subject-specific departments at the main school – five of them for less than six periods per week. For timetabling reasons, eleven of the thirty groups had more than one teacher. Indeed, one group was taught each week by three different teachers. These factors – school on twin sites, large numbers of teachers, and multiple teaching of classes – were basic constraints on the science teaching.

Conditions were further exacerbated at Simpson by teacher absences; by the relative shortage of apparatus; by the lack of laboratory accommodation appropriate to the needs of Curriculum Paper Seven; and, not least, by the fact that integrated science was only in its first full year of operation at the school.

The essential problem with such a large number of teachers was one of communication. At no time were all ten teachers in the building together. There was no natural opportunity for general discussion of the new scheme or for discussion of pupil progress. For some of the teachers the only channel of communication was a record book kept in the preparation room where each of them indicated the work or work-sheet completed each lesson. At times, unfortunately, this task was forgotten.

When classes were taught by more than one teacher the communication problem was more acute. At Simpson, teachers sharing classes tried to maintain continuous progress through the integrated course. (The alternative strategy was to subdivide the courses – usually along subject lines – with one teacher, say, doing all the 'chemistry' sections.) Thus each teacher was required week by week to begin where the previous one had left off and to finish at a recognisable point. In a situation like this there was little scope for free-wheeling. As one teacher described it, 'All you can do is paddle along.'

For certain demonstrations or experiments there was sometimes only enough apparatus for it to be used by one class at a time. As several groups were taught simultaneously, complicated organisational bartering took place to avoid localised shortages. If it was a teacher's turn to use a certain piece of apparatus he had to use it when available or, as sometimes happened, forfeit the opportunity. The fact that some of the apparatus had to be ferried from the main school further added to this difficulty.

Finally, teacher absence was a reality at Simpson school. On such occasions it was customary for the absent teacher's class to be split among the remaining classes rather than to be taken by another teacher. Sometimes teachers did not return from their periods of absence. In the previous year, four science groups had been taught by a succession of five different temporary teachers. When a further teacher left without being replaced, another five groups were distributed among the teachers that remained.

Each of these factors suggests why the teachers were under some pressure to stick to the course. In the circumstances it is reasonable to assume that anyone who had sought to develop his own ideas or even to fulfil the prescriptions of Curriculum Paper Seven was likely to receive little sympathy from his or her colleagues – particularly if it involved their co-operation. As most of the teachers spent so little time teaching at the Annexe, their priorities did not lie with the integrated scheme, but with their own subject courses higher up the school.

De facto responsibility for integrated science at Simpson Annexe was retained by the only science teacher in residence there full-time. The fact, however, that he had no formal authority, nor yet a responsibility allowance, undermined the efforts that he made. Most of his free time was spent easing the organisational workload of the teachers who commuted from the main school.

Much of the day to day co-ordination was not in the full-time teacher's hands but the responsibility of the laboratory assistant. As she performed the essential task of ensuring the maintenance of entries in the work diary, and as she was the only person at any given time to know where everything was, her position was a key one. Her role belied her designation as 'ancillary'.

Finally, the staffing problems at Simpson school (and particularly at the Annexe) had produced an instability that effectively precluded any long term planning or development of the integrated science teaching. It was public knowledge in the school that the teacher 'in charge' of integrated science was actively seeking promotion.

Maxwell is a new suburban comprehensive school serving an area of mixed private and public housing. Set in its own playing fields, the school comprises a central three-storey building surrounded by smaller satellite blocks serving specialised functions such as craft, home economics and science. The science department is a one-storey block made up of sixteen laboratories built around a central store, lecture theatre, workshop and darkroom. While different in detail, each laboratory had a fixed teacher's bench (not raised) and movable tables for the pupils. Compared to Simpson the provision of sinks and electrical socket-outlets was two to three times more generous. Although integrated science was taught from the time the school opened, eight out of the sixteen labs were architecturally subject-specific. For example, some labs had fume-cupboards (chemistry), others were south-facing (biology).

At the time of the first year's observation there were no pupils in years four to six and only about 700 pupils in years one to three (60 per cent of the final complement for those years). Integrated science in the first and second years was organised around sixteen mixed ability groups in each year. For this number of children there were three heads of department (physics, biology and chemistry), two assistant science teachers and three laboratory staff. No one had special responsibility for science; the heads of department rotated the task termly.

As the school had not been fully opened when the staff were recruited, the new headmaster was assisted by the local science adviser in making his choice of teachers. As the adviser had been very active in the preparation of Curriculum Paper Seven, he had recommended teachers who would be keen to develop integrated science. None of them, however, had previously taught together.

Conscious of their position (working in a 'show' school) and their commitment to implementing Curriculum Paper Seven, the teaching staff at

Maxwell recognised many of the problems involved in setting up a new department and running a new integrated science scheme. To meet the difficulties they soon established a sophisticated organisational structure to facilitate the introduction of what, for most of them, was an untried scheme. At weekly staff meetings, held after school, strategies were developed for keeping pupil records; for monitoring the use of apparatus; for preparing multiple choice examinations; for making the most economical use of technical staff; and for generally programming the succeeding sections of Curriculum Paper Seven (arranging dates for out-of-school visits, making advance bookings for films and so on).

At the staff meetings (of which I attended the three that took place during the course of the first year's observation) considerable discussion centred on the presentation of the course and the best possible use of the worksheets. Even the content and form of written work was discussed. Needless to say, as a result of this activity, the members of the science department spent a considerable time preparing materials, work-sheets and examinations outside school hours. It is obvious in such a situation that the staff meetings played an important part in the organisation of the department. Much of the long term planning of work, and the negotiation of responsibility was performed on these occasions.

In most respects this system functioned successfully. It helped to resolve many of the day to day problems of the integrated course (see below). However, the organisational structure also created a number of problems when it began to exert its own hegemony over the work of the individual teacher. As one teacher put it: 'We're so well organised, at times I don't know what I'm doing.'

One problem that arose concerned the devolution of responsibility. Considerable time was spent at the staff meetings discussing who should be responsible for preparing the succeeding sections of the course; or who, for example, should be responsible for liaison with the laboratory staff. Typically, these discussions revolved around subject loyalties and responsibilities. Was a 'biology' section really a biology section or was it a 'chemistry' section? Was a malfunctioning fish tank the responsibility of the head of biology, the head of science or the person whose room it was in? Who reported it to the lab assistants? Which assistant? In situations like this there appeared to be an organisational tension between the informal parity among the staff and the formal hierarchical structure within the science department. Thus, while the preparation of additional materials was shared out equally among all the teachers, only the heads of department had keys to the science block (which was kept locked outside lesson time).

A second problem arising at the staff meetings concerned timing. In the interests of organisational clarity (and maintenance of a 'common ped-agogy') dates were fixed well in advance for the completion of the various sections and for the setting of the multiple choice section tests. However, as various factors usually intervened, time had to be spent at successive meetings rescheduling deadlines fixed previously.

A third problem concerned furthering the aims of the course. However explicitly they are expressed in curriculum papers or teachers' guides, aims and objectives require re-interpretation in practice. Considerable discussion took place at Maxwell around what should be done to fulfil the objectives. In the interests of presenting a unified course, this generally meant seeking agreed common ground rather than allowing divergence of content and method.

By the nature of this research it was possible to take a further look at the organisational structure of Simpson and Maxwell in the following year. (The data for Simpson were collected during a half-day return visit. The data for Maxwell during an eight week observation period.) Not unexpectedly the position at Simpson had changed very little since the first year. If anything, it had moved a little closer towards the integrated idea. In particular, all the staff who taught integrated science now met every six weeks during school time. In two other respects conditions had also changed marginally towards integration. Multiple teaching of single groups had been reduced from eleven to seven groups and no teacher taught at the Annexe for less than five periods. (In the previous year five out of the ten teachers had taught there for less than six periods per week.) Each of these changes enhanced the possibility of integrated science at Simpson gradually beginning to develop an identity of its own.

At Maxwell the position had changed more noticeably. Over the whole school, the numbers of staff and pupils had risen by over 40 per cent (without an equivalent all-round increase of equipment in the science department). The number of first year science groups had risen from sixteen to twenty-four and third and fourth year public examination courses were well under way. The initial response on the part of the teachers to the apparent decrease in apparatus was to reprogramme the sections of the course. To ease the burden on specific items of equipment (for example, the Van de Graaf generator), sections two ('looking at living things') and three ('energy: the basic ideas'), and sections four ('matter as particles') and seven ('electricity') of the scheme were juxtaposed for half of the twenty-four first year groups. In practice this was only partially successful as section seven leans heavily on ideas supposedly developed in section four.

The response to the increase in staff was to change the committee structure within the science department. General meetings attended by all the staff were replaced by a system of meetings based on four domains of responsibility: (1) meetings of the three heads of department (biology, physics and chemistry), (2) meetings of staff within departments, (3) meetings of all science staff, and (4) meetings for those (usually one teacher from each subject department) concerned with the preparation of the materials and tests used in the various sections of the course.

Since only the departmental and heads of department meetings were scheduled during school time, and since the 'science' meetings took place rarely (none during the eight weeks of the observation), this organisational form served to reinforce a subject-specific rather than an integrated identity within the science department.

A third development in the teaching was that three of the new assistant staff were appointed as subject specialists rather than to teach integrated science. When they began teaching they found to their evident unease that almost 70 per cent of their teaching time was spent on integrated science. While being interviewed they made such comments as 'Teaching biology I'm lost, . . . I feel the chemistry and biology lessons are pretty empty' (physicist); 'I'd rather teach biology . . . I think you should keep it as an integrated course but with different teachers' (biologist); 'I find it difficult teaching other than biology. . . . I don't have enough background. . . . Botany I can talk about off the cuff' (second biologist). In teaching predominantly integrated science, however, they were no different from the other teachers, all of whom spent upwards of 64 per cent of their time similarly engaged (that is, teaching years one and two).

A final factor which suggested a change of emphasis in the department was that a proposal had been made that subject specialists should teach their 'own' sections of the scheme. Yet, of the eight sections in the first year part of the scheme, only three sections are given unique subject labels by Curriculum Paper Seven. The majority are described as including subject matter from more than one discipline. For example section four, 'energy: the basic idea' is described as including 'physics with chemistry and biology'.

From the data presented it is apparent that certain features of the model proposed by Bernstein were exemplified by Simpson and Maxwell. At both schools there was a conflict of interest between the integrated and the collection modes of organisation. At Simpson this conflict was apparent from the outset. At Maxwell this same conflict – though originally latent – increasingly became an important feature of department life as time passed.

In their own ways – as quite different schools – Simpson and Maxwell represent two distinct types. Simpson is a school where a new integrated collection was assimilated and then *redefined* in terms of an older collection curriculum. (Walker and Adelman have aptly named this form of integration 'disguised collection'.)[7] Thus, despite a superficial display of integration (for example, using the published worksheets), Simpson retained certain important features of a collection curriculum: didactic (factual) instruction predominated; teachers retained their subject identities; and in addition, since horizontal relationships among staff were weak, effective control rested with the only full-time teacher [. . .]. As foreshadowed earlier, this general 'collection' effect tended to swamp attempts at introducing the integrated idea.

Maxwell, by contrast, is a school where the opportunity existed for establishing an integrated curriculum. As a new school Maxwell had a hand-picked staff and an abundance of resources. Yet, faced with increased staff and student numbers, and more intense utilisation of resources the science department at Maxwell were having difficulty in fulfilling their aim of implementing Curriculum Paper Seven.

The fact that there were still two or three years before it achieved a 'stable state' (full quota of staff and students), and the fact that it intended developing collection curricula in years three to six, meant that Maxwell could easily fall back on traditional subject-specific patterns of organisation in years one and two. Clearly, in a school like this, later years present a qualitatively different situation. For the first time the possibility exists for establishing a division of labour and (paid) 'responsibility' based on the integrated science/non-integrated science distinction. Integrated science would become a fourth science subject with its own department, specialists, equipment and laboratories. In this event a polarisation of curriculum identities takes place. At the time of writing (October 1973) this has not occurred at Maxwell since certain countervailing strategies have been deployed. For example, the local authority promotion policy deliberately precludes the appointment of principal teachers of 'integrated science'. Also, the authority actively encourages its teachers to attend 'management' courses which – by using educational simulation exercises – discuss and explore the kind of problems raised at Maxwell.

III

So far this paper has documented aspects of the learning milieu related to the departmental organisation of the Scottish Integrated Science Scheme. In the remaining section I want to look at the classroom impact of two features of the integrated science milieu at Maxwell: the timetable and the testing.

   In the context I studied – as will become clear – each of these institutions was taken for granted. That is, it was accepted without comment and did not feature prominently in the perceived business of the department. Here I would like to demonstrate that both timetable and testing were in fact problematic, and that they had a differential impact across the four classes I observed. In each case I shall argue that the public 'reality' sustained at departmental level concealed quite different and sometimes opposing 'realities' within each science class. This section also serves to demonstrate how an instructional system like the Scottish Integrated Science Scheme is successively transformed as its wisdom is filtered through the organisational structure of the school, science department and classrooms. Throughout, a number of 'interference' 'boundary' and 'mediating' effects can be discerned.

   Each of the four classes I observed during the second year of fieldwork had the same amount of time set aside for science: five [35 minute] periods per week. The class differed, however, in the way their time was allocated. One class, for example, had one treble period and one double period; others had their science time broken down into smaller units. Some double periods were uninterrupted; others had the morning interval halfway through. In addition each class was taught by a different teacher (see Table 1). Within this broad framework the teaching and the course work were disseminated day by day.

   In accordance with the structure laid out in Curriculum Paper Seven, first year course work in science at Maxwell was divided into eight sections. [. . .] Theoretically, the teachers could follow them in any order they wished. However, as the integrated course was very much a departmental concern, a

Table 1 Distribution of first year science lessons of four classes at Maxwell school

	Monday a.m.	Monday p.m.	Tuesday a.m.	Tuesday p.m.	Wednesday a.m.	Wednesday p.m.	Thursday a.m.	Thursday p.m.	Friday a.m.	Friday p.m.
Mr Spencer's class		2					3			
Mr Darwin's class	2*		1							2
Mr Rutherford's class	2						2	1		
Mr Dalton's class				2*	3*					

* Lesson split by mid-morning break.

number of factors – emanating from departmental decisions – affected its classroom organisation. These decisions did not always map neatly onto the timetable. As a result, a series of 'interference' effects became apparent.

First, the science department's 'notes for the guidance of staff' contained an integrated science 'calendar' that gave suggested dates for the completion of each section, and included the following among the 'duties' of each course planning subcommittee:

(b) allocate the content, period-by-period if possible, but within the overall time allocation suggested in CP7.
(c) write down specific teaching objectives with suitable experiments and workcards to fulfil them. . . .
(d) compare these prepared objectives with the more general ones in CP7. This list may be longer and should be more precise than that in CP7. . . .
(i) prepare a homework schedule for the section on the basis of an average of one written exercise per fortnight. . . .
(j) prepare suitable revision and summary material. . . .
(m) as it is important to keep everyone informed, each section group must duplicate the results of their discussions under headings a, b, c, e, f, g, h, i, j above and these will be supplied to every teacher concerned.

These directives – each concerned with time and content – sought to promote a uniform pacing and patterning of the integrated scheme throughout the department.

Second, as noted above, it was decided that half of the twenty-four first year classes should do section seven of the scheme while the other half did section four. When the work in the sections was completed, the 'twinned' classes were to exchange their equipment. Thus, to facilitate a uniform departmental change-over from section to section, each teacher was asked to pay close attention to the time allocation for each of these sections.

A third influence prompting a lock-step effect was the fact that the tests which punctuated the sections were scheduled to take place across the department as close as possible to a given date. As will become apparent later this was to render the test results comparable. (The phasing of testing was to ensure the teaching time for each group was equivalent.)

A fourth and final influence was that each teacher was required to complete three sections of the integrated science course by a certain date. This was to comply with a school request for 'grades' to enter in school reports.

These departmental decisions were based on the assumption that the teaching time for each class was the same. Although in principle this was true, in practice there were a number of important discrepancies between the classes.

For example, 'twinned' sections which were conducted over the same period of time should have been equivalent in length. But [. . .] the recommended time for section seven was 33 per cent more than that for section four. Not only did this affect the pacing of teaching, it also affected the manner in which the teachers presented their lessons.

Towards the end of my observation – having tried to conceptualise and codify the teaching I had seen – I made the following comments in my field notes: 'Style of teaching depends on the time available. Have noticed that each teacher skates [over the work] when in a hurry. If the bell has gone the teacher is more directive and more curt in calling to order.' Earlier I had noticed further examples of this phenomenon (examples taken from different teachers):

Inclement weather. [Teacher] dictating names of trees (rather than allowing children out onto the school grounds to find out for themselves – as was the original intention). Also wants to get finished and have section 2 tests before half-term.
Emphasis or de-emphasis [of content] is used in certain sections.
Mr Darwin has missed a number of lessons. He is hurrying through this section. Assumed that the kids had done more energy experiments than they had. Only two groups had done more than two (out of a possible five).

Besides being affected in this way by the vagaries of time (and weather), the distribution of teaching time within each week also had its effect on the overall pattern of teaching:

Mr Dalton raised the question of having a split double period the day before a treble [see Table 1]. He said it created problems of (a) continuity, (b) bittiness and (c) organisation. Said he would have to treat the split doubles as two singles.

Mr Dalton raised this issue without any prompting. He was referring to the fact that he had only one true double period. He also pointed out that this double lesson came at the end of his week's teaching with that group (he did not see them again for another six days). Mr Dalton felt that each of the first three lessons on his timetable was too short to launch any new work satisfactorily. (Essentially, he regarded them as too brief for any large scale practical work of the kind that typically began each integrated science worksheet.)

The distribution of lessons within each week also affected Mr Darwin's teaching. He too had three single lessons early in the week together with a double lesson on Friday afternoon. As Mr Darwin was also 'head' of the science department at that time he missed lessons through being absent at various meetings both in and out of school. Thus, when he was able to take his classes he was under pressure to make up time. For example, compared with the other teachers I observed (who took upwards of four lessons) Mr Darwin covered the classification system of animals in a double period on Friday afternoon. At that time the increased amount of work required by Mr Darwin caused the following comment in the field notes: 'This was a fascinating lesson as Mr Darwin *attempted to cover* classification. He began with the variety of life and worked up to subdivisions within the vertebrates [emphasis added].'

Although the departmental lock-step effect resulted from a concern with promoting a common pedagogy, it tended, in fact, to exacerbate the differences between the classes. Certain teachers were always trying to keep up to schedule, whereas the others were (not officially) encouraged to 'mark time' by deviating from the prescribed course or providing additional revision materials. Equally, the constant pressure of successive deadlines precluded the 'slower' teachers from adopting a long term strategy for overcoming their difficulties (for example, by totally re-ordering or re-programming the course work for their classes). The science department (led by the respective heads of physics, biology and chemistry) tried to implement a mode of organisation which, publicly, was intended to provide equal opportunities for all the teachers and children. Privately, however, this machinery appeared to abrogate much that it was intended to promote. The mismatch between the instructional system and the learning milieu produced a number of organisational stresses. Some of these could be accommodated within the classroom but others had an impact that reverberated throughout the department and even the school. For example, as noted earlier, the mismatch between expected and actual completion dates for sections was a recurrent item on the agenda of departmental meetings.

While in Curriculum Paper Seven and at the departmental level the equivalence of teaching time was taken for granted, it was manifestly problematic at the classroom level. Like Curriculum Paper Seven, the departmental notes became a 'Bible' (a term actually used for the former). Both represented some kind of handed down wisdom. Despite being prepared by the members of the science department themselves, the notes were objectified and became a departmental prescription – a local instructional system. Depending on their private commitment, however, the teachers accepted, modified or ignored such wisdom. Indeed, the different and diverging standpoints taken by the teachers were reflected in the behaviour of their pupils. This can be more clearly seen in the way that testing and assessment were handled.

As already indicated, the development of new curricula has been associated with a concern for evaluation and assessment. Curriculum Paper Seven reflects this concern: seven of the eleven recommendations specific to the integrated scheme explicitly make reference to 'tests' or 'testing'.

In its general discussion, Curriculum Paper Seven attempts to devalue traditional assessment procedures. It decries, therefore, the 'learning of many associated facts'; the use of test scores for 'making fine distinctions' or 'ranking'; and the examination of the 'correct use of English' as a primary function for tests (paras 41–2 *passim*). Instead, it attempts to point out new directions:

> In this orientation period the only people for whom test results will have any importance will be the school and the pupil himself. Any examinations set should be such that this syllabus is taught as it ought to be; tests should be constructed to examine practical techniques, design of experiments and ability to solve problem situations either by experiment or by describing the experiment in words. *When* written answers are required they should not be long essays about remembered details; instead, questions of the multiple choice and one-word answer type should be used.

Two paragraphs later Curriculum Paper Seven goes on to recommend:

> That any necessary testing at this stage should be only of the informal classroom type discussed above, and that this should be administered at an appropriate stage in the development of the course used, at the end of a section, say, rather than at some prearranged time such as the end of a term [para. 43].

At this point, however, Curriculum Paper Seven neglects its statement that 'tests should be constructed to examine practical techniques, design of experiments and ability to solve problem situations' and, instead, devotes the remainder of its discussion to considering assessment solely in terms of multiple choice tests. The problematic features associated with testing at Maxwell derive from this one-sided emphasis already present in the instructional system.

Overall, Curriculum Paper Seven uses an 'objectives'-based approach to curriculum design. That is, it attempts to specify the 'outcome(s) of learning' in 'behavioural terms' which are 'observable and measureable'. [. . .] It advocates a similar framework for assessing pupil learning. However, despite the fact that the 'general objectives' of Curriculum Paper Seven cover 'knowledge and understanding' as well as 'practical skills' and 'attitudes', discussion of pupil learning is restricted merely to the first of these. By default, therefore, multiple choice testing of knowledge and understanding became the dominant mode of assessment for the integrated scheme.

At Maxwell the one-sided nature of this emphasis in Curriculum Paper Seven went unnoticed. In fact, as can be seen from the following excerpt from the 'notes for guidance of staff', it became heightened. Interests, skills and attitudes became ancillary aspects of the testing programme:

> What is our interpretation of continuous assessment?
> Our syllabus contains 15 sections of varying length covering 300 periods in the first two years. During this time we shall conduct between 15 and 20 separate small attainment tests of the pupil's factual knowledge and reasoning based on the content of, and administered at the conclusion of, each of these 15 sections.
> At half-yearly intervals, or thereabouts, we should also like to give revision tests, covering all of the work up to that point of time.

We shall also try to assess the pupils' awareness, interest, skills and progress, together with their attitudes to science and to their work in general.

Within this definition of assessment, the use of multiple choice tests at Maxwell did not reflect the prescriptions of Curriculum Paper Seven. The tests deployed were 'norm-referenced' and 'discriminatory' rather than 'criterion-referenced' and 'diagnostic' as intended. That is, they were used to discriminate among children on the basis of the total distribution of marks rather than to provide an indication of whether each child had achieved a certain standard.[8]

A number of other critical comments could be made about the tests and their use. In the context of this account, however, such criticisms are as irrelevant as they are true. Here, these data are being presented not to suggest that the teachers are (unknowingly) 'wrong', but to make a different point: that the assessment procedures envisaged by Curriculum Paper Seven were severely modified at Maxwell when translated into practice.

The fact that these procedures involved a range of complex assumptions (for example, a knowledge of the difference between criterion-referenced and norm-referenced testing) which were not fully apprehended by the teachers at Maxwell (nor indeed fully spelled out by Curriculum Paper Seven) meant that their implementation was problematic.

Needless to say, a range of unintended effects flowed from the teachers' misinterpretation. As already discussed, the setting of tests simultaneously (to ensure comparability of classes) prompted a lock-step effect in the department. In addition, such an approach promoted invalid discriminations between classes (and teachers) and produced what one teacher called a 'local hit-parade of results'. In addition, since no account was taken of the poor reliability of such tests or of statistical artefacts (for example, regression effects), they were used to make (statistically) invalid discriminations among individuals. None of these effects was implied by Curriculum Paper Seven.

Finally, some of the pupils picked up the idea that the tests performed a discriminatory (rather than a diagnostic) function. For example, in completing the sentence: 'The main reason we have science tests is that . . .' different children wrote

'the teacher has to give us a mark for our report cards.'
'he has to find a mark for our report cards.'

Certain of this group of children also read a selective function into the assessment procedures, for example:

'So the teacher can put you in groups.'
'Maybe we will go to a higher or lower class and it depends on the mark we get.'

It could be argued, of course, that ideas such as these were picked up outside the science department. However, the fact that there is a real difference between the classes reduces the impact of this objection. Unlike the others, Mr Spencer's class did not see the tests as providing their teacher with discriminatory information.

When observation and interview data are taken into account an explanation can be offered for the differential distribution of the responses. Mr Spencer quite clearly played down the examinations – not only among his colleagues but also in front of the children. My field notes record the following: 'Discussed objective tests with Mr Spencer. He was "against" them. [Said he preferred] written work, essays.' One day, as he gave out an exam, he commented to the children: 'If the questions look a bit crazy to you they look a bit crazy to a few other people.' Mr Spencer reiterated his views during a formal tape-recorded interview. He noted a conflict between the aims of testing at Maxwell:

> The purpose of the tests has never been established. There have been discussions in science departmental meetings about whether they are designed to see whether pupils have attained the objectives. That's one aim that has been put forward for them. But in distinction to that there's been this other aim that they're to select our pupils so that we can give an assessment mark. . . . These are two confusing aims, but they've never been resolved. When I personally write an exam or even when I give it I, er, well, I don't know what I'm doing. . . .

IV

In this paper I have based my discussion on case study material drawn from two schools. The early part supports the argument that the introduction of integrated studies is not merely equivalent to introducing a new syllabus but implies a radical change of emphasis in the organisational context and thinking of secondary education. As a result simple questions of content cannot be separated from complex questions of grouping children by ability, from questions of 'responsibility' and authority, or even from questions of school democracy. That the new forms of organisation may be in opposition to the old adds further potency to these questions.

The current co-existence of integrated and collective curricula in secondary education points, I suggest, to a fundamental dilemma if not a crisis for the comprehensive school. Until recently the role of the secondary school was clearly defined. Each in their own way – junior secondary, secondary modern and senior secondary schools – performed a purely academic (or vocational) function. In this and other ways they exemplified a 'collection' paradigm. Today, however, comprehensive schools are expected to retain this academic/intellectual function while at the same time paying tribute to new patterns of organisation, new boundaries of knowledge and new conceptions of education. In short, they are expected to run collection and·integrated ideas side by side. Thus, teachers are required to be 'inter-disciplinary' *and* subject specialists; to be concerned with teaching sixth-formers *and* 'slow learners'; and to be responsible for both the academic *and* social welfare of their pupils. Some of the tensions that these expectancies promote have been described in this paper.

The second part of the account serves to illustrate certain other, more classroom-based phenomena. First, it shows that an initial mismatch between an instructional system and the learning milieu can create a number of boundary or interference effects. These become particularly noticeable where the two systems fail to intersect or overlap uniformly. In an extreme case such a mismatching can begin as a minor disturbance but, through time, build up into a major (that is, increasingly acknowledged) issue. An instance of this phenomenon at Maxwell arose from the minor discrepancies between the departmental schedule and the individual teacher's time allocation. Eventually, certain teachers were unable to keep up with the others.

Second, it reminds us how the teacher functions: not as a mere agent or curriculum technician, but as an active yet selective amplifier and transmitter of knowledge. The teacher is a critical mediator between the pupil on the one hand, and the institutional context and the instructional system on the other. As a result all are modified extensively in the classroom setting. At Maxwell the children in each class reported their views on testing differently – but in a way that could be linked to the views of their respective teachers. Thus, in his mediating role, the teacher is not merely a 'stage manager' in the classroom, but also a director, designer and, very often, a principal actor.

Third, it shows how the implementation of Curriculum Paper Seven was accompanied by a series of transformations which, ultimately, resulted in its serving ends directly opposed to those intended (norm-referenced rather than criterion-referenced testing). This example is an extreme case. But it suggests confirmation of the assertion made earlier that when an instructional system is adopted it undergoes modifications that are rarely trivial.

Finally, it illustrates that while the teacher's influence is potent, his scope for redefining an instructional system is not limitless. He too is bounded by a series of intervening institutional constraints. At Maxwell, for example, Mr Spencer was required to comply with the grading system that operated across the science department. While his efforts to mitigate its influence were [. . .] moderately successful, he was still unable to distance himself entirely from the departmental norm, and it had a recognisable impact on both himself and his pupils. Eventually, Mr Spencer's capacity to sustain his own classroom ethos in the face of conflicting definitions was exceeded. His ideological position (not only on testing and homework, but also on curriculum integration) became more and more isolated from that of the other members of the science staff. Towards the end of the year he applied for a teaching post elsewhere. In September he took up a post of responsibility in another school where he would be teaching and organising integrated science in a manner which reflected his own interests more clearly.

Notes

1 This account is part of a much larger work. For the complete study, see Hamilton, D. (1973) *At the Classroom Level: Studies in the learning milieu*, unpublished Ph.D. thesis, University of Edinburgh.

2 This description of an 'instructional system' and the subsequent account of the

'learning milieu' are taken, with minor alterations, from Parlett, M. R. and Hamilton, D. (1972) 'Evaluations as Illumination; a new approach to the study of innovations programs'. Occasional paper No. 9. Centre for research in the Educational Sciences, University of Edinburgh.

3 See pp. 157–76 in this Reader.

4 Such distinctions begin while the students are still in training. In at least one Scottish College of Education, honours and ordinary graduates – even though they may end up in the same school with equivalent timetables – are trained separately.

5 The expression 'general science' seems to derive from the idea of 'science for all': the title of a Science Masters' Association pamphlet prepared at the request of the government committee to 'Inquire into the Position of Natural Science in the Education System of Great Britain' (1916, also known as the Thomson Committee). When the committee reported in 1918 it advocated a general course of science for all pupils up to the age of sixteen. Subsequently, 'general science' became substituted for 'science for all' and developed as a scheme for elementary rather than grammar schools.

6 All the organisational features at Simpson and Maxwell have been presented in the past tense. This is deliberate and is an attempt to emphasise the reality of educational change. Since the data collection was completed, important changes have taken and are taking place at both schools.

7 See R. Walker and C. Adelman, *Towards a Sociography of Classrooms*, Research Monograph, Centre for Science Education, Chelsea College, University of London, 1972.

8 Each child was awarded a grade (A–E) on the basis of the distribution of the marks across the department: 10 per cent received grade A, 20 per cent grade B, 40 per cent grade C, 20 per cent grade D and 10 per cent grade E. Had the grades been criterion-referenced it would have been possible for a large number of the children, if not all, to get grade A (instead of only 10 per cent). In the criterion-referenced case 'success' is based on achieving a certain standard, not on the overall distribution of the marks.

3.6 The Evolution of the Continuous Staff Conference

Elizabeth Richardson

[The importance of the social system of the school is emphasised in this extract, from a management study by Elizabeth Richardson, which is concerned with the struggle of the staff to define their roles and relationships. This struggle is treated within the following perspectives: staff relationships and institutional growth; professional advancement; staff experience; consultation and decision-making; the discussions among the staff.]

Staff relationships and institutional growth

It has been my thesis [. . .] that the process of learning about the changing demands of the schools, if it is to be effective in the long run, must be strengthened by the examination of relationships within the staff group itself. We cannot learn about the effects of streaming, setting and banding without examining our own fears that we are somehow grading and assessing one another as 'A', 'B' or 'C' teachers. We cannot learn about curriculum development and the organisation of knowledge without examining the double pull within ourselves from the attraction of a subject area to which we have become committed and from the claims upon us of children or students who may not share our commitment to that subject. We cannot learn to understand the problems of deviant, delinquent or emotionally disturbed children without recognising the elements of deviance, delinquency and emotional disturbance in ourselves as staff members.

[. . .] The effort to identify what is inadequate in the system and to replace it or augment it with something new inevitably brings conflict in its wake. For innovation – be it undertaken by an individual teacher working in isolation, by a group of teachers working together in one school or in a number of different schools, or by the whole staff group in a particular school – is likely to result in some sacrifice of personal security, since to turn from known policies to untried ones demands an act of faith and offers no guarantee of successful outcomes. Consultation about what shall be changed and what shall be preserved unchanged is thus inseparable from the continuous process of re-education within the staff group. And it is in this sense that I am using the concept of 'in-service education' in this final section, not as a substitute for the evolving pattern of college and university education of teachers but as an indispensable part of that pattern.

Source: RICHARDSON, E. (1973) *The Teacher, the School and the Task of Management*. London: Heinemann Educational Books, pp. 312–33.

Every staff group has within it the ingredients of a kind of continuous educational workshop. For it is in the staff group itself that meeting points can be found between student and practitioner, between the young and the middle-aged, between the inexperienced and the experienced, between the enthusiasts and the cynics, the optimists and the pessimists, between the so-called 'pupil-orientated' and the so-called 'subject-orientated' teachers. Some of the paired, yet mutually contradictory, terms I have just used may appear to imply an acceptance of the very dichotomies I have been trying to reconcile in this book [Richardson, 1973]. Are these sub-groups in the staff room imaginary? Or do they really exist? Is the polarisation to which I am drawing attention inevitable? Or can teachers, by recognising some of the unconscious mechanisms that create them, take steps to remove them, so that individual members of a staff group can escape from the kind of trap they are put into by their colleagues? Does it lie within the professional competence of teachers to reduce the element of polarisation in their own working groups? [. . .]

Examination of experience in the staff group

It must by now be apparent that the Nailsea staff, in working with me in the way they did, had to examine the effects of polarisation and the real meaning of ambivalence at many different levels in the system. With the growing sanction to bring out in staff meetings feelings that might formerly have been suppressed, the real educational problems with which people were having to grapple came more clearly into focus. To their own surprise, perhaps, the increasing freedom to acknowledge weakness, uncertainty and bewilderment created a climate in which leadership skills could grow and flourish. For in these situations it became more and more clear that leadership was not being exercised only by the designated leader or chairman in a particular meeting.

Many members of the staff from the most junior to the most senior offered leadership to their colleagues by opening up for investigation important areas of feeling and thought, often at considerable risk to themselves as persons. Nor was it only I, in my role as consultant, who made interpretative comments during staff meetings. The members of the standing committee in particular became increasingly able to do this, not because they arrived at staff meetings armed with prepared comments but because the work they did together during their weekly meetings made them more sensitive to the feelings of their colleagues and to the ideas with which those colleagues were struggling in the larger meetings. It seemed that as the most senior people learned to listen more attentively, they found themselves both intellectually and emotionally in touch with the deeper undercurrents in the staff discussions. Certain people – both in this top-management group and in the rest of the staff group – became less competitive in discussion than they had formerly been; and as the style and content of their contributions changed, quieter and more reserved colleagues found voices where before they had remained silent.

When I look back over the events of the spring and summer of 1970 certain meetings stand out as turning points in the development of a kind of joint capability within the staff group of relating questions about the inner feelings of persons in the sentient system to questions about the outward behaviour, in professional roles, of those same persons as colleagues in the task system. Three meetings in particular during that year appear to me in retrospect to have been crucial: the standing committee meeting of 30 January, the senior staff meeting of 19 May and the full staff meeting of 18 June. Each of these marked a new stage in the progress towards making available for public discussion matters which would, at an earlier stage in the school's history, have been considered private and therefore accessible only to personal friends.

Scrutinising more closely the three occasions I have selected, I find that they show a gradual enlarging of the areas of human concern that can be encompassed in this way. The first of those three meetings, within the small-group boundary of the standing committee, marked a turning point, or sudden development, of a new kind of awareness in the area of interpersonal relationships; the second, within the wider boundary of the fairly large senior staff meeting, marked a turning point in the examination of inter-group relationships; and the third, in the very large group to which all the teaching staff belonged, and at least two of the non-teaching staff as well, marked a new stage of understanding in the area of the relationships between the institution and the outside world.

Significantly, I believe, each of these meetings took place soon after a full staff meeting devoted to open discussion of some aspect of my own gradual move towards the writing and publication of this report. The earliest of these was the meeting of January 1970, at which my internal report to the staff, distributed just before Christmas, was discussed. During that meeting the problem of differentiating between the role and the person was somewhat dramatically highlighted, when I was suddenly taken to task by a part-time teacher in the modern-languages department for allowing my feelings to show in meetings. She told me, with a directness and severity that I found unnerving, yet at the same time strangely reassuring, that she did not think I behaved as a consultant should, that I did not maintain the calmness she felt ought to be part of consultant behaviour, and that in getting 'worked up' (as indeed I had done earlier in that meeting when I felt that people were trying to evade the real task we were there to tackle) I stirred up too much emotional heat in the group. Following this confrontation, the staff began to recognise that I, like any of them, had to come to terms with the person I was, and use, as best I could, my own feelings about a situation as indicators that might help me to understand it better. Thus their struggle to relate themselves to me in my role as consultant could not be separated from the problem of relating themselves to me as a person, any more than their pupils could entirely separate them as the persons *they* were from them in their roles as teachers in that school. Both the staff and I had to acknowledge that another consultant, even if he or she had striven to behave consistently within the same role as I had tried to take, would have brought different personal characteristics to bear on the task. This problem of distinguishing between the role and the person without denying the effect of each upon the other was to recur in many ways during the coming months, when roles in the staff group and the characteristics of different persons in the same roles came under scrutiny.

It was less than a week after that meeting that the first significant turning point was reached in the standing committee of 30 January, when the members of the committee found themselves recognising, with a considerable sense of shock, that their deliberations with colleagues over curricular matters were making unexpected demands on their capacity to work with the strong feelings exposed by those colleagues, as persons under stress in maintaining their roles in a difficult task. This recognition produced a sudden and dramatic fusion of the thinking and feeling sides of the task of consultation, which must, later, have influenced the way in which the members of the committee were able to help their colleagues to examine more critically the extent to which the staff structure was still forcing a separation between the handling of children as persons and the recognition of those children as learners.

In the senior staff meeting of 19 May there was a second turning point when the place of the house system in the total organisation was discussed. The actual question before the senior staff at that time was not whether houses should continue to be part of the middle-school structure but only whether they should continue to be linked with the lower-school tutorial system. The surprise was that it became possible, even in that early meeting, for questions to be raised about the justification of the house system itself, and that although the house heads were anxious to defend the system, they did not appear to be as threatened in their own roles as might have been expected. This preliminary exploration of some of the issues paved the way for the subsequent discussions, first between the lower-school and middle-school tutorial staff groups later in that same term, then, many months later, between the standing committee and the house heads, and later still in the summer of 1971 in the senior staff group in the context of future reorganisation and of the allocation of posts of special responsibility. These developments made it clear that already by the spring of 1970 the senior staff meeting had begun to provide a framework within which those in middle-management roles, whether technically in the curricular system or technically in the pastoral system, could share with each other and with the top-management group the responsibility for projecting their thinking forward into the future, recognising that their own roles, if they remained in the school, might change radically as a result of this forward thinking, since it concerned broad questions of policy as distinct from immediate questions of implementation.

In the full staff meeting of 18 June 1970, which I now identify as a third turning point, the problem of determining how much of what had hitherto been private could increasingly be made public was explored in another context – that of assessment. In this context 'public' began to mean something more than in the earlier discussion about the house system and the still earlier encounters between the standing committee and certain individual colleagues: for it now involved the boundary between staff and parents, where before it had involved only the internal boundaries between staff groups and between individual staff members.

This was the meeting on assessment, in which problems of trust and distrust between parents and teachers were opened up, along with acknowledgements that the difficulty about arriving at acceptable assessment scales that could be used generally throughout the school and by all staff was closely linked with the wish to preserve the good aspects of a teacher's relationship with pupils by claiming for it a kind of privacy that might be at variance with the teacher's responsibility towards the parents of those pupils.

This progression corresponded with the gradual shift in the staff group's thinking about my written accounts, real or projected, of the Nailsea experience. In the January meeting, preceding the standing committee's first painful awakening to the stresses of top-management responsibility, the shift was towards an examination of their reactions to my first written communication to themselves as a staff group. In the May meeting, preceding the senior-staff group's discussion about role relationships between the lower and middle-school tutorial staff groups, the shift was towards consideration of the possibility that I might publish two articles about the implications for other schools of this school's experience. And in the June meetings, preceding the full staff meeting on the subject of assessment and the communication of information to parents, the shift was towards consideration of the more alarming, because less controllable, presentation of a course of six lectures to Bristol students, each lecture to be followed by a forty-five-minute discussion period.

In fact, in that year, I neither wrote the articles nor gave the lectures. But the opening up of discussion with the staff group about the two possibilities released them, it appeared, to open up new areas of difficult, even painful discussion among themselves. For it was around this time that the house heads were publicly challenged about the nature of their authority in the middle school, that Mike Burnham was publicly challenged about the nature of his authority in the upper school and that Denys John was publicly challenged about the nature of his authority in the school as a whole. And it was during this period that Denys John began to change the style of documentation for staff meetings and to develop a programme of phased discussions that were to lead up to known dates on which decisions about major policy matters would have to be made.

Consultation, documentation and decision-making

Readers of this book [Richardson 1973] may from time to time have wondered whether the reorganisation of the management structure at Nailsea was in the direction of a strengthening or of a weakening of the 'hierarchy'. Now the word 'hierarchy' is very often used as though it were a descriptive term applicable only to those at the 'top'. But in fact the word means a 'graded organisation'. We can therefore speak of a hierarchy of responsibilities that includes every single person in a school staff group; and we must recognise that every sub-section itself implies some hierarchical ordering of responsibilities. Even within the standing committee there were three identifiable orders of responsibility: namely the first-order responsibility of the headmaster, who was ultimately answerable to the outside world for what happened in his institution, the second-order responsibility of the deputy head and the senior mistress, who – notwithstanding all the uncertainties about their respective roles – could and did exercise authority on behalf of the headmaster over the school as a whole, and the third-order responsibilities of the heads of the three main sections of the school, who between them had authority over the lower, middle and upper schools but not over the whole school.

Part of the problem of growth for a large institution is that people are reluctant to acknowledge that such hierarchical divisions are present, or if not present, are needed, in every important sub-section as well as in the management system as a whole. The difficulty seems to arise from the error of perceiving each identifiable sub-group as separate from the rest rather than as interrelated with the rest. The standing committee's separateness from the rest, as a bounded group with the responsibilities of top management, had to be reconciled with its inclusion in the larger 'senior-staff group' that also included within *its* boundary the two dozen or so colleagues in middle management roles. And the senior-staff group in its turn had to be recognised as both a separate consultative body within the organisation and as an integral part of the full staff group (see Figure 1).

The strength of the resistance to the notion of 'hierarchy' as a necessary aspect of efficient organisation was illustrated by Denys John himself on the occasion [. . .] when, in introducing Dawn Castell into the already established Fourth Year Curriculum study group in the autumn of 1968, he assured her that there was 'no hierarchy' in that group. It was illustrated in my hearing again about a year later, in a meeting of the house heads with Clive Vanloo, when consideration was being given to a suggestion that had come from one of the house tutors, that they might learn more about what went on in one another's house groups if they instituted a practice of inter-house visiting, perhaps by rotating tutors between the houses in some assemblies or on some lunch occasions. Peter Chapman remarked that it was difficult to find times when tutors could talk about educational matters, adding rather sadly and also with a touch of exasperation that on those occasions when 'the hierarchy' came to have lunch in one of the houses the conversation, inevitably perhaps, was just social. Later in this discussion Clive Vanloo was assured categorically by Graeme Osborn that he was 'not in the hierarchy'. It was clear from the discussion that all four house heads were thinking of the hierarchy as including Denys John, Robin Thomas and Joan Bradbury, as probably not including the three section heads, and as almost certainly excluding themselves. What was not clear was whether Graeme Osborn, in telling Clive Vanloo that he was not part of it, was offering him a friendly gesture implying solidarity between him and the house heads or a

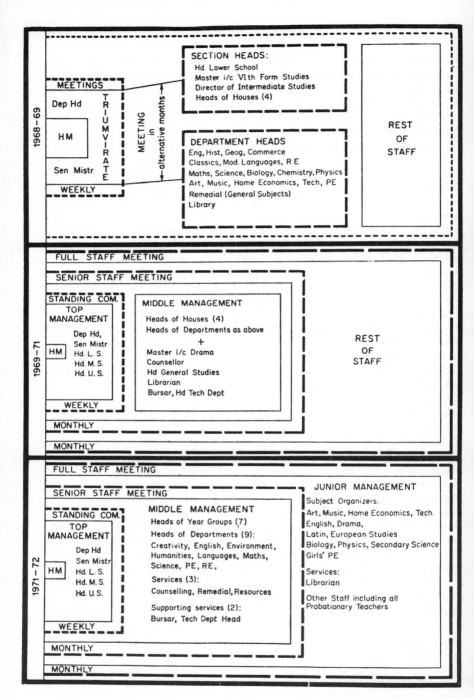

Figure 1 Successive modifications of management and consultative structure

hurtful rebuff implying their rejection of him in his leadership role.

Consultation, participation, discussions about educational matters: all these imply situations in which some people talk and others listen, in which some ask questions and others attempt to answer them (or are expected to do so), in which some throw out challenges or appeals and others respond or fail to respond, in which some offer leads and others follow or turn the other way. Many people assume that ideas are unlikely to be generated during a large meeting unless someone writes a paper as a focus for discussion. Others believe that the important writing is done after a meeting when the ideas that have been generated are recorded, analysed and interpreted. In the earlier months of this three-year study the staff, more often than not, were provided either with a speculative or theoretical paper written by Denys John or with tabulated proposals, very often concerned with curriculum organisation or time-tabling, drawn up sometimes by himself and sometimes by Robin Thomas and Joan Bradbury. In the later months, the staff were more likely to find themselves offered the more challenging task of responding to a broad theme, such as 'the tutorial function' or 'the role of the school counsellor' or 'lower-school organisation' or 'assessment and relations with parents'. The effect of introducing this more open kind of discussion was that the old style of pre-meeting manifesto based on the head's ideas gave way to a new style of post-meeting summary, based on the verbal contributions of the staff during their meetings.

The staff experienced this change on one occasion quite suddenly and, perhaps for many of them, unexpectedly. In March 1970, following the January and February meetings on curriculum development when twenty-eight people had talked with the standing committee, Denys John issued to all his colleagues a document that must have been perceived by them to be radically different in tone and content from those he had circulated from time to time in the past. This document took the form of a collated summary of the suggestions yielded by those meetings, each item linked with the initials of the staff member who had been responsible for it, some being accompanied by the head's own comment or interpretation. To the seventeen separate items drawn from the meetings of the standing committee, he added two that were based on discussions he had had, outside the standing-committee meetings, with Tina Bateman and Margaret Fisher, who had put before him some of the problems of leadership and teamwork that they predicted might arise for them in the complex overlapping areas of humanities, religious education and counselling. The inclusion of these two additional items must have implied, both to the two persons concerned and to the rest of the staff that although Denys John as headmaster could not (and would not wish to) refuse to be accessible to individual staff members who were anxious about any particular aspect of a developing situation, he could not, as chairman of the standing committee, go into collusion with attempts to create 'private' conversations about staff-wide problems unless it was understood that the content of such conversations must be part of the available data for the public discussions in the senior-staff and full-staff meetings during the period of consultation.

The sequel to this new way of following up staff discussions was the evolution of a new way of preparing for them. In the summer term of that year the staff were given a framework in which the phases of consultation were clearly related, first to specific problems that need to be examined by all staff, secondly to the differentiation between the standing-committee, senior-staff and full-staff meetings, and thirdly to the dates upon which any particular decisions would have to be made. The phasing of discussion on three different problems – namely, 'lower-school organisation', 'third-year curriculum and time allocation', and 'assessments and objectives' – over the fifteen weeks of that summer term is shown in Figure 2, which has been reproduced from Denys John's own circular distributed to all staff at the beginning of the term. The special full staff meeting of 1 June, arranged unexpectedly to discuss my proposed lecture course, has been added to the diagram, but no other alteration has been made.

Did this schedule of phased discussions turn out to be an answer to all the problems of consultation? By no means. The special meeting to discuss the third-year curriculum, which took place on 7 July, affords an illustration of the inevitable gap between intention and actuality – a meeting that I described in the previous chapter as being focused on a curious 'exchange of boasts and confessions' about the use of time. In fact the standing committee, despite the forecast that decisions would be reached by 25 June, were still trying to find some way of providing an additional five hours for the options that were to start in Year III instead of in Year IV as they had formerly done; and when Denys John postponed his decisions he posted a notice in the staff common-room to make this known. A schedule, clearly, is not infallible. It is at best a forecast of the kind of sequence that may prove helpful in controlling the boundaries of debate and in regulating the relations between the sentient and task systems so that the need to preserve known advantages or comfortable situations does not militate against necessary change. The schedule does not protect the headmaster, or any of his colleagues, from the unpredictable difficulties that may interfere with the process. Nor should it insulate the staff group against unexpected creative ideas that may necessitate a modification of the schedule.

Sub-group discussion and plenary discussion in general staff meetings

One of the constraints upon creativeness in the general staff discussions was the sheer size of the full staff group, which, by 1970, numbered seventy-five, including the ten part-time staff who were, of course, entitled to attend staff meetings. The discussions about the possible substitution of sectional staff meetings, based on the tutorial teams in the lower, middle and upper schools, had exposed the fears of being over-identified with one particular age group of pupils in the school, and this particular solution to the problem of size was not reconsidered. But the need to find ways of tackling the difficulties of exchanging useful information and ideas in the large group was now being openly acknowledged. Sometimes this acknowledgement would take the form of accusatory remarks – surprise that colleagues within the same staff group should be unable to enter into a face-to-face relationship or deal openly with one another, impatience with adults who, although accustomed to exercising authority in the classroom, could be so inarticulate, or even totally silent, with their peers, indignant denial that there could be anything to fear in a group of people whom one knew and worked with every day. At other times there would be a far greater acceptance of the reality that even a group of known colleagues could be intimidating, that experience of communicating effectively with children in a classroom was no guarantee of ability to communicate, in a meeting, with fellow teachers in the staff room. Sometimes it appeared that it was some of those in middle-management roles who wished to deny the difficulties and that the most senior and the most junior members of the staff group could most easily find a meeting ground in a willingness to tolerate their own insecurity and inadequacy in face of the difficulties.

There was one staff meeting in particular, during the spring of 1970, that revealed a great deal of anxiety about risking experience and opinion in the public arena of a full staff meeting. This was a meeting devoted to the subject of tutorial work – an area of teaching that was clearly felt to be so personal that any exploration of real experiences would make tutors feel exposed and vulnerable. The anxiety showed itself in the first few minutes when someone broke the silence by announcing that John Phillips, although unable to attend the meeting, had left a list of the tutorial functions that he considered to be the most important. This list – read out to the meeting – recalled vividly to me the written manifesto which Denys John had offered to the section heads about ten months earlier, and which had aroused from them a veiled but unmistakable hostility. The use of John Phillips as a kind of absent leader also recalled another senior staff meeting of that period – the department heads' meeting at which the absent Lewis Smith had been used, and indeed had offered himself, in much the same way, when 'the role of a department head' had been the theme for discussion. It seemed that, faced with the need to scrutinise their own roles in public, the staff were very liable to resist any kind of laying down of a law by the head: yet, when he refrained from laying down any law, they looked round for a substitute who might offer to do so in his place. The particular difficulty of probing into the area of tutorial work turned out to be linked with fears lest some colleagues, in their other roles as subject teachers, particularly if they were involved with English or religious education, might be encroaching on the work of tutors. There was also anxiety about the developing programme of Human Relationships work, which, because it required the splitting of tutor groups, was proving divisive, giving rise to assumptions that most members of staff were 'good' at one aspect of tutorial work and 'bad' at another, and that the Human Relationships tutor was perhaps being perceived, by children and by colleagues, and possibly also by parents, as compensating for a tutor's weakness in handling

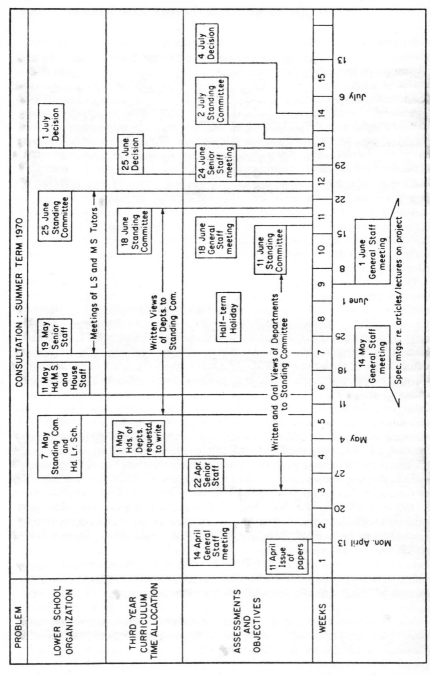

Figure 2 Schedule of staff meetings in relation to consultation and decision making

problems of human relationships as they might be arising in his own tutor group.

Eventually, out of the exploration of these problems, a creative idea emerged. In the autumn of 1970, one of the new members of staff suggested to Denys John a new form of staff meeting [. . .] which came into effect almost immediately. The proposal was that the first hour or so of the full staff meeting should be spent in small groups which would contain members from a cross-section of departments and sections and from all levels of responsibility, and that the groups should then come together into a plenary session for the last half-hour of the meeting and work as a total group. This suggestion provided a much more acceptable alternative to the earlier notion of having separate meetings of the lower, middle and upper-school tutorial staff groups, since it did not threaten people with loss of the already tenuous sense of belonging to the whole school and therefore to a corporate body of staff.

The staff now had the opportunity, in its monthly general meetings, to explore important problems of policy, as well as immediate problems of implementing agreed policies, in groups that were small enough to offer support so that people felt more prepared to risk exposing their ideas and sharing bad experiences as well as good ones. But the new-style staff meeting went further than this. It also provided a work pattern in which the problems of bringing back, not the content necessarily, but the resultant learning into the large and increasingly complex staff group, including both its full-time and its part-time members, could really be examined. For people could now test out their ideas both in the intimate setting of a small but diverse group of colleagues and in the public arena of the full staff group, when 'colleagues' had so often appeared to be 'strangers'. It also raised a number of questions about role definition, group cohesion and commitment to a new set of relationships, questions that could be used as pointers to comparable problems arising every day in the management of learning situations in classroom, laboratory, workshop and gymnasium.

Unexpectedly the standing committee found themselves having to examine again in this new context how the role of the head differed from and related to the roles of his five most senior colleagues, for it was these five who had to take on the responsibility for accepting in the small groups a role that was consistent with their task as members of top management. And immediately new questions presented themselves. Were the members of the committee to be 'leaders', 'consultants' or just 'ordinary members' of the groups? Should there be six groups or only five? If the headmaster did not actually take a group himself, should he move around from one to another to 'get a feel of the discussions'? And if he did this what effect would his presence or absence have on the groups and on the members of the standing committee as they tried to work out their own roles in relation to the task of the groups? Should each standing-committee member remain with the same group throughout the school year, or should they rotate? Ought the groups themselves to be reshuffled at intervals or perhaps for every meeting in the interest of variety of experience, or ought they to persist with the same membership so that some identity could be established that would assist their work at the task?

Surprisingly, yet in another way predictably, there was pressure from the staff for movement, variety and impermanence. This pressure was surprising because so many had experienced the difficulties of communicating effectively with colleagues who were not well known to them; it was, nevertheless, predictable in face of the evidence (shared by many members) that commitment to task-centred working groups over a long period could prove exacting and even painful. The standing committee – again surprisingly at one level and predictably at another – found themselves very ready at first to collude with those who wanted to keep the groups fluid, thus both depriving themselves of the opportunity to work through authority problems with comparable cross-sections of the staff group, and protecting themselves from the need to test their own leadership skills beyond the known limits of their competence.

Even Denys John with the experience of the Human Relationships staff study group behind him and knowing that his role as headmaster would inevitably affect his leadership of any one small group in the situation, nevertheless chose to take one of the groups himself in the first meeting. In the later meetings, when he relinquished this role, he decided to go in and out of his colleagues' groups rather than accept the much greater strain of staying out of them during the first hour. Yet had he stayed out – as on an earlier occasion he had been able to stay out of the special meeting of the lower and middle-school tutorial teams chaired by Robin Thomas – he would probably have freed himself to work more creatively in the follow-up session with the whole staff group, and would have freed the other five members of the top-management group to carry a greater authority in working with the sub-groups during the preceding hour.

Again, my own experience in this situation, as in so many others, illuminated for me the nature of a headmaster's dilemma in making these decisions. For when I attended one of these new-style staff meetings I too found myself uncertain what I ought to do during that first hour when the staff were dispersed and working in five different places with five different leaders or co-ordinators. Like Denys John, I decided to 'visit' groups. In the time available I visited three, the third for only the last few minutes of its time. I scarcely knew whether it was joining a group or leaving it that made me more anxious, since the first felt like intruding on privacy and the second felt like expressing rejection or boredom, however much I really wanted to remain.

Examining the situation in the standing committee the following week, we learned that the arrival of either Denys John or myself in a group produced an immediately inhibiting effect upon the members, as sensed by the five standing-committee members who had been leading or interpreting the discussions. Yet neither of us had been aware of any particular change in the atmosphere as we moved in on a group and sat down to listen to its deliberations. Nor had we any means of knowing, except at second hand through the reports of the standing-committee members, how the quality or content of the discussion before the entrance of either of us had differed from what happened while either of us was present. As for any discomfiture, nervousness or sense of being intruders that he or I might have felt, this had evidently passed unnoticed by the members, just as their sudden inhibitedness had passed unnoticed by us. There was a further problem for Denys John in deciding whether or not he would continue the 'visiting' or 'sitting-in' pattern in later meetings. For a decision to visit groups could be interpreted either as 'the head taking an interest' or 'the head keeping tabs on us', even perhaps as 'the head interfering'; conversely, however, a decision *not* to visit them could be interpreted either as indifference or as trust.

Having decided to delegate responsibility for the small-group sessions entirely to the other five members of the standing committee, Denys John then had to face the assembled staff group without any knowledge of what had been going on during the previous hour and a quarter. The natural defence against the discomfort of this situation, for himself and for the large staff group, was to build in a reporting session, which in fact he did, at the urgent written request of one of the younger men on the staff. But the reporting back – undertaken, appropriately, by the standing committee members – quickly reduced the time available for discussion from forty-five minutes to about twenty-five, since it was difficult in practice for anyone to give a coherent account in less than four minutes of a discussion that had only just ended, leaving no time for any considered preparation of a more condensed report. Thus the standing-committee found themselves forced into a sort of collective monologue, which was time-consuming and repetitive, however competent the individual reporting might be, and which forced the rest of the staff into the roles of audience, with consequent frustration on all sides.

The removal of this defence in the meeting of November 1971, a meeting devoted to problems of staff-pupil relationships within the school, left the staff feeling exposed and unprotected. The standing-committee was taken to task for having 'abdicated' from the responsibility of reporting back to the meeting; some argument followed about the value or futility of such reporting; and again, as on the two earlier occasions to which I referred above, there was resort to an absent leader, this time Pip Ridgwell, who had been unable to attend the meeting but had furnished his group with a written statement giving his views about the present troubles the school was experiencing. Nevertheless, it required only a quiet but provocative question from Denys John – 'Are we evading the real topic?' and an acknowledgement from Pat Richardson (who had initiated the protest at the beginning) that they had now wasted ten minutes, for the real discussion to get under way. As it turned out, the removal of the ritual reporting did, after the initial resistance, free the staff to open up some of their real anxieties about how they were operating as the adults responsible for the work and general climate of feeling in the school. Repeatedly it seemed that these anxieties were focused on the fear that they could not match their concern for the children and young people in their care with the skill needed to stimulate them to effective work and learning.

It was hard for Denys John to close a meeting in which so much frustration and inadequacy was being expressed. And in fact there was a burst of discussion at the very end of the time available which made it very difficult for him to close it, as he suddenly found himself under attack for interpreting the questions about 'sanctions' as references to the need to punish children. Yet to close it on all this uncertainty – knowing that it would be another month before he could hold another full staff meeting – must itself have been an indication to the staff of his own belief that the staff had strengths as well as the weaknesses they had been acknowledging, and that there was leadership available to them in the intervening days and weeks if they could find ways of mobilising it, not only in the section heads and in the year-group and department heads, but within teaching and tutorial teams. For the evidence that even some of the youngest members of staff could offer such leadership had been there in the meeting for all to see.

The oldness and newness of a school

Sometimes one hears in one context the formulation of an idea that quite suddenly illuminates another. A few months ago, by chance, listening to a radio talk by Hans Keller about the music of Beethoven, I heard him say: 'We cannot understand the newness of Beethoven's mind except in the context of the oldness of his creative memory'. A week or so later, in another radio talk, he illustrated over and over again his belief that at the very moment when Beethoven was exhibiting one characteristic he was also exhibiting the opposite. If we transfer these insights to the field of education, we find they are just as applicable in helping us to understand schools as in helping us to listen more sensitively to music. For a school, too, must reconcile creatively its newness and its oldness, and its staff have to learn to recognise in one another not only the obvious and familiar behaviour that everyone has learned to expect but also the less obvious, often unseen or unheard dual of that behaviour. We have to try to acknowledge the latent radicalism of the 'conservative' teacher and the latent conservatism of the 'radical' teacher, and so avoid the mutual stereotyping that is so destructive of personality and therefore so impoverishing to the work of the institution.

The tension between nostalgia for the past and hope for the future could at times produce an effect almost like a collision. For the wish to return to a past that had been, in fantasy, trouble-free, was inevitably accompanied by a scarcely acknowledged wish to punish those who offended against that image – a wish that might express itself in a rather desperate search for certainty about what 'sanctions' were available to staff when they found themselves baffled by the defiant or merely casual attitudes of pupils, or in futile longings for assurance that seventy-five colleagues working in the same school could be relied on to agree about standards and to be entirely consistent in the demands they made on pupils. But almost in the same breath could come a challenge that they ought rather to be examining self-critically their own deficiencies in setting up learning situations for these bored, indifferent or rebellious pupils and that they should be devising ways of engaging these pupils in work that they might find satisfying.

There was some evidence that at least one member of the staff, apart from Denys John himself, feared that the reorganisation of the departments might prove to be only 'another aspirin', and that fundamental rethinking had yet to be started in the area of curriculum change. Yet this same member of the staff, despite the at times despairing talk about declining standards of behaviour, felt that real progress in understanding had been made on the caring side of the school's work, if only, perhaps, because far more attention was being given to the personal needs of those very pupils who gave the staff most trouble.

Because the sharing of a caring concern for children and young people brings into play the parent or potential parent in every man or woman, the members of a staff group can risk more exposure to one another in the pursuit of a more effective organisation for caring. But the professional training in a subject or group of subjects that every student has to undergo before he can take on the role of a teacher, places him in a situation of rivalry with many of his colleagues and is thus a divisive agent in the staff group. Real exposure of 'teaching' problems is therefore more difficult to tolerate than exposure of problems that can be described as 'tutorial'. Paradoxically, the area in which both the teacher and the pupil are presumed to perceive one another most clearly as persons, may after all prove less difficult to talk about in public than the area in which those same persons as learners and as promoters of learning have to confront and evaluate one another. For the ability to handle in one's own classes the day-to-day consequences of curriculum development is still perceived as the real test of professional competence, as though it were not indissolubly bound up with the other, more elusive, kind of tutorial competence, where personal awareness of children as children is more easily acknowledged to be of primary importance.

Experienced teachers are being judged in both roles by their pupils, by the students who come into the school for limited periods to carry out their assigned school practice, by young probationary teachers who join their departments or houses or year groups, by parents who build up images of them from the slender evidence of children's conversations about what goes on in their classes and tutor groups and from the other kind of evidence afforded by their own discussions with them during parents' evening or in special interviews at times of crucial decision-making or at times of crisis. The school is constantly under pressure, from outside as well as from inside, to review its own methods of evaluating its own work.

The stability of a staff group is never certain. Every school of any size or importance experiences annually the fluctuating intake and output of students in training, the inward flow of new colleagues and the inevitable loss of old colleagues. In addition there may be the temporary withdrawal of experienced staff on secondment to the universities to pursue further studies in education, and the consequent necessity to assimilate their new ideas, often critical of school values and practices formerly taken for granted. Every school must therefore accept a three-fold responsibility to work at the task of reconciling the old and the new, first in its own internal arrangements for the planning and implementation of policy (which has really been the main theme of this book), secondly in its relations with the colleges and departments of education that carry responsibility for the initial training of teachers, and thirdly in its relations with other educational institutions through the experienced teachers it exports, either to pursue advanced studies or to take up responsible posts in other parts of the educational system (see Figure 3).

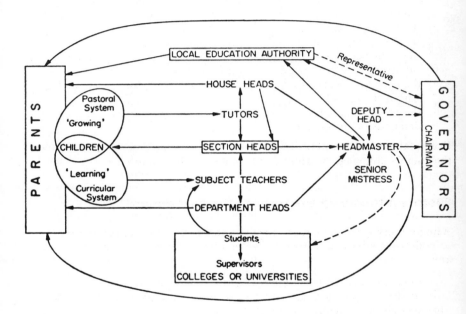

Figure 3 Patterns of accountability

3.7   A Theory of Curriculum Change

William Reid

We can [. . .] postulate that the curriculum offered by the school will be to a great extent dependent on:

(i)   the stocks of knowledge, ideas, images, styles and models available in its environment (for most schools, in society at large);

(ii) the nature of the input of students it receives;

(iii) the nature of the output of students (their destinations);

(iv) the influence channelled towards the school by other institutions;

(v) the strength of the boundary around the school;

(vi) the need for congruence between theory, social system and technology within the school;

(vii) the need for congruence between the activities of the school and the demands of outside forces.

Each of these factors will be briefly considered, and indications given of how they act to influence the kinds of curricula which schools offer.

Factors influencing the form of the curriculum

A major limiting factor on the form of any particular curriculum is the variety of models available to influence it. Models relevant to the shaping of curricula are:

(i)   models of the nature of knowledge and knowing;

(ii) models of truth-seeking strategies within the subjects to be taught;

(iii) models of the nature of children;

(iv) models of desirable adult characteristics;

(v) models of relationships between people and particularly between adults and children;

(vi) models of the role of the teacher and of effective teaching;

(vii) models of the curriculum itself.

Fundamental to any consideration of why curricula take the forms they do is the question, what ways of conceptualising the nature of knowledge and the process of acquiring it exist in the surrounding society? And to what extent are these available for inclusion in the theory of the school? Schools do not necessarily have to wait until ideas about learning are generally accepted before adopting them, but there has to be some degree of acceptance of them

Source: REID, W. A. (1978) *Thinking about the Curriculum*. London: Routledge and Kegan Paul, pp. 83–9.

before they can be successfully incorporated. Exactly how far they have to spread before they become influential on schools will depend on the strength of the boundary between the school and the outside world and on the school's relationship to institutions that generate and diffuse ideas on knowledge and learning. If a stage has not yet been reached when there are generally available technologies and social systems to support the theory, then disequilibrium and rejection may result. It is often the case that the school is operating on a theory of knowledge which, though popularly held, is rejected by philosophers and psychologists. Teaching continues to be dominated in most schools by passive models of knowledge acquisition based on a 'naive theory of vision'. According to this,

> the eye does not contribute anything to the object seen; it simply registers the object. Similarly, when understanding is treated as a kind of seeing, the mind simply registers the idea. . . . It follows from the supposed passivity of the eye that the object seen is wholly there, with all its *visual* properties, colour, shape, size. It exists prior to the act of seeing, and is unaffected by the act of seeing. . . . The vision-based theory of understanding states that direct inspection, or intuition, results in clear ideas. . . . Common-sense theories of understanding are still based on common-sense theories of seeing[1] (Schon, 1963).

The content of the curriculum will reflect the range of knowledge thought to be important and, in the case of academic 'subjects', the way they are conceived and practised in industry, higher education or learned societies. The biology curriculum in the nineteenth century had to be 'taxonomic' in character because that was the state of the research paradigm on which it was modelled (Medaway, 1967). Chemistry, on the other hand, presented several different possibilities, but it was the one subscribed to by those high in the social structure of the discipline that became almost universally adopted (Layton, 1973). Recent curriculum reform movements have been concerned to persuade schools to respond to alternative models, either because they are clinging to an outdated conception of the 'approved' model, or in order to promote the acceptance of a variety of models capable of serving a wider range of purposes. Examples would be the introduction of new science curricula. The early Nuffield schemes in England were indicators to the schools that science's image of itself was changing and that more emphasis should be placed on the innovative rather than the normative aspects of scientific activity. Later projects were more concerned with suggesting roles for school science other than that of inducting students into science as a professional activity.

Though the nineteenth century generally saw children as subordinate creatures, in need of moral correction and inspiration, and having to be disciplined in order to be taught, notions of the child as autonomous learner were not lacking. However, their entry into the language of educators and teachers was a very gradual process which can be charted through analysis of the language of official reports (Cheverst, 1972). Similarly, there are, at any time, a variety of images of the desirable adults that children, as a result of education, should grow into, and of the relations that should exist between children and adults. The view that is projected in the school may be one that relates to a particular section of society, if that is what the school serves, or it may be one that is widely accepted. A few schools deliberately set out to promote models which are not generally admired. An example of shifts in the accepted models of behaviour on the part of children and adults, and of relations between them, is documented by Mandel (Mandel, 1964), who discusses and compares two series of reading books for younger children, one the 'Rollo' series, popular in the nineteenth century, and the other the present day 'Dick and Jane' series:

In the first group of books, the world is full of dangers and evil temptations, and the child himself is full of evil impulses that he must learn to control. In the second group, the world is full of good possibilities, and the child himself has only good impulses which should be given rein and encouragement. . . . With all the potential for badness outside and inside Rollo, it is natural that he should be given some sort of mechanism to protect himself from danger. From the first, Rollo is being taught a code of Christian virtues which he is to adopt in order to resist the evil around and within him. . . . The first step in inculcating such a set of rules for behavior is to impress the child with the wisdom and sanctity of authority. Rollo himself must be taught to obey his parents unquestioningly. . . .

While Rollo is adopting precepts, Dick is adapting to social experience . . . Dick's world requires no constant watchfulness with confirmed inner virtues always on hand to protect him . . . his world is distinct from the world of adults. Indeed adults foster the autonomy of Dick and his group. Each individual finds self-confirmation and a source of meaning in social interaction with his peers. . . . The children spend their time having fun while playing with one another, while going to school, or while participating in humorous little incidents described as funny or silly (Mandel, 1964, pp. 193, 197 and 199).

Mandel's discussion sums up well the curricular implications of the endorsement by the school of particular models of the child, the adult, and the relationships that should exist between them, and it is particularly useful in that it takes its example from what is apparently the learning of a value neutral skill – how to read.

Models of the role of the teacher and of effective teaching will be adopted to accord with images of adult and child, and with preferred styles of relationships. But they will also depend on the value placed by society on teaching, which in turn will affect the type of person who becomes a teacher, and the experiences he is given to prepare him for the task. A view of effective teaching will also reflect the state of knowledge about technologies for implementing theoretical conceptions of the purposes of the curriculum. If effective teaching is extended to include planning as well as implementing the curriculum, then account must also be taken of what models are available for exemplifying a curriculum. In the last century, the curriculum could only be conceived as a schedule of content – facts to be learned or skills to be mastered, generally ranged under subject headings. Today we have discovered other possibilities: the curriculum can be seen in terms of aims and objectives, exploits or experiences, initiations or cultural confrontations. Also, broader definitions have been accepted for what can legitimately be part of a curriculum. Not only can 'subjects' appear in different forms, or be assimilated to one another in schemes of integration, but new areas of knowledge and experience, not before considered as material for a curriculum, can be imported – community service, black studies, making TV programmes, carrying out social and ecological surveys, to mention only some of the less extreme examples of innovation in curricular activities.

But, as has been pointed out, it is seldom the case that the choice of model is totally constrained by the total absence of alternatives. One of the factors which plays a large part in deciding which set of models will, in practice, be adopted is the nature of the school's input and output of students. Who are they, and where do they come from? Where will they go when they leave and what expectations will be held of them by those who will continue their education or give them employment? According to their family and community background, students will be more or less accepting of the school's valuation of what is suitable knowledge, more or less prepared to fit in with new definitions of proper social relationships, more or less ready to acquire new images of what they might become as adults. The extent to which the school accepts and encourages the inclinations of its entering students, or tries to change them, is largely a function of where they will go when they leave, and how far the new environments they will enter are capable of influencing the school. If the success of a secondary school is judged by the number of students it sends to universities and into prestigious occupations, then the demands of these institutions may outweigh the influence of the local community in determining where the school looks for appropriate models.

Moderating any interaction of pressures to adopt particular definitions of its task is the school's boundary – the psychological frontier that exists between the members of the organisation and their activities, and the outside world in the form of local and national communities and of institutions capable of influencing what the school does. Generally speaking, schools have strong boundaries, because inputs of resources into them are not directly linked to the sale of a product. The thought was well expressed by Edward Thring over a century ago:

The old foundations [are] a great saving power in the land. Whatever their faults may be, they are generally free from meddling, free from the necessity of producing some show, something saleable. They are able to stand a storm without shrinking, and to face with calmness the morning letter-bag and the penny post (Thring, 1864, p. 118).

The worthy ambition of many a head teacher – 'to face with calmness the morning letter-bag' – is, as Thring perceptively observed, to be realised only if his output is not defined as 'saleable'. The desire to avoid commitment to a saleable output is one reason why schools strive to identify themselves with scholarly traditions and are reluctant to implement curricula which pursue overtly vocational objectives. However, schools are not always able to command this privileged position. At about the time that Thring was writing,

English elementary schools were administered under a system of 'payment by results' which allowed them very little autonomy. But as well as boundary control which regulates the imposition of specific performance demands on the school, there may be control over the selection of students and teachers. It was commonly the case in the English secondary school that the entry of students could be limited to those most likely to import ideas, behaviours and aspirations consonant with the established 'theory' of the institution.

Since the school functions as a single organisation, and its ability to function depends on keeping dissonance and conflict within reasonable bounds, an overall determinant of the character of the curriculum is the way in which accommodation is achieved between technology, task group and theory. This can be best illustrated by examples. The English elementary school in the nineteenth century used a mass production technology, based on formal classrooms and simple teacher/pupil interaction with little use of technical aids to learning. The social system was paternal and authoritarian. Children were expected to follow instructions and to be in all ways subordinate to and respectful of the wishes of teachers who themselves were products of authoritarian and rule-bound training colleges. The theory of the task was that it was the job of the school to inculcate basic moral values, as propagated by the established church, and the basic skills of reading, writing and simple calculation. The three elements of theory, social system and technology were in harmony. It is difficult to see how a major shift could have taken place in any one of them without setting up an intolerable dissonance. Formal methods reflected the commonly held definition of the task and of the nature of children. The established style of social relationships allowed that task to be carried out effectively. The modern primary school presents a balance of a different type. The technology is seen in much more interactive terms with liberal use of teaching aids – not necessarily in the form of film strips and tape-recorders, more often in the shape of scissors, paste and *papier mâché*. The social system tends to the maternal and the familial, while the theory construes children as active learners and teaching as an engagement in a humanistic activity which attends to basic skill requirements but also stresses, through concepts of growth, harmony and discovery, the need to foster the developing social and intellectual capacities of the child. Here too, the technology, social system and theory are consonant, but produce an arena for the enactment of curriculum that is supportive of quite different knowledge and values. Again, the whole would seem to be dependent on the harmony of the parts. The theory could not be implemented by the technology of the nineteenth century, nor could a nineteenth-century technology be sustained by the social system as it now exists.

Finally, the school will tend to reduce conflict between its methods of operation and the demands and constraints laid upon it by other institutions and by society at large. This is another aspect of the boundary question. Conflict can be reduced by conformity, but it can also be avoided by isolating the school, or some part of it, from outside forces. The latter response is less likely when demands are mediated through the inputs or outputs of students.

These must cross the boundary, and control is difficult. When there was widespread selection for different types of secondary education at age eleven, primary schools had to shape their activities according to the pressures of the secondary sector. Internal and external consonance are mutually dependent. External forces that provide a means of establishing internal harmony will be acceded to. English primary schools in the 1960s were ready to accept new approaches to mathematics teaching which were being pressed by academics and HMIs because this provided them with the shift in technology that was needed to harmonise it with shifts in theory and in the social system. However, it is unlikely that schools will change their internal elements in ways that will result in severe disequilibrium with environmental forces. The cases where this does occur are exceptional. A recent example was that of the William Tyndale Junior School in London where severe curricular disagreements between staff, parents, managers and local authority led to an official enquiry and to dismissals, resignations and disciplinary proceedings. The root of the problem was that the curriculum of the school, under the influence of a new head and deputy appointed from outside, had become far removed from the concept of a suitable curriculum held by many parents. The actual breakdown came through the special circumstance that, being in an area of urban depopulation and declining rolls, the school was unable to defend its boundaries and parents exercised their right to send their children to other schools in the neighbourhood.

Note

1 You may compare Schon's view with Karl Popper's discussion of a 'bucket' theory of knowledge in *Objective Knowledge: an evolutionary approach* (1972) Oxford, Oxford University Press.

References

CHEVERST, W. J. (1972) 'The role of the metaphor in educational thought: an essay in content analysis' in *Journal of Curriculum Studies*, *4*, pp. 71–82.

LAYTON, D. (1973) *Science for the People: the origins of the school science curriculum in England*. London: Allen and Unwin.

MANDEL, R. (1964) 'Children's books: mirrors of social development' in *Elementary School Journal*, *64*, pp. 190–9.

MEDAWAY, P. B. (1967) *The Art of the Soluble*. London: Methuen, pp. 114–15.

SCHON, D. A. (1963) *The Displacement of Concepts*. London: Tavistock, pp. 173–4 and 176.

THRING, E. (1864) *Education and School*. Cambridge: Macmillan, p. 118.

Index

Main entries are shown in *italics*.

Acknowledgments

The editors and publisher wish to thank the following for permission to reprint copyright material in this book:

The Open University Press for 'Three educational ideologies' by Malcolm Skilbeck from E203 – *Curriculum Design and Development*, Unit 3, copyright © 1976; Routledge and Kegan Paul Ltd for an extract from *Culture, Industrialization and Education* (1968) by G. H. Bantock, an extract from *Class Culture and the Curriculum* (1975) by Denis Lawton, an extract from *Teachers, Ideology and Control* (1978) by G. Grace, 'Handling Innovation in the Classroom' by David Hamilton from *Case Studies in Curriculum Change* (1975) edited by W. A. Reid and D. F. Walker and for an extract from *Thinking about the Curriculum* (1978) by William Reid; *New Society* for 'The curriculum mongers: education in reverse' by John White from *New Society* No. 336, 6 March 1969; Uldis Ozolins for his article 'Lawton's "refutation" of a working-class curriculum' from *Melbourne Working Papers* 1979 edited by L. Johnson and U. Ozolins; Sage Publications and Gabriel Chanan for 'The curriculum transaction' from *Reorganizing Education* (1977) edited by E. King; BBC Publications for an extract by Daniel Boorstin from *Exploring Spirit* (1975); Hutchinson Publishing Group Ltd for an extract from *The Politics of Curriculum Change* (1980) by T. Becher and S. Maclure; The Controller of Her Majesty's Stationery Office for an extract from Section 1 of *Curriculum 11–16* (1977) and for an extract from Volume 1 of *Children and their Primary Schools* (The Plowden Report) (1963); The Curriculum Development Centre, Canberra for an extract from *Core Curriculum for Australian Schools* (1980); Dr William Taylor for his article 'Innovation without Growth' from *Educational Administration*, 4 (2) Spring 1976; OECD, Paris and Per Dalin for 'Strategies of Innovation' from *Case Studies in Educational Innovation IV* (1974); The Council for Educational Technology for 'The Utilisation of Educational Research and Development' by Ronald Havelock from *British Journal of Educational Technology* 2 (2) 1972; Macmillan, London and Basingstoke and the Schools Council, London for an extract from *Science 5–13: A Formative Evaluation* (1975); Collier Macmillan Ltd for 'On the classification and framing of educational knowledge' by B. Bernstein from *Knowledge and Control* (1971) edited by M. F. D. Young; Heinemann Educational Books and Bolt and Watson Ltd for an extract from *The Teacher, the School and the Task of Management* (1973) by E. Richardson.